300 quantitative que~~stions~~ ~~in~~ this guide

P9-CDU-455

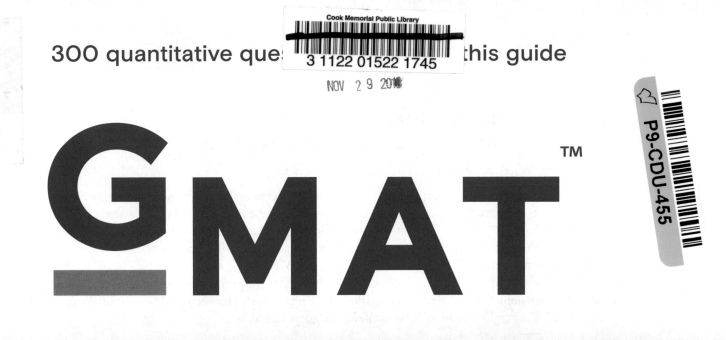

GMAT™

Official Guide Quantitative Review 2019

📖 Book + 💻 Online

The ONLY source of real GMAT® questions from past exams

This edition includes
45 never-before-seen questions

NEW! Index of questions by subject area and difficulty

IMPROVED! Online question bank offers better performance metrics

GMAT® Official Guide Quantitative Review 2019

Table of Contents

Dear GMAT Test-Taker,

Thank you for your interest in graduate management education. Taking the GMAT® exam lets schools know that you're serious about your educational goals. By using the *Official Guide* to prepare for the GMAT exam, you're taking a very important step toward achieving your goals and pursuing admission to the MBA or business master's program that is the best fit for you.

This book, *GMAT® Official Guide Quantitative Review 2019*, is designed to help you prepare for and build confidence to do your best on the GMAT exam. It's the only guide of its kind on the market that includes real GMAT exam questions published by the Graduate Management Admission Council (GMAC), the makers of the exam.

In 1954, leading business schools joined together to launch a standardized way of assessing candidates for business school programs. For 65 years, the GMAT exam has helped people demonstrate their command of the skills needed for success in the classroom. Schools use and trust the GMAT exam as part of their admissions process because it's a proven predictor of classroom success and your ability to excel in your chosen program.

Today more than 7,000 graduate programs around the world use the GMAT exam to establish their MBA, graduate-level management degrees and specialized business master's programs as hallmarks of excellence. Nine out of 10 new MBA enrollments globally are made using a GMAT score.*

We are driven to keep improving the GMAT exam as well as to help you find and gain admission to the best school or program for you. We're committed to ensuring that no talent goes undiscovered and that more people around the world can pursue opportunities in graduate management education.

I applaud your commitment to educational success, and I know that this book and the other GMAT Official Prep materials available at mba.com will give you the confidence to achieve your personal best on the GMAT exam and launch or reinvigorate a rewarding career.

I wish you success on all your educational and professional endeavors in the future.

Sincerely,

Sangeet Chowfla
President & CEO of the Graduate Management Admission Council

GMAT® Official Guide 2019 Quantitative Review

1.0 What Is the GMAT® Exam?

1.0 What Is the GMAT® Exam?

The Graduate Management Admission Test® (GMAT®) exam is a standardized exam used in admissions decisions by more than 7,000 graduate management programs worldwide, at approximately 2,300 graduate business schools worldwide. It helps you gauge, and demonstrate to schools, your academic potential for success in graduate-level management studies.

The four-part exam measures your Analytical Writing, Integrated Reasoning, Verbal, and Quantitative Reasoning skills—higher-order reasoning skills that management faculty worldwide have identified as important for incoming students to have. "Higher-order" reasoning skills involve complex judgments, and include critical thinking, analysis, and problem solving. Unlike undergraduate grades and curricula, which vary in their meaning across regions and institutions, your GMAT scores provide a standardized, statistically valid, and reliable measure of how you are likely to perform academically in the core curriculum of a graduate management program. The GMAT exam's validity, fairness, and value in admissions have been well-established through numerous academic studies.

The GMAT exam is delivered entirely in English and solely on a computer. It is not a test of business knowledge, subject-matter mastery, English vocabulary, or advanced computational skills. The GMAT exam also does not measure other factors related to success in graduate management study, such as job experience, leadership ability, motivation, and interpersonal skills. Your GMAT score is intended to be used as one admissions criterion among other, more subjective, criteria, such as admissions essays and interviews.

1.1 Why Take the GMAT® Exam?

Launched in 1954 by a group of nine business schools to provide a uniform measure of the academic skills needed to succeed in their programs, the GMAT exam is now used by more than 7,000 graduate management programs at approximately 2,300 institutions worldwide.

Taking the GMAT exam helps you stand out in the admissions process and demonstrate your readiness and commitment to pursuing graduate management education. Schools use GMAT scores to help them select the most qualified applicants—because they know that candidates who take the GMAT exam are serious about earning a graduate business degree, and it's a proven predictor of a student's ability to succeed in his or her chosen program. When you consider which programs to apply to, you can look at a school's use of the GMAT exam as one indicator of quality. Schools that use the GMAT exam typically list score ranges or average scores in their class profiles, so you may also find these profiles helpful in gauging the academic competitiveness of a program you are considering and how well your performance on the exam compares with that of the students enrolled in the program.

> ### Myth -vs- **FACT**
>
> $\mathcal{M}$ – **If I don't achieve a high score on the GMAT, I won't get into my top choice schools.**
>
> F – **There are great schools available for candidates at any GMAT score range.**
>
> Fewer than 50 of the more than 250,000 people taking the GMAT exam each year get a perfect score of 800; and many more get into top business school programs around the world each year. Admissions Officers use GMAT scores as one component in their admissions decisions, in conjunction with undergraduate records, application essays, interviews, letters of recommendation, and other information when deciding whom to accept into their programs. Visit School Finder on mba.com to learn about schools that are the best fit for you.

No matter how you perform on the GMAT exam, you should contact the schools that interest you to learn more and to ask how they use GMAT scores and other criteria (such as your undergraduate grades, essays, and letters of recommendation) in their admissions processes. School admissions offices, web sites, and materials published by schools are the key sources of information when you are doing research about where you might want to go to business school.

For more information on the GMAT, test preparation materials, registration, how to use and send your GMAT scores to schools, and applying to business school, please visit mba.com.

1.2 GMAT® Exam Format

The GMAT exam consists of four separately timed sections (see the table on the next page). The Analytical Writing Assessment (AWA) section consists of one essay. The Integrated Reasoning section consists of graphical and data analysis questions in multiple response formats. The Quantitative and Verbal Reasoning sections consist of multiple-choice questions.

The Verbal and Quantitative sections of the GMAT exam are computer adaptive, which means that the test draws from a large bank of questions to tailor itself to your ability level, and you won't get many questions that are too hard or too easy for you. The first question will be of medium difficulty. As you answer each question, the computer scores your answer and uses it—as well as your responses to all preceding questions—to select the next question.

Computer-adaptive tests become more difficult the more questions you answer correctly, but if you get a question that seems easier than the last one, it does not necessarily mean you answered the last question incorrectly. The test has to cover a range of content, both in the type of question asked and the subject matter presented.

> ## Myth -vs- FACT
>
> M – **Getting an easier question means I answered the last one wrong.**
>
> F – **You should not become distracted by the difficulty level of a question.**
>
> Most people are not skilled at estimating question difficulty, so don't worry when taking the test or waste valuable time trying to determine the difficulty of the question you are answering.
>
> To ensure that everyone receives the same content, the test selects a specific number of questions of each type. The test may call for your next problem to be a relatively hard data sufficiency question involving arithmetic operations. But, if there are no more relatively difficult data sufficiency questions involving arithmetic, you might be given an easier question.

Because the computer uses your answers to select your next questions, you may not skip questions or go back and change your answer to a previous question. If you don't know the answer to a question, try to eliminate as many choices as possible, then select the answer you think is best.

Though the individual questions are different, the mix of question types is the same for every GMAT exam. Your score is determined by the difficulty and statistical characteristics of the questions you answer as well as the number of questions you answer correctly. By adapting to each test-taker, the GMAT exam is able to accurately and efficiently gauge skill levels over a full range of abilities, from very high to very low.

The test includes the types of questions found in this book and online at gmat.wiley.com, but the format and presentation of the questions are different on the computer. When you take the test:

- Only one question or question prompt at a time is presented on the computer screen.
- The answer choices for the multiple-choice questions will be preceded by circles, rather than by letters.

- Different question types appear in random order in the multiple-choice and Integrated Reasoning sections.

- You must select your answer using the computer.

- You must choose an answer and confirm your choice before moving on to the next question.

- You may not go back to previous screens to change answers to previous questions.

Format of the GMAT® Exam		
	Questions	Timing
Analytical Writing Assessment	1	30 min.

Integrated Reasoning
    Multi-Source Reasoning
    Table Analysis
    Graphics Interpretation
    Two-Part Analysis
	12	30 min.

Quantitative Reasoning
    Problem Solving
    Data Sufficiency
	31	62 min.

Verbal Reasoning
    Reading Comprehension
    Critical Reasoning
    Sentence Correction
	36	65 min.

	Total Time:	187 min.

You will now have the flexibility to select the order for the section of the GMAT exam from three options.

Order #1	Order #2	Order #3
Analytical Writing Assessment	Verbal	Quantitative
Integrated Reasoning		
Optional 8-minute break		
Quantitative	Quantitative	Verbal
Optional 8-minute break		
Verbal	Integrated Reasoning	Integrated Reasoning
	Analytical Writing Assessment	Analytical Writing Assessment

The section order selection will take place at the test center on exam date, immediately prior to the start of the GMAT exam.

1.3 What Is the Content of the Exam Like?

The GMAT exam measures higher-order analytical skills encompassing several types of reasoning. The Analytical Writing Assessment asks you to analyze the reasoning behind an argument and respond in writing; the Integrated Reasoning section asks you to interpret and synthesize information from multiple sources and in different formats to make reasoned conclusions; the Quantitative section asks you to reason quantitatively using basic arithmetic, algebra, and geometry; and the Verbal section asks you to read and comprehend written material and to reason and evaluate arguments.

Test questions may address a variety of subjects, but all of the information you need to answer the questions will be included on the exam, with no outside knowledge of the subject matter necessary. The GMAT exam is not a test of business knowledge, English vocabulary, or advanced computational skills. You will need to read and write in English and have basic math and English skills to perform well on the test, but its difficulty comes from analytical and critical thinking abilities.

The questions in this book are organized by question type and from easiest to most difficult, but keep in mind that when you take the test, you may see different types of questions in any order within each section.

1.4 Analytical Writing Assessment

The Analytical Writing Assessment (AWA) consists of one 30-minute writing task: Analysis of an Argument. The AWA measures your ability to think critically, communicate your ideas, and formulate an appropriate and constructive critique. You will type your essay on a computer keyboard.

1.5 Integrated Reasoning Section

The Integrated Reasoning section highlights the relevant skills that business managers in today's data-driven world need in order to analyze sophisticated streams of data and solve complex problems. It measures your ability to understand and evaluate multiple sources and types of information—graphic, numeric, and verbal—as they relate to one another. This section will require you to use both quantitative and verbal reasoning to solve complex problems and solve multiple problems in relation to one another.

Four types of questions are used in the Integrated Reasoning section:

- Multi-Source Reasoning
- Table Analysis
- Graphics Interpretation
- Two-Part Analysis

Integrated Reasoning questions may be quantitative, verbal, or a combination of both. You will have to interpret graphics and sort tables to extract meaning from data, but advanced statistical knowledge and spreadsheet manipulation skills are not necessary. You will have access to an on-screen calculator with basic functions for the Integrated Reasoning section, but note that the calculator is *not* available on the Quantitative section.

1.6 Quantitative Section

The GMAT Quantitative section measures your ability to reason quantitatively, solve quantitative problems, and interpret graphic data.

Two types of multiple-choice questions are used in the Quantitative section:

- Problem Solving
- Data Sufficiency

Both are intermingled throughout the Quantitative section, and require basic knowledge of arithmetic, elementary algebra, and commonly known concepts of geometry.

To review the basic mathematical concepts that you will need to answer Quantitative questions, see the math review in chapter 3. For test-taking tips specific to the question types in the Quantitative section, practice questions, and answer explanations, see chapters 4 and 5.

1.7 Verbal Section

The GMAT Verbal section measures your ability to read and comprehend written material and to reason and evaluate arguments. The Verbal section includes reading sections from several different content areas. Although you may be generally familiar with some of the material, neither the reading passages nor the questions assume detailed knowledge of the topics discussed.

Three types of multiple-choice questions are intermingled throughout the Verbal section:

- Reading Comprehension
- Critical Reasoning
- Sentence Correction

All three require basic knowledge of the English language, but the Verbal section is not a test of advanced vocabulary.

For test-taking tips specific to each question type in the Verbal section, practice questions, and answer explanations, see *GMAT® Official Guide 2019*, or *GMAT® Official Guide Verbal Review 2019*; both are available for purchase at mba.com

1.8 What Computer Skills Will I Need?

The GMAT exam requires only basic computer skills. You will type your AWA essay on the computer keyboard using standard word-processing keystrokes. In the Integrated Reasoning and multiple-choice sections, you will select your responses using either your computer mouse or the keyboard. The Integrated Reasoning section includes basic computer navigation and functions, such as clicking on tabs and using drop-down menus to sort tables and select answers. You will also have access to an on-screen calculator in the Integrated Reasoning section (calculator is not available in any other section of the exam).

1.9 What Are the Test Centers Like?

The GMAT exam is administered under standardized conditions at test centers worldwide. Each test center has a proctored testing room with individual computer workstations that allow you to sit for the exam under quiet conditions and with some privacy. You will be able to take two optional 8-minute breaks during the course of the exam. You may not take notes or scratch paper with you into the testing room, but an erasable notepad and marker will be provided for you to use during the test. For more information about exam day visit mba.com.

1.10 How Are Scores Calculated?

Verbal and Quantitative sections are scored on a scale of 6 to 51, in one-point increments. The Total GMAT score ranges from 200 to 800 and is based on your performance in these two sections. Your score is determined by:

- The number of questions you answer

- The number of questions you answer correctly or incorrectly

- The level of difficulty and other statistical characteristics of each question

Your Verbal, Quantitative, and Total GMAT scores are determined by an algorithm that takes into account the difficulty of the questions that were presented to you and how you answered them. When you answer the easier questions correctly, you get a chance to answer harder questions, making it possible to earn a higher score. After you have completed all the questions on the test, or when your time is expired, the computer will calculate your scores. Your scores on the Verbal and Quantitative sections are combined to produce your Total score which ranges from 200 to 800 in 10-point increments.

The Analytical Writing Assessment consists of one writing task. Your essay will be scored two times independently. Essays are evaluated by college and university faculty members from a variety of disciplines, including management education, who rate the overall quality of your critical thinking and writing. (For details on how readers are qualified, visit mba.com.) In addition, your response is also scored by an automated scoring program designed to reflect the judgment of expert readers.

Your essay is scored on a scale of 0 to 6, in half-point increments, with 6 being the highest score and 0 the lowest. A score of zero is given for responses that are off topic, are in a foreign language, merely attempt to copy the topic, consist only of keystroke characters, or are blank. Your AWA score is typically the average of two independent ratings. If the independent scores vary by more than a point, a third reader adjudicates, but because of ongoing training and monitoring, discrepancies are rare.

Your Integrated Reasoning section is scored on a scale of 1 to 8, in one-point increments. Many questions have multiple parts, and you must answer all parts of a question correctly to receive credit; partial credit will not be given.

Your Analytical Writing Assessment and Integrated Reasoning scores are computed and reported separately from the other sections of the test and have no effect on your Verbal, Quantitative, or Total scores. The schools that you have designated to receive your scores may receive a copy of your Analytical Writing Assessment essay with your score report. Your own copy of your score report will not include your essay.

Your GMAT score includes a percentile ranking that compares your skill level with other test-takers from the past three years. The percentile rank of your score shows the percentage of tests taken with scores lower than your score. Every July, percentile ranking tables are updated. Visit mba.com to view the most recent percentile rankings tables.

1.11 Test Development Process

The GMAT exam is developed by experts who use standardized procedures to ensure high-quality, widely-appropriate test material. All questions are subjected to independent reviews and are revised or discarded as necessary. Multiple-choice questions are tested during GMAT exam administrations. Analytical Writing Assessment tasks are tested on mba.com registrants and then assessed for their fairness and reliability. For more information on test development, visit mba.com.

2.0 How to Prepare

2.0 How to Prepare

2.1 How Should I Prepare to Take the Test?

The GMAT® exam is designed specifically to measure reasoning skills needed for management education, and the test contains several question formats unique to the GMAT exam. At a minimum, you should be familiar with the test format and the question formats before you sit for the test. Because the GMAT exam is a timed exam, you should practice answering test questions, not only to better understand the question formats and the skills they require, but also to help you learn to pace yourself so you can finish each section when you sit for the exam.

Because the exam measures reasoning rather than subject-matter knowledge, you most likely will not find it helpful to memorize facts. You do not need to study advanced mathematical concepts, but you should be sure your grasp of basic arithmetic, algebra, and geometry is sound enough that you can use these skills in quantitative problem solving. Likewise, you do not need to study advanced vocabulary words, but you should have a firm understanding of basic English vocabulary and grammar for reading, writing, and reasoning.

This book and other study materials released by the Graduate Management Admission Council (GMAC) are the ONLY source of questions that have been retired from the GMAT exam. All questions that appear or have appeared on the GMAT exam are copyrighted and owned by GMAC, which does not license them to be reprinted elsewhere. Accessing live Integrated Reasoning, Quantitative, or Verbal test questions in advance or sharing test content during or after you take the test is a serious violation, which could cause your scores to be canceled and schools to be notified. In cases of a serious violation, you may be banned from future testing and other legal remedies may be pursued.

> *Myth* -vs- **FACT**
>
> $\mathcal{M}$ – **You need very advanced math skills to get a high GMAT score.**
>
> F – **The GMAT measures your reasoning and critical thinking abilities, rather than your advanced math skills.**
>
> The GMAT exam only requires basic quantitative skills. You should review the math skills (algebra, geometry, basic arithmetic) presented in this guide (chapter 3). The difficulty of GMAT Quantitative questions stems from the logic and analysis used to solve the problems and not the underlying math skills.

2.2 What About Practice Tests?

The Quantitative and Verbal sections of the GMAT exam are computer adaptive, and the Integrated Reasoning section includes questions that require you to use the computer to sort tables and navigate to different sources of information. Our official practice materials will help you get comfortable with the format of the test and better prepare for exam day. Two full-length GMAT practice exams are available at no charge for those who have created an account on mba.com. The practice exams include computer-adaptive Quantitative and Verbal sections, plus additional practice questions, information about the test, and tutorials to help you become familiar with how the GMAT exam will appear on the computer screen at the test center.

To maximize your studying efforts with the free practice exams, you should leverage official practice materials as you start to prepare for the test. Take one practice test to make yourself familiar with the exam and to get a baseline score. After you have studied using this book and other study materials, take the second practice test to determine whether you need to shift your focus to other areas you need to strengthen. Note that the free practice tests may include questions that are also published in this book. As your test day approaches, consider taking more official practice tests to help measure your progress and give you a better idea of how you might score on exam day.

2.3 Where Can I Get Additional Practice?

If you would like additional practice, you may want to purchase *GMAT® Official Guide 2019* and/or *GMAT® Official Guide Verbal Review 2019* . You can also find more Quantitative, Verbal, and Integrated Reasoning practice questions, full-length, computer-adaptive practice exams, Analytical Writing Assessment practice prompts, and other helpful study materials at mba.com.

2.4 General Test-Taking Suggestions

Specific test-taking strategies for individual question types are presented later in this book. The following are general suggestions to help you perform your best on the test.

1. **Use your time wisely.**
   Although the GMAT exam stresses accuracy more than speed, it is important to use your time wisely. On average, you will have about 1¾ minutes for each Verbal question, about 2 minutes for each Quantitative question, and about 2½ minutes for each Integrated Reasoning question, some of which have multiple questions. Once you start the test, an onscreen clock will show the time you have left. You can hide this display if you want, but it is a good idea to check the clock periodically to monitor your progress. The clock will automatically alert you when 5 minutes remain for the section you are working on.

2. **Answer practice questions ahead of time.**
   After you become generally familiar with all question types, use the practice questions in this book and online at gmat.wiley.com to prepare for the actual test. It may be useful to time yourself as you answer the practice questions to get an idea of how long you will have for each question when you sit for the actual test, as well as to determine whether you are answering quickly enough to finish the test in the allotted time.

3. **Read all test directions carefully.**
   The directions explain exactly what is required to answer each question type. If you read hastily, you may miss important instructions and impact your ability to answer correctly. To review directions during the test, click on the Help icon. But be aware that the time you spend reviewing directions will count against your time allotment for that section of the test.

4. **Read each question carefully and thoroughly.**
   Before you answer a question, determine exactly what is being asked and then select the best choice. Never skim a question or the possible answers; skimming may cause you to miss important information or nuances.

Myth -vs- FACT

M – **It is more important to respond correctly to the test questions than it is to finish the test.**

F – **There is a significant penalty for not completing the GMAT exam.**

Pacing is important. If you are stumped by a question, give it your best guess and move on. If you guess incorrectly, the computer program will likely give you an easier question, which you are likely to answer correctly, and the computer will rapidly return to giving you questions matched to your ability. If you don't finish the test, your score will be reduced. Failing to answer five verbal questions, for example, could reduce your score from the 91st percentile to the 77th percentile.

5. **Do not spend too much time on any one question.**

    If you do not know the correct answer, or if the question is too time consuming, try to eliminate choices you know are wrong, select the best of the remaining answer choices, and move on to the next question.

    Not completing sections and randomly guessing answers to questions at the end of each test section can significantly lower your score. As long as you have worked on each section, you will receive a score even if you do not finish one or more sections in the allotted time. You will not earn points for questions you never get to see.

6. **Confirm your answers ONLY when you are ready to move on.**

    On the Quantitative and Verbal sections, once you have selected your answer to a multiple-choice question, you will be asked to confirm it. Once you confirm your response, you cannot go back and change it. You may not skip questions. In the Integrated Reasoning section, there may be several questions based on information provided in the same question prompt. When there is more than one response on a single screen, you can change your response to any of the questions on the screen before moving on to the next screen. However, you may not navigate back to a previous screen to change any responses.

7. **Plan your essay answer before you begin to write.**

    The best way to approach the Analysis of an Argument section is to read the directions carefully, take a few minutes to think about the question, and plan a response before you begin writing. Take time to organize your ideas and develop them fully but leave time to reread your response and make any revisions that you think would improve it.

Myth -vs- FACT

𝕄 – **The first 10 questions are critical and you should invest the most time on those.**

F – **All questions count.**

The computer-adaptive testing algorithm uses each answered question to obtain an *initial* estimate. However, as you continue to answer questions, the algorithm self-corrects by computing an updated estimate on the basis of all the questions you have answered, and then administers items that are closely matched to this new estimate of your ability. Your final score is based on all your responses and considers the difficulty of all the questions you answered. Taking additional time on the first 10 questions will not game the system and can hurt your ability to finish the test.

3.0 Math Review

3.0 Math Review

To answer quantitative reasoning questions on the GMAT exam, you will need to be familiar with basic mathematical concepts and formulas. This chapter contains a list of the basic mathematical concepts, terms, and formulas that may appear or can be useful for answering quantitative reasoning questions on the GMAT exam. This chapter offers only a high-level overview, so if you find unfamiliar terms or concepts, you should consult other resources for a more detailed discussion and explanation.

Keep in mind that this knowledge of basic math, while necessary, is seldom sufficient in answering GMAT questions. Unlike traditional math problems that you may have encountered in school, GMAT quantitative reasoning questions require you to *apply* your knowledge of math. For example, rather than asking you to demonstrate your knowledge of prime factorization by listing the prime factors of a number, a GMAT question may require you to apply your knowledge of prime factorization and properties of exponents to simplify an algebraic expression with a radical.

To prepare for the GMAT Quantitative Reasoning section, we recommend starting with a review of the basic mathematical concepts and formulas to ensure that you have the foundational knowledge necessary for solving the questions, before moving on to practicing the application of this knowledge on real GMAT questions from past exams.

Section 3.1, "Arithmetic," includes the following topics:

1. Properties of Integers
2. Fractions
3. Decimals
4. Real Numbers
5. Ratio and Proportion
6. Percents
7. Powers and Roots of Numbers
8. Descriptive Statistics
9. Sets
10. Counting Methods
11. Discrete Probability

Section 3.2, "Algebra," does not extend beyond what is usually covered in a first-year high school algebra course. The topics included are as follows:

1. Simplifying Algebraic Expressions
2. Equations
3. Solving Linear Equations with One Unknown
4. Solving Two Linear Equations with Two Unknowns
5. Solving Equations by Factoring
6. Solving Quadratic Equations
7. Exponents
8. Inequalities
9. Absolute Value
10. Functions

Section 3.3, "Geometry," is limited primarily to measurement and intuitive geometry or spatial visualization. Extensive knowledge of theorems and the ability to construct proofs, skills that are usually developed in a formal geometry course, are not tested. The topics included in this section are the following:

1. Lines
2. Intersecting Lines and Angles
3. Perpendicular Lines
4. Parallel Lines
5. Polygons (Convex)
6. Triangles
7. Quadrilaterals
8. Circles
9. Rectangular Solids and Cylinders
10. Coordinate Geometry

Section 3.4, "Word Problems," presents examples of and solutions to the following types of word problems:

1. Rate Problems
2. Work Problems
3. Mixture Problems
4. Interest Problems
5. Discount

6. Profit
7. Sets
8. Geometry Problems
9. Measurement Problems
10. Data Interpretation

3.1 Arithmetic

1. Properties of Integers

An *integer* is any number in the set $\{\ldots -3, -2, -1, 0, 1, 2, 3, \ldots\}$. If x and y are integers and $x \neq 0$, then x is a *divisor* (*factor*) of y provided that $y = xn$ for some integer n. In this case, y is also said to be *divisible* by x or to be a *multiple* of x. For example, 7 is a divisor or factor of 28 since $28 = (7)(4)$, but 8 is not a divisor of 28 since there is no integer n such that $28 = 8n$.

If x and y are positive integers, there exist unique integers q and r, called the *quotient* and *remainder*, respectively, such that $y = xq + r$ and $0 \leq r < x$. For example, when 28 is divided by 8, the quotient is 3 and the remainder is 4 since $28 = (8)(3) + 4$. Note that y is divisible by x if and only if the remainder r is 0; for example, 32 has a remainder of 0 when divided by 8 because 32 is divisible by 8. Also, note that when a smaller integer is divided by a larger integer, the quotient is 0 and the remainder is the smaller integer. For example, 5 divided by 7 has the quotient 0 and the remainder 5 since $5 = (7)(0) + 5$.

Any integer that is divisible by 2 is an *even integer*; the set of even integers is $\{\ldots -4, -2, 0, 2, 4, 6, 8, \ldots\}$. Integers that are not divisible by 2 are *odd integers*; $\{\ldots -3, -1, 1, 3, 5, \ldots\}$ is the set of odd integers.

If at least one factor of a product of integers is even, then the product is even; otherwise the product is odd. If two integers are both even or both odd, then their sum and their difference are even. Otherwise, their sum and their difference are odd.

A *prime* number is a positive integer that has exactly two different positive divisors, 1 and itself. For example, 2, 3, 5, 7, 11, and 13 are prime numbers, but 15 is not, since 15 has four different positive divisors, 1, 3, 5, and 15. The number 1 is not a prime number since it has only one positive divisor. Every integer greater than 1 either is prime or can be uniquely expressed as a product of prime factors. For example, $14 = (2)(7)$, $81 = (3)(3)(3)(3)$, and $484 = (2)(2)(11)(11)$.

The numbers $-2, -1, 0, 1, 2, 3, 4, 5$ are *consecutive integers*. Consecutive integers can be represented by $n, n + 1, n + 2, n + 3, \ldots$, where n is an integer. The numbers $0, 2, 4, 6, 8$ are *consecutive even integers*, and $1, 3, 5, 7, 9$ are *consecutive odd integers*. Consecutive even integers can be represented by $2n, 2n + 2, 2n + 4, \ldots$, and consecutive odd integers can be represented by $2n + 1, 2n + 3, 2n + 5, \ldots$, where n is an integer.

Properties of the integer 1. If n is any number, then $1 \cdot n = n$, and for any number $n \neq 0$, $n \cdot \dfrac{1}{n} = 1$.

The number 1 can be expressed in many ways; for example, $\dfrac{n}{n} = 1$ for any number $n \neq 0$.

Multiplying or dividing an expression by 1, in any form, does not change the value of that expression.

Properties of the integer 0. The integer 0 is neither positive nor negative. If n is any number, then $n + 0 = n$ and $n \cdot 0 = 0$. Division by 0 is not defined.

2. Fractions

In a fraction $\frac{n}{d}$, n is the *numerator* and d is the *denominator*. The denominator of a fraction can never be 0, because division by 0 is not defined.

Two fractions are said to be *equivalent* if they represent the same number. For example, $\frac{8}{36}$ and $\frac{14}{63}$ are equivalent since they both represent the number $\frac{2}{9}$. In each case, the fraction is reduced to lowest terms by dividing both numerator and denominator by their *greatest common divisor* (gcd). The gcd of 8 and 36 is 4 and the gcd of 14 and 63 is 7.

Addition and subtraction of fractions.

Two fractions with the same denominator can be added or subtracted by performing the required operation with the numerators, leaving the denominators the same. For example, $\frac{3}{5}+\frac{4}{5}=\frac{3+4}{5}=\frac{7}{5}$ and $\frac{5}{7}-\frac{2}{7}=\frac{5-2}{7}=\frac{3}{7}$. If two fractions do not have the same denominator, express them as equivalent fractions with the same denominator. For example, to add $\frac{3}{5}$ and $\frac{4}{7}$, multiply the numerator and denominator of the first fraction by 7 and the numerator and denominator of the second fraction by 5, obtaining $\frac{21}{35}$ and $\frac{20}{35}$, respectively; $\frac{21}{35}+\frac{20}{35}=\frac{41}{35}$.

For the new denominator, choosing the *least common multiple* (lcm) of the denominators usually lessens the work. For $\frac{2}{3}+\frac{1}{6}$, the lcm of 3 and 6 is 6 (not $3\times6=18$), so $\frac{2}{3}+\frac{1}{6}=\frac{2}{3}\times\frac{2}{2}+\frac{1}{6}=\frac{4}{6}+\frac{1}{6}=\frac{5}{6}$.

Multiplication and division of fractions.

To multiply two fractions, simply multiply the two numerators and multiply the two denominators.

For example, $\frac{2}{3}\times\frac{4}{7}=\frac{2\times4}{3\times7}=\frac{8}{21}$.

To divide by a fraction, invert the divisor (that is, find its *reciprocal*) and multiply. For example, $\frac{2}{3}\div\frac{4}{7}=\frac{2}{3}\times\frac{7}{4}=\frac{14}{12}=\frac{7}{6}$.

In the problem above, the reciprocal of $\frac{4}{7}$ is $\frac{7}{4}$. In general, the reciprocal of a fraction $\frac{n}{d}$ is $\frac{d}{n}$, where n and d are not zero.

Mixed numbers.

A number that consists of a whole number and a fraction, for example, $7\frac{2}{3}$, is a mixed number: $7\frac{2}{3}$ means $7+\frac{2}{3}$.

To change a mixed number into a fraction, multiply the whole number by the denominator of the fraction and add this number to the numerator of the fraction; then put the result over the denominator of the fraction. For example, $7\frac{2}{3}=\frac{(3\times7)+2}{3}=\frac{23}{3}$.

3. Decimals

In the decimal system, the position of the period or *decimal point* determines the place value of the digits. For example, the digits in the number 7,654.321 have the following place values:

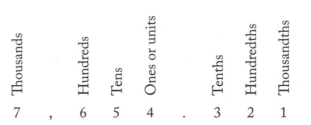

Some examples of decimals follow.

$$0.321 = \frac{3}{10} + \frac{2}{100} + \frac{1}{1,000} = \frac{321}{1,000}$$

$$0.0321 = \frac{0}{10} + \frac{3}{100} + \frac{2}{1,000} + \frac{1}{10,000} = \frac{321}{10,000}$$

$$1.56 = 1 + \frac{5}{10} + \frac{6}{100} = \frac{156}{100}$$

Sometimes decimals are expressed as the product of a number with only one digit to the left of the decimal point and a power of 10. This is called *scientific notation*. For example, 231 can be written as 2.31×10^2 and 0.0231 can be written as 2.31×10^{-2}. When a number is expressed in scientific notation, the exponent of the 10 indicates the number of places that the decimal point is to be moved in the number that is to be multiplied by a power of 10 in order to obtain the product. The decimal point is moved to the right if the exponent is positive and to the left if the exponent is negative. For example, 2.013×10^4 is equal to 20,130 and 1.91×10^{-4} is equal to 0.000191.

Addition and subtraction of decimals.

To add or subtract two decimals, the decimal points of both numbers should be lined up. If one of the numbers has fewer digits to the right of the decimal point than the other, zeros may be inserted to the right of the last digit. For example, to add 17.6512 and 653.27, set up the numbers in a column and add:

$$
\begin{array}{r}
17.6512 \\
+ 653.2700 \\
\hline
670.9212
\end{array}
$$

Likewise for 653.27 minus 17.6512:

$$
\begin{array}{r}
653.2700 \\
-17.6512 \\
\hline
635.6188
\end{array}
$$

Multiplication of decimals.

To multiply decimals, multiply the numbers as if they were whole numbers and then insert the decimal point in the product so that the number of digits to the right of the decimal point is equal to the sum of the numbers of digits to the right of the decimal points in the numbers being multiplied. For example:

$$2.09 \quad \text{(2 digits to the right)}$$

$$\underline{\times 1.3} \quad \text{(1 digit to the right)}$$

$$627$$

$$\underline{2090}$$

$$2.717 \quad (2+1=3 \text{ digits to the right})$$

Division of decimals.

To divide a number (the dividend) by a decimal (the divisor), move the decimal point of the divisor to the right until the divisor is a whole number. Then move the decimal point of the dividend the same number of places to the right, and divide as you would by a whole number. The decimal point in the quotient will be directly above the decimal point in the new dividend. For example, to divide 698.12 by 12.4:

$$12.4\overline{)698.12}$$

will be replaced by:

$$124\overline{)6981.2}$$

and the division would proceed as follows:

$$
\begin{array}{r}
56.3 \\
124\overline{)6981.2} \\
\underline{620} \\
781 \\
\underline{744} \\
372 \\
\underline{372} \\
0
\end{array}
$$

4. Real Numbers

All *real* numbers correspond to points on the number line and all points on the number line correspond to real numbers. All real numbers except zero are either positive or negative.

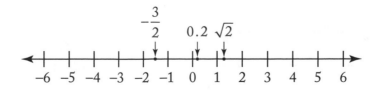

On a number line, numbers corresponding to points to the left of zero are negative and numbers corresponding to points to the right of zero are positive. For any two numbers on the number line, the number to the left is less than the number to the right; for example, $-4 < -3 < -\frac{3}{2} < -1$, and $1 < \sqrt{2} < 2$.

To say that the number n is between 1 and 4 on the number line means that $n > 1$ and $n < 4$, that is, $1 < n < 4$. If n is "between 1 and 4, inclusive," then $1 \le n \le 4$.

The distance between a number and zero on the number line is called the *absolute value* of the number. Thus 3 and -3 have the same absolute value, 3, since they are both three units from zero. The absolute value of 3 is denoted $|3|$. Examples of absolute values of numbers are

$$|-5| = |5| = 5, \left|-\frac{7}{2}\right| = \frac{7}{2}, \text{ and } |0| = 0.$$

Note that the absolute value of any nonzero number is positive.

Here are some properties of real numbers that are used frequently. If x, y, and z are real numbers, then

(1) $x + y = y + x$ and $xy = yx$.
For example, $8 + 3 = 3 + 8 = 11$, and $(17)(5) = (5)(17) = 85$.

(2) $(x + y) + z = x + (y + z)$ and $(xy)z = x(yz)$.
For example, $(7 + 5) + 2 = 7 + (5 + 2) = 7 + (7) = 14$, and $\left(5\sqrt{3}\right)\left(\sqrt{3}\right) = (5)\left(\sqrt{3}\sqrt{3}\right) = (5)(3) = 15$.

(3) $xy + xz = x(y + z)$.
For example, $718(36) + 718(64) = 718(36 + 64) = 718(100) = 71,800$.

(4) If x and y are both positive, then $x + y$ and xy are positive.

(5) If x and y are both negative, then $x + y$ is negative and xy is positive.

(6) If x is positive and y is negative, then xy is negative.

(7) If $xy = 0$, then $x = 0$ or $y = 0$. For example, $3y = 0$ implies $y = 0$.

(8) $|x + y| \le |x| + |y|$. For example, if $x = 10$ and $y = 2$, then $|x + y| = |12| = 12 = |x| + |y|$; and if $x = 10$ and $y = -2$, then $|x + y| = |8| = 8 < 12 = |x| + |y|$.

5. Ratio and Proportion

The *ratio* of the number a to the number b ($b \ne 0$) is $\frac{a}{b}$.

A ratio may be expressed or represented in several ways. For example, the ratio of 2 to 3 can be written as 2 to 3, 2:3, or $\frac{2}{3}$. The order of the terms of a ratio is important. For example, the ratio of the number of months with exactly 30 days to the number with exactly 31 days is $\frac{4}{7}$, not $\frac{7}{4}$.

A *proportion* is a statement that two ratios are equal; for example, $\frac{2}{3} = \frac{8}{12}$ is a proportion. One way to solve a proportion involving an unknown is to cross multiply, obtaining a new equality. For example, to solve for n in the proportion $\frac{2}{3} = \frac{n}{12}$, cross multiply, obtaining $24 = 3n$; then divide both sides by 3, to get $n = 8$.

6. Percents

Percent means *per hundred* or *number out of 100*. A percent can be represented as a fraction with a denominator of 100, or as a decimal. For example:

$$37\% = \frac{37}{100} = 0.37.$$

To find a certain percent of a number, multiply the number by the percent expressed as a decimal or fraction. For example:

$$20\% \text{ of } 90 = 0.2 \times 90 = 18$$

or

$$20\% \text{ of } 90 = \frac{20}{100} \times 90 = \frac{1}{5} \times 90 = 18.$$

Percents greater than 100%.

Percents greater than 100% are represented by numbers greater than 1. For example:

$$300\% = \frac{300}{100} = 3$$

$$250\% \text{ of } 80 = 2.5 \times 80 = 200.$$

Percents less than 1%.

The percent 0.5% means $\frac{1}{2}$ of 1 percent. For example, 0.5% of 12 is equal to $0.005 \times 12 = 0.06$.

Percent change.

Often a problem will ask for the percent increase or decrease from one quantity to another quantity. For example, "If the price of an item increases from \$24 to \$30, what is the percent increase in price?" To find the percent increase, first find the amount of the increase; then divide this increase by the original amount, and express this quotient as a percent. In the example above, the percent increase would be found in the following way: the amount of the increase is $(30 - 24) = 6$. Therefore, the percent increase is $\frac{6}{24} = 0.25 = 25\%$.

Likewise, to find the percent decrease (for example, the price of an item is reduced from \$30 to \$24), first find the amount of the decrease; then divide this decrease by the original amount, and express this quotient as a percent. In the example above, the amount of decrease is $(30 - 24) = 6$.

Therefore, the percent decrease is $\frac{6}{30} = 0.20 = 20\%$.

Note that the percent increase from 24 to 30 is not the same as the percent decrease from 30 to 24.

In the following example, the increase is greater than 100 percent: If the cost of a certain house in 1983 was 300 percent of its cost in 1970, by what percent did the cost increase?

If n is the cost in 1970, then the percent increase is equal to $\dfrac{3n-n}{n} = \dfrac{2n}{n} = 2$, or 200%.

7. Powers and Roots of Numbers

When a number k is to be used n times as a factor in a product, it can be expressed as k^n, which means the nth power of k. For example, $2^2 = 2 \times 2 = 4$ and $2^3 = 2 \times 2 \times 2 = 8$ are powers of 2.

Squaring a number that is greater than 1, or raising it to a higher power, results in a larger number; squaring a number between 0 and 1 results in a smaller number. For example:

$$3^2 = 9 \qquad (9 > 3)$$
$$\left(\frac{1}{3}\right)^2 = \frac{1}{9} \qquad \left(\frac{1}{9} < \frac{1}{3}\right)$$
$$(0.1)^2 = 0.01 \qquad (0.01 < 0.1)$$

A *square root* of a number n is a number that, when squared, is equal to n. The square root of a negative number is not a real number. Every positive number n has two square roots, one positive and the other negative, but $\sqrt{n}$ denotes the positive number whose square is n. For example, $\sqrt{9}$ denotes 3. The two square roots of 9 are $\sqrt{9} = 3$ and $-\sqrt{9} = -3$.

Every real number r has exactly one real *cube root*, which is the number s such that $s^3 = r$. The real cube root of r is denoted by $\sqrt[3]{r}$. Since $2^3 = 8$, $\sqrt[3]{8} = 2$. Similarly, $\sqrt[3]{-8} = -2$, because $(-2)^3 = -8$.

8. Descriptive Statistics

A list of numbers, or numerical data, can be described by various statistical measures. One of the most common of these measures is the *average*, or *(arithmetic) mean*, which locates a type of "center" for the data. The average of n numbers is defined as the sum of the n numbers divided by n. For example, the average of 6, 4, 7, 10, and 4 is $\dfrac{6+4+7+10+4}{5} = \dfrac{31}{5} = 6.2$.

The *median* is another type of center for a list of numbers. To calculate the median of n numbers, first order the numbers from least to greatest; if n is odd, the median is defined as the middle number, whereas if n is even, the median is defined as the average of the two middle numbers. In the example above, the numbers, in order, are 4, 4, 6, 7, 10, and the median is 6, the middle number.

For the numbers 4, 6, 6, 8, 9, 12, the median is $\dfrac{6+8}{2} = 7$. Note that the mean of these numbers is 7.5.

The median of a set of data can be less than, equal to, or greater than the mean. Note that for a large set of data (for example, the salaries of 800 company employees), it is often true that about half of the data is less than the median and about half of the data is greater than the median; but this is not always the case, as the following data show.

3, 5, 7, 7, 7, 7, 7, 7, 8, 9, 9, 9, 9, 10, 10

Here the median is 7, but only $\dfrac{2}{15}$ of the data is less than the median.

The *mode* of a list of numbers is the number that occurs most frequently in the list. For example, the mode of 1, 3, 6, 4, 3, 5 is 3. A list of numbers may have more than one mode. For example, the list 1, 2, 3, 3, 3, 5, 7, 10, 10, 10, 20 has two modes, 3 and 10.

The degree to which numerical data are spread out or dispersed can be measured in many ways. The simplest measure of dispersion is the *range,* which is defined as the greatest value in the numerical data minus the least value. For example, the range of 11, 10, 5, 13, 21 is $21 - 5 = 16$. Note how the range depends on only two values in the data.

One of the most common measures of dispersion is the *standard deviation.* Generally speaking, the more the data are spread away from the mean, the greater the standard deviation. The standard deviation of n numbers can be calculated as follows: (1) find the arithmetic mean, (2) find the differences between the mean and each of the n numbers, (3) square each of the differences, (4) find the average of the squared differences, and (5) take the nonnegative square root of this average. Shown below is this calculation for the data 0, 7, 8, 10, 10, which have arithmetic mean 7.

x	$x - 7$	$(x - 7)^2$
0	−7	49
7	0	0
8	1	1
10	3	9
10	3	9
	Total	68

Standard deviation $\sqrt{\dfrac{68}{5}} \approx 3.7$

Notice that the standard deviation depends on every data value, although it depends most on values that are farthest from the mean. This is why a distribution with data grouped closely around the mean will have a smaller standard deviation than will data spread far from the mean. To illustrate this, compare the data 6, 6, 6.5, 7.5, 9, which also have mean 7. Note that the numbers in the second set of data seem to be grouped more closely around the mean of 7 than the numbers in the first set. This is reflected in the standard deviation, which is less for the second set (approximately 1.1) than for the first set (approximately 3.7).

There are many ways to display numerical data that show how the data are distributed. One simple way is with a *frequency distribution,* which is useful for data that have values occurring with varying frequencies. For example, the 20 numbers

$$
\begin{array}{cccccccccc}
-4 & 0 & 0 & -3 & -2 & -1 & -1 & 0 & -1 & -4 \\
-1 & -5 & 0 & -2 & 0 & -5 & -2 & 0 & 0 & -1
\end{array}
$$

are displayed on the next page in a frequency distribution by listing each different value x and the frequency f with which x occurs.

Data Value x	Frequency f
−5	2
−4	2
−3	1
−2	3
−1	5
0	7
Total	20

From the frequency distribution, one can readily compute descriptive statistics:

$$\text{Mean:} = \frac{(-5)(2)+(-4)(2)+(-3)(1)+(-2)(3)+(-1)(5)+(0)(7)}{20} = -1.6$$

Median: −1 (the average of the 10th and 11th numbers)

Mode: 0 (the number that occurs most frequently)

Range: $0 - (-5) = 5$

$$\text{Standard deviation:} \quad \sqrt{\frac{(-5+1.6)^2(2)+(-4+1.6)^2(2)+\ldots+(0+1.6)^2(7)}{20}} \approx 1.7$$

9. Sets

In mathematics a *set* is a collection of numbers or other objects. The objects are called the *elements* of the set. If S is a set having a finite number of elements, then the number of elements is denoted by $|S|$. Such a set is often defined by listing its elements; for example, $S = \{-5, 0, 1\}$ is a set with $|S| = 3$. The order in which the elements are listed in a set does not matter; thus $\{-5, 0, 1\} = \{0, 1, -5\}$. If all the elements of a set S are also elements of a set T, then S is a *subset* of T; for example, $S = \{-5, 0, 1\}$ is a subset of $T = \{-5, 0, 1, 4, 10\}$.

For any two sets A and B, the *union* of A and B is the set of all elements that are in A or in B or in both. The *intersection* of A and B is the set of all elements that are both in A and in B. The union is denoted by $A \cup B$ and the intersection is denoted by $A \cap B$. As an example, if $A = \{3, 4\}$ and $B = \{4, 5, 6\}$, then $A \cup B = \{3, 4, 5, 6\}$ and $A \cap B = \{4\}$. Two sets that have no elements in common are said to be *disjoint* or *mutually exclusive*.

The relationship between sets is often illustrated with a *Venn diagram* in which sets are represented by regions in a plane. For two sets S and T that are not disjoint and neither is a subset of the other, the intersection $S \cap T$ is represented by the shaded region of the diagram below.

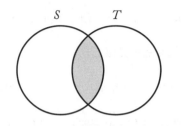

This diagram illustrates a fact about any two finite sets S and T: the number of elements in their union equals the sum of their individual numbers of elements minus the number of elements in their intersection (because the latter are counted twice in the sum); more concisely,

$$|S \cup T| = |S| + |T| - |S \cap T|.$$

This counting method is called the general addition rule for two sets. As a special case, if S and T are disjoint, then

$$|S \cup T| = |S| + |T|$$

since $|S \cap T| = 0$.

10. Counting Methods

There are some useful methods for counting objects and sets of objects without actually listing the elements to be counted. The following principle of multiplication is fundamental to these methods.

If an object is to be chosen from a set of m objects and a second object is to be chosen from a different set of n objects, then there are mn ways of choosing both objects simultaneously.

As an example, suppose the objects are items on a menu. If a meal consists of one entree and one dessert and there are 5 entrees and 3 desserts on the menu, then there are $5 \times 3 = 15$ different meals that can be ordered from the menu. As another example, each time a coin is flipped, there are two possible outcomes, heads and tails. If an experiment consists of 8 consecutive coin flips, then the experiment has 2^8 possible outcomes, where each of these outcomes is a list of heads and tails in some order.

A symbol that is often used with the multiplication principle is the *factorial*. If n is an integer greater than 1, then n factorial, denoted by the symbol $n!$, is defined as the product of all the integers from 1 to n. Therefore,

$$2! = (1)(2) = 2,$$
$$3! = (1)(2)(3) = 6,$$
$$4! = (1)(2)(3)(4) = 24, \text{ etc.}$$

Also, by definition, $0! = 1! = 1$.

The factorial is useful for counting the number of ways that a set of objects can be ordered. If a set of n objects is to be ordered from 1st to nth, then there are n choices for the 1st object, $n - 1$ choices for the 2nd object, $n - 2$ choices for the 3rd object, and so on, until there is only 1 choice for the nth object.

Thus, by the multiplication principle, the number of ways of ordering the n objects is

$$n(n-1)(n-2)\cdots(3)(2)(1) = n!.$$

For example, the number of ways of ordering the letters A, B, and C is 3!, or 6:

ABC, ACB, BAC, BCA, CAB, and CBA.

These orderings are called the *permutations* of the letters A, B, and C.

A permutation can be thought of as a selection process in which objects are selected one by one in a certain order. If the order of selection is not relevant and only k objects are to be selected from a larger set of n objects, a different counting method is employed.

Specifically, consider a set of n objects from which a complete selection of k objects is to be made without regard to order, where $0 \le k \le n$. Then the number of possible complete selections of k objects is called the number of *combinations* of n objects taken k at a time and is denoted by $\binom{n}{k}$.

The value of $\binom{n}{k}$ is given by $\binom{n}{k} = \dfrac{n!}{k!(n-k)!}$.

Note that $\binom{n}{k}$ is the number of k-element subsets of a set with n elements. For example, if $S = \{A, B, C, D, E\}$, then the number of 2-element subsets of S, or the number of combinations of 5 letters taken 2 at a time, is $\binom{5}{2} = \dfrac{5!}{2!3!} = \dfrac{120}{(2)(6)} = 10$.

The subsets are $\{A, B\}, \{A, C\}, \{A, D\}, \{A, E\}, \{B, C\}, \{B, D\}, \{B, E\}, \{C, D\}, \{C, E\}$, and $\{D, E\}$. Note that $\binom{5}{2} = 10 = \binom{5}{3}$ because every 2-element subset chosen from a set of 5 elements corresponds to a unique 3-element subset consisting of the elements *not* chosen.

In general, $\binom{n}{k} = \binom{n}{n-k}$.

11. Discrete Probability

Many of the ideas discussed in the preceding three topics are important to the study of discrete probability. Discrete probability is concerned with *experiments* that have a finite number of *outcomes*. Given such an experiment, an *event* is a particular set of outcomes. For example, rolling a number cube with faces numbered 1 to 6 (similar to a 6-sided die) is an experiment with 6 possible outcomes: 1, 2, 3, 4, 5, or 6. One event in this experiment is that the outcome is 4, denoted $\{4\}$; another event is that the outcome is an odd number: $\{1, 3, 5\}$.

The probability that an event E occurs, denoted by $P(E)$, is a number between 0 and 1, inclusive. If E has no outcomes, then E is *impossible* and $P(E) = 0$; if E is the set of all possible outcomes of the experiment, then E is *certain* to occur and $P(E) = 1$. Otherwise, E is possible but uncertain, and $0 < P(E) < 1$. If F is a subset of E, then $P(F) \le P(E)$. In the example above, if the probability of each of the 6 outcomes is the same, then the probability of each outcome is $\dfrac{1}{6}$, and the outcomes are said to be *equally likely.* For experiments in which all the individual outcomes are equally likely, the probability of an event E is

$$P(E) = \frac{\text{The number of outcomes in } E}{\text{The total number of possible outcomes}}.$$

In the example, the probability that the outcome is an odd number is

$$P(\{1,3,5\}) = \frac{|\{1,3,5\}|}{6} = \frac{3}{6} = \frac{1}{2}.$$

Given an experiment with events E and F, the following events are defined:
"not E" is the set of outcomes that are not outcomes in E;
"E or F" is the set of outcomes in E or F or both, that is, $E \cup F$;
"E and F" is the set of outcomes in both E and F, that is, $E \cap F$.

The probability that E does not occur is $P(\text{not } E) = 1 - P(E)$. The probability that "$E$ or F" occurs is $P(E \text{ or } F) = P(E) + P(F) - P(E \text{ and } F)$, using the general addition rule at the end of section 4.1.9 ("Sets"). For the number cube, if E is the event that the outcome is an odd number, $\{1, 3, 5\}$, and F is the event that the outcome is a prime number, $\{2, 3, 5\}$, then $P(E \text{ and } F) = P(\{3,5\}) = \frac{2}{6} = \frac{1}{3}$ and so

$$P(E \text{ or } F) = P(E) + P(F) - P(E \text{ and } F) = \frac{3}{6} + \frac{3}{6} - \frac{2}{6} = \frac{4}{6} = \frac{2}{3}.$$

Note that the event "E or F" is $E \cup F = \{1, 2, 3, 5\}$, and hence $P(E \text{ or } F) = \frac{|\{1,2,3,5\}|}{6} = \frac{4}{6} = \frac{2}{3}$.

If the event "E and F" is impossible (that is, $E \cap F$ has no outcomes), then E and F are said to be *mutually exclusive* events, and $P(E \text{ and } F) = 0$. Then the general addition rule is reduced to $P(E \text{ or } F) = P(E) + P(F)$.

This is the special addition rule for the probability of two mutually exclusive events.

Two events A and B are said to be *independent* if the occurrence of either event does not alter the probability that the other event occurs. For one roll of the number cube, let $A = \{2, 4, 6\}$ and let $B = \{5, 6\}$. Then the probability that A occurs is $P(A) = \frac{|A|}{6} = \frac{3}{6} = \frac{1}{2}$, while, *presuming B occurs,* the probability that A occurs is

$$\frac{|A \cap B|}{|B|} = \frac{|\{6\}|}{|\{5,6\}|} = \frac{1}{2}.$$

Similarly, the probability that B occurs is $P(B) = \frac{|B|}{6} = \frac{2}{6} = \frac{1}{3}$, while, *presuming A occurs,* the probability that B occurs is

$$\frac{|B \cap A|}{|A|} = \frac{|\{6\}|}{|\{2,4,6\}|} = \frac{1}{3}.$$

Thus, the occurrence of either event does not affect the probability that the other event occurs. Therefore, A and B are independent.

The following multiplication rule holds for any independent events E and F: $P(E \text{ and } F) = P(E)P(F)$.

For the independent events A and B above, $P(A \text{ and } B) = P(A)P(B) = \left(\dfrac{1}{2}\right)\left(\dfrac{1}{3}\right) = \left(\dfrac{1}{6}\right)$.

Note that the event "A and B" is $A \cap B = \{6\}$, and hence $P(A \text{ and } B) = P(\{6\}) = \dfrac{1}{6}$. It follows from the general addition rule and the multiplication rule above that if E and F are independent, then

$$P(E \text{ or } F) = P(E) + P(F) - P(E)P(F).$$

For a final example of some of these rules, consider an experiment with events A, B, and C for which $P(A) = 0.23$, $P(B) = 0.40$, and $P(C) = 0.85$. Also, suppose that events A and B are mutually exclusive and events B and C are independent. Then

$$P(A \text{ or } B) = P(A) + P(B) \text{ (since } A \text{ or } B \text{ are mutually exclusive)}$$
$$= 0.23 + 0.40$$
$$= 0.63$$
$$P(B \text{ or } C) = P(B) + P(C) - P(B)P(C) \text{ (by independence)}$$
$$= 0.40 + 0.85 - (0.40)(0.85)$$
$$= 0.91$$

Note that $P(A \text{ or } C)$ and $P(A \text{ and } C)$ cannot be determined using the information given. But it can be determined that A and C are *not* mutually exclusive since $P(A) + P(C) = 1.08$, which is greater than 1, and therefore cannot equal $P(A \text{ or } C)$; from this it follows that $P(A \text{ and } C) \geq 0.08$. One can also deduce that $P(A \text{ and } C) \leq P(A) = 0.23$, since $A \cap C$ is a subset of A, and that $P(A \text{ or } C) \geq P(C) = 0.85$ since C is a subset of $A \cup C$. Thus, one can conclude that $0.85 \leq P(A \text{ or } C) \leq 1$ and $0.08 \leq P(A \text{ and } C) \leq 0.23$.

3.2 Algebra

Algebra is based on the operations of arithmetic and on the concept of an *unknown quantity*, or *variable*. Letters such as x or n are used to represent unknown quantities. For example, suppose Pam has 5 more pencils than Fred. If F represents the number of pencils that Fred has, then the number of pencils that Pam has is $F + 5$. As another example, if Jim's present salary S is increased by 7%, then his new salary is $1.07S$. A combination of letters and arithmetic operations, such as

$F + 5, \dfrac{3x^2}{2x - 5}$, and $19x^2 - 6x + 3$, is called an *algebraic expression*.

The expression $19x^2 - 6x + 3$ consists of the *terms* $19x^2$, $-6x$, and 3, where 19 is the *coefficient* of x^2, -6 is the coefficient of x^1, and 3 is a *constant term* (or coefficient of $x^0 = 1$). Such an expression is called a *second degree* (or *quadratic*) *polynomial in x* since the highest power of x is 2. The expression $F + 5$ is a *first degree* (or *linear*) *polynomial in F* since the highest power of F is 1. The expression $\dfrac{3x^2}{2x - 5}$ is not a polynomial because it is not a sum of terms that are each powers of x multiplied by coefficients.

1. Simplifying Algebraic Expressions

Often when working with algebraic expressions, it is necessary to simplify them by factoring or combining *like* terms. For example, the expression $6x + 5x$ is equivalent to $(6 + 5)x$, or $11x$. In the expression $9x - 3y$, 3 is a factor common to both terms: $9x - 3y = 3(3x - y)$. In the expression $5x^2 + 6y$, there are no like terms and no common factors.

If there are common factors in the numerator and denominator of an expression, they can be divided out, provided that they are not equal to zero.

For example, if $x \neq 3$, then $\dfrac{x-3}{x-3}$ is equal to 1; therefore,

$$\frac{3xy - 9y}{x - 3} = \frac{3y(x-3)}{x-3}$$
$$= (3y)(1)$$
$$= 3y$$

To multiply two algebraic expressions, each term of one expression is multiplied by each term of the other expression. For example:

$$(3x - 4)(9y + x) = 3x(9y + x) - 4(9y + x)$$
$$= (3x)(9y) + (3x)(x) + (-4)(9y) + (-4)(x)$$
$$= 27xy + 3x^2 - 36y - 4x$$

An algebraic expression can be evaluated by substituting values of the unknowns in the expression. For example, if $x = 3$ and $y = -2$, then $3xy - x^2 + y$ can be evaluated as

$$3(3)(-2) - (3)^2 + (-2) = -18 - 9 - 2 = -29$$

2. Equations

A major focus of algebra is to solve equations involving algebraic expressions. Some examples of such equations are

$$5x - 2 = 9 - x \quad \text{(a linear equation with one unknown)}$$
$$3x + 1 = y - 2 \quad \text{(a linear equation with two unknowns)}$$
$$5x^2 + 3x - 2 = 7x \quad \text{(a quadratic equation with one unknown)}$$
$$\frac{x(x-3)(x^2+5)}{x-4} = 0 \quad \text{(an equation that is factored on one side with 0 on the other)}$$

The *solutions* of an equation with one or more unknowns are those values that make the equation true, or "satisfy the equation," when they are substituted for the unknowns of the equation. An equation may have no solution or one or more solutions. If two or more equations are to be solved together, the solutions must satisfy all the equations simultaneously.

Two equations having the same solution(s) are *equivalent equations*. For example, the equations

$$2 + x = 3$$
$$4 + 2x = 6$$

each have the unique solution $x = 1$. Note that the second equation is the first equation multiplied by 2. Similarly, the equations

$$3x - y = 6$$
$$6x - 2y = 12$$

have the same solutions, although in this case each equation has infinitely many solutions. If any value is assigned to x, then $3x - 6$ is a corresponding value for y that will satisfy both equations; for example, $x = 2$ and $y = 0$ is a solution to both equations, as is $x = 5$ and $y = 9$.

3. Solving Linear Equations with One Unknown

To solve a linear equation with one unknown (that is, to find the value of the unknown that satisfies the equation), the unknown should be isolated on one side of the equation. This can be done by performing the same mathematical operations on both sides of the equation. Remember that if the same number is added to or subtracted from both sides of the equation, this does not change the equality; likewise, multiplying or dividing both sides by the same nonzero number does not change the equality. For example, to solve the equation $\dfrac{5x - 6}{3} = 4$ for x, the variable x can be isolated using the following steps:

$$5x - 6 = 12 \quad \text{(multiplying by 3)}$$
$$5x = 18 \quad \text{(adding 6)}$$
$$x = \frac{18}{5} \quad \text{(dividing by 5)}$$

The solution, $\dfrac{18}{5}$, can be checked by substituting it for x in the original equation to determine whether it satisfies that equation:

$$\frac{5\left(\dfrac{18}{5}\right) - 6}{3} = \frac{18 - 6}{3} = \frac{12}{3} = 4$$

Therefore, $x = \dfrac{18}{5}$ is the solution.

4. Solving Two Linear Equations with Two Unknowns

For two linear equations with two unknowns, if the equations are equivalent, then there are infinitely many solutions to the equations, as illustrated at the end of section 4.2.2 ("Equations"). If the equations are not equivalent, then they have either one unique solution or no solution. The latter case is illustrated by the two equations:

$$3x + 4y = 17$$
$$6x + 8y = 35$$

Note that $3x + 4y = 17$ implies $6x + 8y = 34$, which contradicts the second equation. Thus, no values of x and y can simultaneously satisfy both equations.

There are several methods of solving two linear equations with two unknowns. With any method, if a contradiction is reached, then the equations have no solution; if a trivial equation such as $0 = 0$ is reached, then the equations are equivalent and have infinitely many solutions. Otherwise, a unique solution can be found.

One way to solve for the two unknowns is to express one of the unknowns in terms of the other using one of the equations, and then substitute the expression into the remaining equation to obtain an equation with one unknown. This equation can be solved and the value of the unknown substituted into either of the original equations to find the value of the other unknown. For example, the following two equations can be solved for x and y.

$$(1) \quad 3x + 2y = 11$$
$$(2) \quad x - y = 2$$

In equation (2), $x = 2 + y$. Substitute $2 + y$ in equation (1) for x:

$$3(2 + y) + 2y = 11$$
$$6 + 3y + 2y = 11$$
$$6 + 5y = 11$$
$$5y = 5$$
$$y = 1$$

If $y = 1$, then $x - 1 = 2$ and $x = 2 + 1 = 3$.

There is another way to solve for x and y by eliminating one of the unknowns. This can be done by making the coefficients of one of the unknowns the same (disregarding the sign) in both equations and either adding the equations or subtracting one equation from the other. For example, to solve the equations

$$(1) \quad 6x + 5y = 29$$
$$(2) \quad 4x - 3y = -6$$

by this method, multiply equation (1) by 3 and equation (2) by 5 to get

$$18x + 15y = 87$$
$$20x - 15y = -30$$

Adding the two equations eliminates y, yielding $38x = 57$, or $x = \dfrac{3}{2}$. Finally, substituting $\dfrac{3}{2}$ for x in one of the equations gives $y = 4$. These answers can be checked by substituting both values into both of the original equations.

5. Solving Equations by Factoring

Some equations can be solved by factoring. To do this, first add or subtract expressions to bring all the expressions to one side of the equation, with 0 on the other side. Then try to factor the nonzero side into a product of expressions. If this is possible, then using property (7) in section 4.1.4 ("Real Numbers") each of the factors can be set equal to 0, yielding several simpler equations that possibly can be solved. The solutions of the simpler equations will be solutions of the factored equation. As an example, consider the equation $x^3 - 2x^2 + x = -5(x-1)^2$:

$$x^3 - 2x^2 + x + 5(x-1)^2 = 0$$
$$x(x^2 - 2x + 1) + 5(x-1)^2 = 0$$
$$x(x-1)^2 + 5(x-1)^2 = 0$$
$$(x+5)(x-1)^2 = 0$$
$$x + 5 = 0 \text{ or } (x-1)^2 = 0$$
$$x = -5 \text{ or } x = 1.$$

For another example, consider $\dfrac{x(x-3)(x^2+5)}{x-4} = 0$. A fraction equals 0 if and only if its numerator equals 0. Thus, $x(x-3)(x^2+5) = 0$:

$$x = 0 \text{ or } x - 3 = 0 \text{ or } x^2 + 5 = 0$$
$$x = 0 \text{ or } x = 3 \text{ or } x^2 + 5 = 0.$$

But $x^2 + 5 = 0$ has no real solution because $x^2 + 5 > 0$ for every real number. Thus, the solutions are 0 and 3.

The solutions of an equation are also called the *roots* of the equation. These roots can be checked by substituting them into the original equation to determine whether they satisfy the equation.

6. Solving Quadratic Equations

The standard form for a *quadratic equation* is

$$ax^2 + bx + c = 0,$$

where a, b, and c are real numbers and $a \neq 0$; for example:

$$x^2 + 6x + 5 = 0$$
$$3x^2 - 2x = 0, \text{ and}$$
$$x^2 + 4 = 0$$

Some quadratic equations can easily be solved by factoring. For example:

$$(1) \qquad x^2 + 6x + 5 = 0$$
$$(x+5)(x+1) = 0$$
$$x + 5 = 0 \text{ or } x + 1 = 0$$
$$x = -5 \text{ or } x = -1$$

$$(2) \qquad 3x^2 - 3 = 8x$$

$$3x^2 - 8x - 3 = 0$$

$$(3x + 1)(x - 3) = 0$$

$$3x + 1 = 0 \text{ or } x - 3 = 0$$

$$x = -\frac{1}{3} \text{ or } x = 3$$

A quadratic equation has at most two real roots and may have just one or even no real root. For example, the equation $x^2 - 6x + 9 = 0$ can be expressed as $(x - 3)^2 = 0$, or $(x - 3)(x - 3) = 0$; thus the only root is 3. The equation $x^2 + 4 = 0$ has no real root; since the square of any real number is greater than or equal to zero, $x^2 + 4$ must be greater than zero.

An expression of the form $a^2 - b^2$ can be factored as $(a - b)(a + b)$.

For example, the quadratic equation $9x^2 - 25 = 0$ can be solved as follows.

$$(3x - 5)(3x + 5) = 0$$

$$3x - 5 = 0 \text{ or } 3x + 5 = 0$$

$$x = \frac{5}{3} \text{ or } x = -\frac{5}{3}$$

If a quadratic expression is not easily factored, then its roots can always be found using the *quadratic formula:* If $ax^2 + bx + c = 0$ $(a \neq 0)$, then the roots are

$$x = \frac{-b + \sqrt{b^2 - 4ac}}{2a} \text{ and } x = \frac{-b - \sqrt{b^2 - 4ac}}{2a}$$

These are two distinct real numbers unless $b^2 - 4ac \leq 0$. If $b^2 - 4ac = 0$, then these two expressions for x are equal to $-\dfrac{b}{2a}$, and the equation has only one root. If $b^2 - 4ac < 0$, then $\sqrt{b^2 - 4ac}$ is not a real number and the equation has no real roots.

7. Exponents

A positive integer exponent of a number or a variable indicates a product, and the positive integer is the number of times that the number or variable is a factor in the product. For example, x^5 means $(x)(x)(x)(x)(x)$; that is, x is a factor in the product 5 times.

Some rules about exponents follow.

Let x and y be any positive numbers, and let r and s be any positive integers.

(1) $(x^r)(x^s) = x^{(r+s)}$; for example, $(2^2)(2^3) = 2^{(2+3)} = 2^5 = 32$.

(2) $\dfrac{x^r}{x^s} = x^{(r-s)}$; for example, $\dfrac{4^5}{4^2} = 4^{5-2} = 4^3 = 64$.

(3) $(x^r)(y^r) = (xy)^r$; for example, $(3^3)(4^3) = 12^3 = 1{,}728$.

(4) $\left(\dfrac{x}{y}\right)^r = \dfrac{x^r}{y^r}$; for example, $\left(\dfrac{2}{3}\right)^3 = \dfrac{2^3}{3^3} = \dfrac{8}{27}$.

(5) $(x^r)^s = x^{rs} = (x^s)^r$; for example, $(x^3)^4 = x^{12} = (x^4)^3$.

(6) $x^{-r} = \dfrac{1}{x^r}$; for example, $3^{-2} = \dfrac{1}{3^2} = \dfrac{1}{9}$.

(7) $x^0 = 1$; for example, $6^0 = 1$.

(8) $x^{\frac{r}{s}} = \left(x^{\frac{1}{s}}\right)^r = \left(x^r\right)^{\frac{1}{s}} = \sqrt[s]{x^r}$; for example, $8^{\frac{2}{3}} = \left(8^{\frac{1}{3}}\right)^2 = \left(8^2\right)^{\frac{1}{3}} = \sqrt[3]{8^2} = \sqrt[3]{64} = 4$ and $9^{\frac{1}{2}} = \sqrt{9} = 3$.

It can be shown that rules 1 – 6 also apply when r and s are not integers and are not positive, that is, when r and s are any real numbers.

8. Inequalities

An *inequality* is a statement that uses one of the following symbols:

$\neq$ not equal to

$>$ greater than

$\geq$ greater than or equal to

$<$ less than

$\leq$ less than or equal to

Some examples of inequalities are $5x - 3 < 9$, $6x \geq y$, and $\dfrac{1}{2} < \dfrac{3}{4}$. Solving a linear inequality with one unknown is similar to solving an equation; the unknown is isolated on one side of the inequality. As in solving an equation, the same number can be added to or subtracted from both sides of the inequality, or both sides of an inequality can be multiplied or divided by a positive number without changing the truth of the inequality. However, multiplying or dividing an inequality by a negative number reverses the order of the inequality. For example, $6 > 2$, but $(-1)(6) < (-1)(2)$.

To solve the inequality $3x - 2 > 5$ for x, isolate x by using the following steps:

$$3x - 2 > 5$$
$$3x > 7 \quad \text{(adding 2 to both sides)}$$
$$x > \frac{7}{3} \quad \text{(dividing both sides by 3)}$$

To solve the inequality $\dfrac{5x - 1}{-2} < 3$ for x, isolate x by using the following steps:

$$\frac{5x - 1}{-2} < 3$$
$$5x - 1 > -6 \quad \text{(multiplying both sides by } -2)$$
$$5x > -5 \quad \text{(adding 1 to both sides)}$$
$$x > -1 \quad \text{(dividing both sides by 5)}$$

9. Absolute Value

The absolute value of x, denoted $|x|$, is defined to be x if $x \geq 0$ and $-x$ if $x < 0$. Note that $\sqrt{x^2}$ denotes the nonnegative square root of x^2, and so $\sqrt{x^2} = |x|$.

10. Functions

An algebraic expression in one variable can be used to define a *function* of that variable. A function is denoted by a letter such as f or g along with the variable in the expression. For example, the expression $x^3 - 5x^2 + 2$ defines a function f that can be denoted by

$$f(x) = x^3 - 5x^2 + 2.$$

The expression $\dfrac{2z+7}{\sqrt{z+1}}$ defines a function g that can be denoted by

$$g(z) = \frac{2z+7}{\sqrt{z+1}}.$$

The symbols "$f(x)$" or "$g(z)$" do not represent products; each is merely the symbol for an expression, and is read "f of x" or "g of z."

Function notation provides a short way of writing the result of substituting a value for a variable. If $x = 1$ is substituted in the first expression, the result can be written $f(1) = -2$, and $f(1)$ is called the "value of f at $x = 1$." Similarly, if $z = 0$ is substituted in the second expression, then the value of g at $z = 0$ is $g(0) = 7$.

Once a function $f(x)$ is defined, it is useful to think of the variable x as an input and $f(x)$ as the corresponding output. In any function there can be no more than one output for any given input. However, more than one input can give the same output; for example, if $h(x) = |x + 3|$, then $h(-4) = 1 = h(-2)$.

The set of all allowable inputs for a function is called the *domain* of the function. For f and g defined above, the domain of f is the set of all real numbers and the domain of g is the set of all numbers greater than -1. The domain of any function can be arbitrarily specified, as in the function defined by "$h(x) = 9x - 5$ for $0 \leq x \leq 10$." Without such a restriction, the domain is assumed to be all values of x that result in a real number when substituted into the function.

The domain of a function can consist of only the positive integers and possibly 0. For example, $a(n) = n^2 + \dfrac{n}{5}$ for $n = 0, 1, 2, 3, \ldots$.

Such a function is called a *sequence* and $a(n)$ is denoted by a_n. The value of the sequence a_n at $n = 3$ is $a_3 = 3^2 + \dfrac{3}{5} = 9.60$. As another example, consider the sequence defined by $b_n = (-1)^n (n!)$ for $n = 1, 2, 3, \ldots$. A sequence like this is often indicated by listing its values in the order $b_1, b_2, b_3, \ldots, b_n, \ldots$ as follows:

$-1, 2, -6, \ldots, (-1)^n(n!), \ldots$, and $(-1)^n(n!)$ is called the nth term of the sequence.

3.3 Geometry

1. Lines

In geometry, the word "line" refers to a straight line that extends without end in both directions.

The line above can be referred to as line PQ or line ℓ. The part of the line from P to Q is called a *line segment*. P and Q are the *endpoints* of the segment. The notation $\overline{PQ}$ is used to denote line segment PQ and PQ is used to denote the length of the segment.

2. Intersecting Lines and Angles

If two lines intersect, the opposite angles are called *vertical angles* and have the same measure. In the figure

$\angle PRQ$ and $\angle SRT$ are vertical angles and $\angle QRS$ and $\angle PRT$ are vertical angles. Also, $x + y = 180°$ since PRS is a straight line.

3. Perpendicular Lines

An angle that has a measure of 90° is a *right angle*. If two lines intersect at right angles, the lines are *perpendicular*. For example:

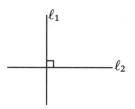

ℓ_1 and ℓ_2 above are perpendicular, denoted by $\ell_1 \perp \ell_2$. A right angle symbol in an angle of intersection indicates that the lines are perpendicular.

4. Parallel Lines

If two lines that are in the same plane do not intersect, the two lines are *parallel*. In the figure

lines ℓ_1 and ℓ_2 are parallel, denoted by $\ell_1 \parallel \ell_2$. If two parallel lines are intersected by a third line, as shown below, then the angle measures are related as indicated, where $x + y = 180°$.

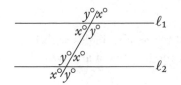

5. Polygons (Convex)

A *polygon* is a closed plane figure formed by three or more line segments, called the *sides* of the polygon. Each side intersects exactly two other sides at their endpoints. The points of intersection of the sides are *vertices*. The term "polygon" will be used to mean a convex polygon, that is, a polygon in which each interior angle has a measure of less than 180°.

The following figures are polygons:

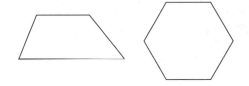

The following figures are not polygons:

A polygon with three sides is a *triangle*; with four sides, a *quadrilateral*; with five sides, a *pentagon*; and with six sides, a *hexagon*.

The sum of the interior angle measures of a triangle is 180°. In general, the sum of the interior angle measures of a polygon with n sides is equal to $(n - 2)180°$. For example, this sum for a pentagon is $(5 - 2)180° = (3)180° = 540°$.

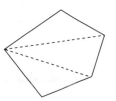

Note that a pentagon can be partitioned into three triangles and therefore the sum of the angle measures can be found by adding the sum of the angle measures of three triangles.

The *perimeter* of a polygon is the sum of the lengths of its sides.

The commonly used phrase "area of a triangle" (or any other plane figure) is used to mean the area of the region enclosed by that figure.

6. Triangles

There are several special types of triangles with important properties. But one property that all triangles share is that the sum of the lengths of any two of the sides is greater than the length of the third side, as illustrated below.

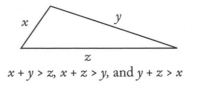

$x + y > z$, $x + z > y$, and $y + z > x$

An *equilateral* triangle has all sides of equal length. All angles of an equilateral triangle have equal measure. An *isosceles* triangle has at least two sides of the same length. If two sides of a triangle have the same length, then the two angles opposite those sides have the same measure. Conversely, if two angles of a triangle have the same measure, then the sides opposite those angles have the same length. In isosceles triangle *PQR* below, $x = y$ since $PQ = QR$.

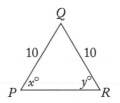

A triangle that has a right angle is a *right* triangle. In a right triangle, the side opposite the right angle is the *hypotenuse*, and the other two sides are the *legs*. An important theorem concerning right triangles is the *Pythagorean theorem*, which states: In a right triangle, the square of the length of the hypotenuse is equal to the sum of the squares of the lengths of the legs.

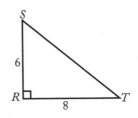

In the figure above, $\triangle RST$ is a right triangle, so $(RS)^2 + (RT)^2 = (ST)^2$. Here, $RS = 6$ and $RT = 8$, so $ST = 10$, since $6^2 + 8^2 = 36 + 64 = 100 = (ST)^2$ and $ST = \sqrt{100}$. Any triangle in which the lengths of the sides are in the ratio 3:4:5 is a right triangle. In general, if a, b, and c are the lengths of the sides of a triangle and $a^2 + b^2 = c^2$, then the triangle is a right triangle.

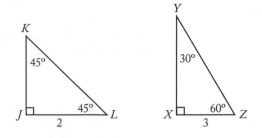

In 45°– 45°– 90° triangles, the lengths of the sides are in the ratio $1:1:\sqrt{2}$. For example, in $\triangle JKL$, if $JL = 2$, then $JK = 2$ and $KL = 2\sqrt{2}$. In 30°– 60°– 90° triangles, the lengths of the sides are in the ratio $1:\sqrt{3}:2$. For example, in $\triangle XYZ$, if $XZ = 3$, then $XY = 3\sqrt{3}$ and $YZ = 6$.

The *altitude* of a triangle is the segment drawn from a vertex perpendicular to the side opposite that vertex. Relative to that vertex and altitude, the opposite side is called the *base*.

The area of a triangle is equal to:

$$\frac{(\text{the length of the altitude}) \times (\text{the length of the base})}{2}$$

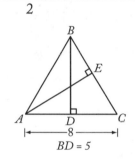

In $\triangle ABC$, $\overline{BD}$ is the altitude to base $\overline{AC}$ and $\overline{AE}$ is the altitude to base $\overline{BC}$. The area of $\triangle ABC$ is equal to

$$\frac{BD \times AC}{2} = \frac{5 \times 8}{2} = 20.$$

The area is also equal to $\frac{AE \times BC}{2}$. If $\triangle ABC$ above is isosceles and $AB = BC$, then altitude $\overline{BD}$ bisects the base; that is, $AD = DC = 4$. Similarly, any altitude of an equilateral triangle bisects the side to which it is drawn.

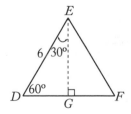

In equilateral triangle DEF, if $DE = 6$, then $DG = 3$ and $EG = 3\sqrt{3}$. The area of $\triangle DEF$ is equal to $\frac{3\sqrt{3} \times 6}{2} = 9\sqrt{3}$.

7. Quadrilaterals

A polygon with four sides is a *quadrilateral*. A quadrilateral in which both pairs of opposite sides are parallel is a *parallelogram*. The opposite sides of a parallelogram also have equal length.

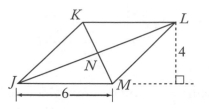

In parallelogram *JKLM*, $\overline{JK} \parallel \overline{LM}$ and *JK* = *LM*; $\overline{KL} \parallel \overline{JM}$ and *KL* = *JM*.

The diagonals of a parallelogram bisect each other (that is, *KN* = *NM* and *JN* = *NL*).

The area of a parallelogram is equal to

(the length of the altitude) × (the length of the base).

The area of *JKLM* is equal to $4 \times 6 = 24$.

A parallelogram with right angles is a *rectangle,* and a rectangle with all sides of equal length is a *square.*

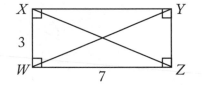

The perimeter of *WXYZ* = 2(3) + 2(7) = 20 and the area of *WXYZ* is equal to $3 \times 7 = 21$. The diagonals of a rectangle are equal; therefore $WY = XZ = \sqrt{9+49} = \sqrt{58}$.

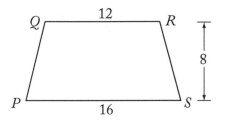

A quadrilateral with two sides that are parallel, as shown above, is a *trapezoid*. The area of trapezoid *PQRS* may be calculated as follows:

$$\frac{1}{2}(\text{the sum of the lengths of the bases})(\text{the height}) = \frac{1}{2}(QR+PS)(8) = \frac{1}{2}(28 \times 8) = 112.$$

8. Circles

A *circle* is a set of points in a plane that are all located the same distance from a fixed point (the *center* of the circle).

A *chord* of a circle is a line segment that has its endpoints on the circle. A chord that passes through the center of the circle is a *diameter* of the circle. A *radius* of a circle is a segment from the center of the circle to a point on the circle. The words "diameter" and "radius" are also used to refer to the lengths of these segments.

The *circumference* of a circle is the distance around the circle. If r is the radius of the circle, then the circumference is equal to $2\pi r$, where π is approximately $\frac{22}{7}$ or 3.14. The *area* of a circle of radius r is equal to πr^2.

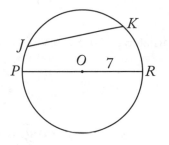

In the circle above, O is the center of the circle and $\overline{JK}$ and $\overline{PR}$ are chords. $\overline{PR}$ is a diameter and $\overline{OR}$ is a radius. If $OR = 7$, then the circumference of the circle is $2\pi(7) = 14\pi$ and the area of the circle is $\pi(7)^2 = 49\pi$.

The number of degrees of arc in a circle (or the number of degrees in a complete revolution) is 360.

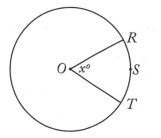

In the circle with center O above, the length of arc RST is $\frac{x}{360}$ of the circumference of the circle; for example, if $x = 60$, then arc RST has length $\frac{1}{6}$ of the circumference of the circle.

A line that has exactly one point in common with a circle is said to be *tangent* to the circle, and that common point is called the *point of tangency*. A radius or diameter with an endpoint at the point of tangency is perpendicular to the tangent line, and, conversely, a line that is perpendicular to a radius or diameter at one of its endpoints is tangent to the circle at that endpoint.

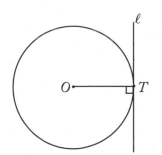

The line ℓ above is tangent to the circle and radius $\overline{OT}$ is perpendicular to ℓ.

If each vertex of a polygon lies on a circle, then the polygon is *inscribed* in the circle and the circle is *circumscribed* about the polygon. If each side of a polygon is tangent to a circle, then the polygon is *circumscribed* about the circle and the circle is *inscribed* in the polygon.

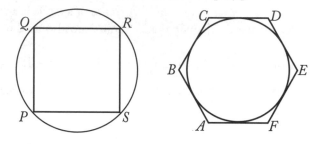

In the figure above, quadrilateral *PQRS* is inscribed in a circle and hexagon *ABCDEF* is circumscribed about a circle.

If a triangle is inscribed in a circle so that one of its sides is a diameter of the circle, then the triangle is a right triangle.

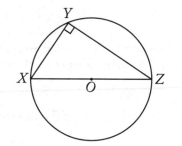

In the circle above, $\overline{XZ}$ is a diameter and the measure of $\angle XYZ$ is 90°.

9. Rectangular Solids and Cylinders

A *rectangular solid* is a three-dimensional figure formed by 6 rectangular surfaces, as shown below. Each rectangular surface is a *face*. Each solid or dotted line segment is an *edge*, and each point at which the edges meet is a *vertex*. A rectangular solid has 6 faces, 12 edges, and 8 vertices. Opposite faces are parallel rectangles that have the same dimensions. A rectangular solid in which all edges are of equal length is a *cube*.

The *surface area* of a rectangular solid is equal to the sum of the areas of all the faces. The *volume* is equal to

$$(\text{length}) \times (\text{width}) \times (\text{height});$$

in other words, (area of base) × (height).

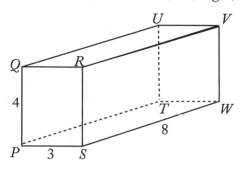

In the rectangular solid above, the dimensions are 3, 4, and 8. The surface area is equal to $2(3 \times 4) + 2(3 \times 8) + 2(4 \times 8) = 136$. The volume is equal to $3 \times 4 \times 8 = 96$.

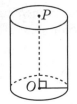

The figure above is a right circular *cylinder*. The two bases are circles of the same size with centers O and P, respectively, and altitude (height) $\overline{OP}$ is perpendicular to the bases. The surface area of a right circular cylinder with a base of radius r and height h is equal to $2(\pi r^2) + 2\pi rh$ (the sum of the areas of the two bases plus the area of the curved surface).

The volume of a cylinder is equal to $\pi r^2 h$, that is,

$$(\text{area of base}) \times (\text{height}).$$

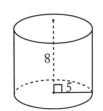

In the cylinder above, the surface area is equal to

$$2(25\pi) + 2\pi(5)(8) = 130\pi,$$

and the volume is equal to

$$25\pi(8) = 200\pi.$$

10. Coordinate Geometry

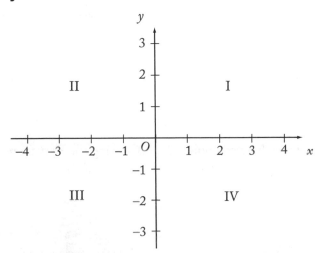

The figure above shows the (rectangular) *coordinate plane*. The horizontal line is called the *x-axis* and the perpendicular vertical line is called the *y-axis*. The point at which these two axes intersect, designated O, is called the *origin*. The axes divide the plane into four quadrants, I, II, III, and IV, as shown.

Each point in the plane has an *x-coordinate* and a *y-coordinate*. A point is identified by an ordered pair (x,y) of numbers in which the x-coordinate is the first number and the y-coordinate is the second number.

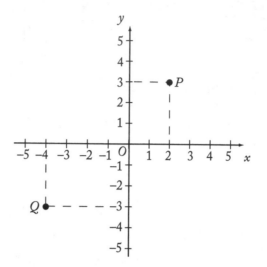

In the graph above, the (x,y) coordinates of point P are (2,3) since P is 2 units to the right of the y-axis (that is, $x = 2$) and 3 units above the x-axis (that is, $y = 3$). Similarly, the (x,y) coordinates of point Q are (−4,−3). The origin O has coordinates (0,0).

One way to find the distance between two points in the coordinate plane is to use the Pythagorean theorem.

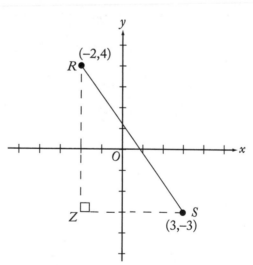

To find the distance between points R and S using the Pythagorean theorem, draw the triangle as shown. Note that Z has (x,y) coordinates (−2,−3), $RZ = 7$, and $ZS = 5$. Therefore, the distance between R and S is equal to

$$\sqrt{7^2 + 5^2} = \sqrt{74}.$$

For a line in the coordinate plane, the coordinates of each point on the line satisfy a linear equation of the form $y = mx + b$ (or the form $x = a$ if the line is vertical). For example, each point on the line on the next page satisfies the equation $y = -\frac{1}{2}x + 1$. One can verify this for the points (−2,2), (2,0), and (0,1) by substituting the respective coordinates for x and y in the equation.

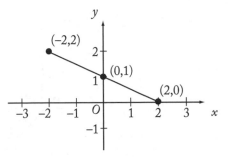

In the equation $y = mx + b$ of a line, the coefficient m is the *slope* of the line and the constant term b is the *y-intercept* of the line. For any two points on the line, the slope is defined to be the ratio of the difference in the y-coordinates to the difference in the x-coordinates. Using $(-2, 2)$ and $(2, 0)$ above, the slope is

$$\frac{\text{The difference in the } y\text{-coordinates}}{\text{The difference in the } x\text{-coordinates}} = \frac{0-2}{2-(-2)} = \frac{-2}{4} = -\frac{1}{2}.$$

The y-intercept is the y-coordinate of the point at which the line intersects the y-axis. For the line above, the y-intercept is 1, and this is the resulting value of y when x is set equal to 0 in the equation $y = -\frac{1}{2}x + 1$. The *x-intercept* is the x-coordinate of the point at which the line intersects the x-axis. The x-intercept can be found by setting $y = 0$ and solving for x. For the line $y = -\frac{1}{2}x + 1$, this gives

$$-\frac{1}{2}x + 1 = 0$$

$$-\frac{1}{2}x = -1$$

$$x = 2.$$

Thus, the x-intercept is 2.

Given any two points (x_1, y_1) and (x_2, y_2) with $x_1 \neq x_2$, the equation of the line passing through these points can be found by applying the definition of slope. Since the slope is $m = \frac{y_2 - y_1}{x_2 - x_1}$, then using a point known to be on the line, say (x_1, y_1), any point (x, y) on the line must satisfy $\frac{y - y_1}{x - x_1} = m$, or

$y - y_1 = m(x - x_1)$. (Using (x_2, y_2) as the known point would yield an equivalent equation.) For example, consider the points $(-2, 4)$ and $(3, -3)$ on the line below.

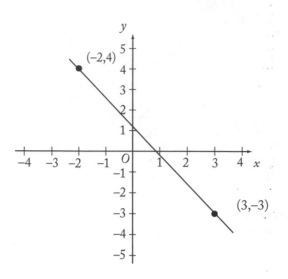

The slope of this line is $\dfrac{-3-4}{3-(-2)} = \dfrac{-7}{5}$, so an equation of this line can be found using the point $(3,-3)$ as follows:

$$y-(-3) = -\frac{7}{5}(x-3)$$

$$y+3 = -\frac{7}{5}x + \frac{21}{5}$$

$$y = -\frac{7}{5}x + \frac{6}{5}$$

The y-intercept is $\dfrac{6}{5}$. The *x-intercept* can be found as follows:

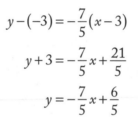

Both of these intercepts can be seen on the graph.

If the slope of a line is negative, the line slants downward from left to right; if the slope is positive, the line slants upward. If the slope is 0, the line is horizontal; the equation of such a line is of the form $y = b$ since $m = 0$. For a vertical line, slope is not defined, and the equation is of the form $x = a$, where a is the x-intercept.

There is a connection between graphs of lines in the coordinate plane and solutions of two linear equations with two unknowns. If two linear equations with unknowns x and y have a unique solution, then the graphs of the equations are two lines that intersect in one point, which is the solution. If the equations are equivalent, then they represent the same line with infinitely many points or solutions. If the equations have no solution, then they represent parallel lines, which do not intersect.

There is also a connection between functions (see section 4.2.10) and the coordinate plane. If a function is graphed in the coordinate plane, the function can be understood in different and useful ways. Consider the function defined by

$$f(x) = -\frac{7}{5}x + \frac{6}{5}.$$

If the value of the function, $f(x)$, is equated with the variable y, then the graph of the function in the xy-coordinate plane is simply the graph of the equation

$$y = -\frac{7}{5}x + \frac{6}{5}$$

shown above. Similarly, any function $f(x)$ can be graphed by equating y with the value of the function:

$$y = f(x).$$

So for any x in the domain of the function f, the point with coordinates $(x, f(x))$ is on the graph of f, and the graph consists entirely of these points.

As another example, consider a quadratic polynomial function defined by $f(x) = x^2 - 1$. One can plot several points $(x, f(x))$ on the graph to understand the connection between a function and its graph:

x	$f(x)$
−2	3
−1	0
0	−1
1	0
2	3

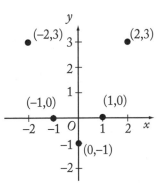

If all the points were graphed for $-2 \le x \le 2$, then the graph would appear as follows.

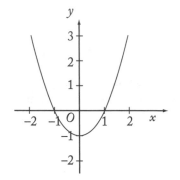

The graph of a quadratic function is called a *parabola* and always has the shape of the curve above, although it may be upside down or have a greater or lesser width. Note that the roots of the equation $f(x) = x^2 - 1 = 0$ are $x = 1$ and $x = -1$; these coincide with the x-intercepts since x-intercepts are found by setting $y = 0$ and solving for x. Also, the y-intercept is $f(0) = -1$ because this is the value of y corresponding to $x = 0$. For any function f, the x-intercepts are the solutions of the equation $f(x) = 0$ and the y-intercept is the value $f(0)$.

3.4 Word Problems

Many of the principles discussed in this chapter are used to solve word problems. The following discussion of word problems illustrates some of the techniques and concepts used in solving such problems.

1. Rate Problems

The distance that an object travels is equal to the product of the average speed at which it travels and the amount of time it takes to travel that distance, that is,

$$\text{Rate} \times \text{Time} = \text{Distance}.$$

Example 1: If a car travels at an average speed of 70 kilometers per hour for 4 hours, how many kilometers does it travel?

Solution: Since rate × time = distance, simply multiply 70 km/hour × 4 hours. Thus, the car travels 280 kilometers in 4 hours.

To determine the average rate at which an object travels, divide the total distance traveled by the total amount of traveling time.

Example 2: On a 400-mile trip, Car X traveled half the distance at 40 miles per hour (mph) and the other half at 50 mph. What was the average speed of Car X ?

Solution: First it is necessary to determine the amount of traveling time. During the first 200 miles, the car traveled at 40 mph; therefore, it took $\dfrac{200}{40} = 5$ hours to travel the first 200 miles.

During the second 200 miles, the car traveled at 50 mph; therefore, it took $\frac{200}{50} = 4$ hours to travel the second 200 miles. Thus, the average speed of Car X was $\frac{400}{9} = 44\frac{4}{9}$ mph. Note that the average speed is *not* $\frac{40+50}{2} = 45$.

Some rate problems can be solved by using ratios.

Example 3: If 5 shirts cost $44, then, at this rate, what is the cost of 8 shirts?

Solution: If c is the cost of the 8 shirts, then $\frac{5}{44} = \frac{8}{c}$. Cross multiplication results in the equation

$$5c = 8 \times 44 = 352$$

$$c = \frac{352}{5} = 70.40$$

The 8 shirts cost $70.40.

2. Work Problems

In a work problem, the rates at which certain persons or machines work alone are usually given, and it is necessary to compute the rate at which they work together (or vice versa).

The basic formula for solving work problems is $\frac{1}{r} + \frac{1}{s} = \frac{1}{h}$, where r and s are, for example, the number of hours it takes Rae and Sam, respectively, to complete a job when working alone, and h is the number of hours it takes Rae and Sam to do the job when working together. The reasoning is that in 1 hour Rae does $\frac{1}{r}$ of the job, Sam does $\frac{1}{s}$ of the job, and Rae and Sam together do $\frac{1}{h}$ of the job.

Example 1: If Machine X can produce 1,000 bolts in 4 hours and Machine Y can produce 1,000 bolts in 5 hours, in how many hours can Machines X and Y, working together at these constant rates, produce 1,000 bolts?

Solution:

$$\frac{1}{4} + \frac{1}{5} = \frac{1}{h}$$

$$\frac{5}{20} + \frac{4}{20} = \frac{1}{h}$$

$$\frac{9}{20} = \frac{1}{h}$$

$$9h = 20$$

$$h = \frac{20}{9} = 2\frac{2}{9}$$

Working together, Machines X and Y can produce 1,000 bolts in $2\frac{2}{9}$ hours.

Example 2: If Art and Rita can do a job in 4 hours when working together at their respective constant rates and Art can do the job alone in 6 hours, in how many hours can Rita do the job alone?

Solution:

$$\frac{1}{6} + \frac{1}{R} = \frac{1}{4}$$

$$\frac{R+6}{6R} = \frac{1}{4}$$

$$4R + 24 = 6R$$

$$24 = 2R$$

$$12 = R$$

Working alone, Rita can do the job in 12 hours.

3. Mixture Problems

In mixture problems, substances with different characteristics are combined, and it is necessary to determine the characteristics of the resulting mixture.

Example 1: If 6 pounds of nuts that cost $1.20 per pound are mixed with 2 pounds of nuts that cost $1.60 per pound, what is the cost per pound of the mixture?

Solution: The total cost of the 8 pounds of nuts is

$$6(\$1.20) + 2(\$1.60) = \$10.40.$$

The cost per pound is

$$\frac{\$10.40}{8} = \$1.30.$$

Example 2: How many liters of a solution that is 15 percent salt must be added to 5 liters of a solution that is 8 percent salt so that the resulting solution is 10 percent salt?

Solution: Let n represent the number of liters of the 15% solution. The amount of salt in the 15% solution $[0.15n]$ plus the amount of salt in the 8% solution $[(0.08)(5)]$ must be equal to the amount of salt in the 10% mixture $[0.10(n + 5)]$. Therefore,

$$0.15n + 0.08(5) = 0.10(n + 5)$$

$$15n + 40 = 10n + 50$$

$$5n = 10$$

$$n = 2 \text{ liters}$$

Two liters of the 15% salt solution must be added to the 8% solution to obtain the 10% solution.

4. Interest Problems

Interest can be computed in two basic ways. With simple annual interest, the interest is computed on the principal only and is equal to (principal) × (interest rate) × (time). If interest is compounded, then interest is computed on the principal as well as on any interest already earned.

Example 1: If $8,000 is invested at 6 percent simple annual interest, how much interest is earned after 3 months?

Solution: Since the annual interest rate is 6%, the interest for 1 year is

$$(0.06)(\$8,000) = \$480.$$

The interest earned in 3 months is $\frac{3}{12}(\$480) = \$120.$

Example 2: If $10,000 is invested at 10 percent annual interest, compounded semiannually, what is the balance after 1 year?

Solution: The balance after the first 6 months would be

$$10,000 + (10,000)(0.05) = \$10,500.$$

The balance after one year would be $\quad 10,500 + (10,500)(0.05) = \$11,025.$

Note that the interest rate for each 6-month period is 5%, which is half of the 10% annual rate. The balance after one year can also be expressed as

$$10,000\left(1 + \frac{0.10}{2}\right)^2 \text{ dollars.}$$

5. Discount

If a price is discounted by n percent, then the price becomes $(100 - n)$ percent of the original price.

Example 1: A certain customer paid $24 for a dress. If that price represented a 25 percent discount on the original price of the dress, what was the original price of the dress?

Solution: If p is the original price of the dress, then $0.75p$ is the discounted price and $0.75p = \$24$, or $p = \$32$. The original price of the dress was $32.

Example 2: The price of an item is discounted by 20 percent and then this reduced price is discounted by an additional 30 percent. These two discounts are equal to an overall discount of what percent?

Solution: If p is the original price of the item, then $0.8p$ is the price after the first discount. The price after the second discount is $(0.7)(0.8)p = 0.56p$. This represents an overall discount of 44 percent $(100\% - 56\%)$.

6. Profit

Gross profit is equal to revenues minus expenses, or selling price minus cost.

Example: A certain appliance costs a merchant $30. At what price should the merchant sell the appliance in order to make a gross profit of 50 percent of the cost of the appliance?

Solution: If s is the selling price of the appliance, then $s - 30 = (0.5)(30)$, or $s = \$45$. The merchant should sell the appliance for $45.

7. Sets

If S is the set of numbers 1, 2, 3, and 4, you can write $S = \{1, 2, 3, 4\}$. Sets can also be represented by Venn diagrams. That is, the relationship among the members of sets can be represented by circles.

Example 1: Each of 25 people is enrolled in history, mathematics, or both. If 20 are enrolled in history and 18 are enrolled in mathematics, how many are enrolled in both history and mathematics?

Solution: The 25 people can be divided into three sets: those who study history only, those who study mathematics only, and those who study history and mathematics. Thus a Venn diagram may be drawn as follows, where n is the number of people enrolled in both courses, $20 - n$ is the number enrolled in history only, and $18 - n$ is the number enrolled in mathematics only.

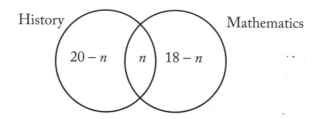

Since there is a total of 25 people, $(20 - n) + n + (18 - n) = 25$, or $n = 13$. Thirteen people are enrolled in both history and mathematics. Note that $20 + 18 - 13 = 25$, which is the general addition rule for two sets (see section 4.1.9).

Example 2: In a certain production lot, 40 percent of the toys are red and the remaining toys are green. Half of the toys are small and half are large. If 10 percent of the toys are red and small, and 40 toys are green and large, how many of the toys are red and large?

Solution: For this kind of problem, it is helpful to organize the information in a table:

	Red	Green	Total
Small	10%		50%
Large			50%
Total	40%	60%	100%

The numbers in the table are the percentages given. The following percentages can be computed on the basis of what is given:

	Red	Green	Total
Small	10%	40%	50%
Large	30%	20%	50%
Total	40%	60%	100%

Since 20% of the number of toys (n) are green and large, $0.20n = 40$ (40 toys are green and large), or $n = 200$. Therefore, 30% of the 200 toys, or $(0.3)(200) = 60$, are red and large.

8. Geometry Problems

The following is an example of a word problem involving geometry.

Example:

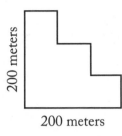

200 meters

200 meters

The figure above shows an aerial view of a piece of land. If all angles shown are right angles, what is the perimeter of the piece of land?

Solution: For reference, label the figure as

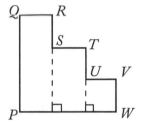

If all the angles are right angles, then $QR + ST + UV = PW$, and $RS + TU + VW = PQ$. Hence, the perimeter of the land is $2PW + 2PQ = 2 \times 200 + 2 \times 200 = 800$ meters.

9. Measurement Problems

Some questions on the GMAT involve metric units of measure, whereas others involve English units of measure. However, except for units of time, if a question requires conversion from one unit of measure to another, the relationship between those units will be given.

Example: A train travels at a constant rate of 25 meters per second. How many kilometers does it travel in 5 minutes? (1 kilometer = 1,000 meters)

Solution: In 1 minute the train travels $(25)(60) = 1,500$ meters, so in 5 minutes it travels 7,500 meters. Since 1 kilometer = 1,000 meters, it follows that 7,500 meters equals $\dfrac{7,500}{1,000}$, or 7.5 kilometers.

10. Data Interpretation

Occasionally a question or set of questions will be based on data provided in a table or graph. Some examples of tables and graphs are given below.

Example 1:

Population by Age Group (in thousands)	
Age	Population
17 years and under	63,376
18–44 years	86,738
45–64 years	43,845
65 years and over	24,054

How many people are 44 years old or younger?

Solution: The figures in the table are given in thousands. The answer in thousands can be obtained by adding 63,376 thousand and 86,738 thousand. The result is 150,114 thousand, which is 150,114,000.

Example 2:

AVERAGE TEMPERATURE AND PRECIPITATION IN CITY X

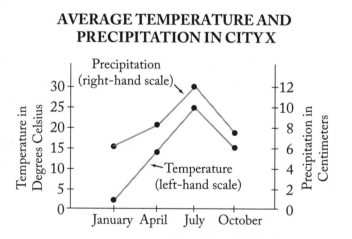

What are the average temperature and precipitation in City X during April?

Solution: Note that the scale on the left applies to the temperature line graph and the one on the right applies to the precipitation line graph. According to the graph, during April the average temperature is approximately 14° Celsius and the average precipitation is approximately 8 centimeters.

Example 3:

DISTRIBUTION OF AL'S WEEKLY NET SALARY

Al's weekly net salary is $350. To how many of the categories listed was at least $80 of Al's weekly net salary allocated?

Solution: In the circle graph, the relative sizes of the sectors are proportional to their corresponding values and the sum of the percents given is 100%. Note that $\frac{80}{350}$ is approximately 23%, so at least $80 was allocated to each of 2 categories—Rent and Utilities, and Savings—since their allocations are each greater than 23%.

4.0 Problem Solving

4.0 Problem Solving

The Quantitative section of the GMAT® exam uses problem solving and data sufficiency questions to gauge your skill level. This chapter focuses on problem solving questions. Remember that quantitative questions require knowledge of the following:

- Arithmetic
- Elementary algebra
- Commonly known concepts of geometry

Problem solving questions are designed to test your basic mathematical skills and understanding of elementary mathematical concepts, as well as your ability to reason quantitatively, solve quantitative problems, and interpret graphic data. The mathematics knowledge required to answer the questions is no more advanced than what is generally taught in secondary school (or high school) mathematics classes.

In these questions, you are asked to solve each problem and select the best of the five answer choices given. Begin by reading the question thoroughly to determine exactly what information is given and to make sure you understand what is being asked. Scan the answer choices to understand your options. If the problem seems simple, take a few moments to see whether you can determine the answer. Then, check your answer against the choices provided.

If you do not see your answer among the choices, or if the problem is complicated, take a closer look at the answer choices and think again about what the problem is asking. See whether you can eliminate some of the answer choices and narrow down your options. If you are still unable to narrow the answer down to a single choice, reread the question. Keep in mind that the answer will be based solely on the information provided in the question—don't allow your own experience and assumptions to interfere with your ability to find the correct answer to the question.

If you find yourself stuck on a question or unable to select the single correct answer, keep in mind that you have about two minutes to answer each quantitative question. You may run out of time if you take too long to answer any one question; you may simply need to pick the answer that seems to make the most sense. Although guessing is generally not the best way to achieve a high GMAT score, making an educated guess is a good strategy for answering questions you are unsure of. Even if your answer to a particular question is incorrect, your answers to other questions will allow the test to accurately gauge your ability level.

The following pages include test-taking strategies, directions that will apply to questions of this type, sample questions, an answer key, and explanations for all the problems. These explanations present problem solving strategies that could be helpful in answering the questions.

4.1 Test-Taking Strategies

1.   **Pace yourself.**

     Consult the on-screen timer periodically. Work as carefully as possible, but do not spend valuable time checking answers or pondering problems that you find difficult.

2.   **Use the erasable notepad provided.**

     Working a problem out may help you avoid errors in solving the problem. If diagrams or figures are not presented, it may help to draw your own.

3.   **Read each question carefully to determine what is being asked.**

     For word problems, take one step at a time, reading each sentence carefully and translating the information into equations or other useful mathematical representations.

4.   **Scan the answer choices before attempting to answer a question.**

     Scanning the answers can prevent you from putting answers in a form that is not given (e.g., finding the answer in decimal form, such as 0.25, when the choices are given in fractional form, such as $\frac{1}{4}$). Also, if the question requires approximations, a shortcut could serve well (e.g., you may be able to approximate 48 percent of a number by using half).

5.   **Don't waste time trying to solve a problem that is too difficult for you.**

     Make your best guess and then move on to the next question.

4.2 The Directions

These directions are very similar to those you will see for problem solving questions when you take the GMAT exam. If you read them carefully and understand them clearly before sitting for the GMAT exam, you will not need to spend too much time reviewing them once the test begins.

Solve the problem and indicate the best of the answer choices given.

Numbers: All numbers used are real numbers.

Figures: A figure accompanying a problem solving question is intended to provide information useful in solving the problem. Figures are drawn as accurately as possible. Exceptions will be clearly noted. Lines shown as straight are straight, and lines that appear jagged are also straight. The positions of points, angles, regions, etc., exist in the order shown, and angle measures are greater than zero. All figures lie in a plane unless otherwise indicated.

4.3 Sample Questions

Solve the problem and indicate the best of the answer choices given.

Numbers: All numbers used are real numbers.

Figures: A figure accompanying a problem solving question is intended to provide information useful in solving the problem. Figures are drawn as accurately as possible. Exceptions will be clearly noted. Lines shown as straight are straight, and lines that appear jagged are also straight. The positions of points, angles, regions, etc., exist in the order shown, and angle measures are greater than zero. All figures lie in a plane unless otherwise indicated.

*PS03439

1. Working at a constant rate, a copy machine makes 20 copies of a one-page document per minute. If the machine works at this constant rate, how many hours does it take to make 4,800 copies of a one-page document?

   (A) 4
   (B) 5
   (C) 6
   (D) 7
   (E) 8

PS11042

2. If $x + y = 2$ and $x^2 + y^2 = 2$, what is the value of xy ?

   (A) −2
   (B) −1
   (C) 0
   (D) 1
   (E) 2

PS02978

3. The sum S of the first n consecutive positive even integers is given by $S = n(n + 1)$. For what value of n is this sum equal to 110 ?

   (A) 10
   (B) 11
   (C) 12
   (D) 13
   (E) 14

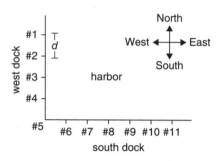

PS08375

4. A certain harbor has docking stations along its west and south docks, as shown in the figure; any two adjacent docking stations are separated by a uniform distance d. A certain boat left the west dock from docking station #2 and moved in a straight line diagonally until it reached the south dock. If the boat was at one time directly east of docking station #4 and directly north of docking station #7, at which docking station on the south dock did the boat arrive?

   (A)   #7
   (B)   #8
   (C)   #9
   (D)   #10
   (E)   #11

PS03887

5. $6(87.30 + 0.65) − 5(87.30) =$

   (A)   3.90
   (B)   39.00
   (C)   90.90
   (D)   91.20
   (E)   91.85

*These numbers correlate with the online test bank question number. See the GMAT Quantitative Review Online Index in the back of this book.

60

PS13800

6. Points A, B, C, and D, in that order, lie on a line. If $AB = 3$ cm, $AC = 4$ cm, and $BD = 6$ cm, what is CD, in centimeters?

(A) 1
(B) 2
(C) 3
(D) 4
(E) 5

PS05292

7. What is the value of $x^2yz - xyz^2$, if $x = -2$, $y = 1$, and $z = 3$?

(A) 20
(B) 24
(C) 30
(D) 32
(E) 48

PS11468

8. A souvenir vendor purchased 1,000 shirts for a special event at a price of $5 each. The vendor sold 600 of the shirts on the day of the event for $12 each and 300 of the shirts in the week following the event for $4 each. The vendor was unable to sell the remaining shirts. What was the vendor's gross profit on the sale of these shirts?

(A) $1,000
(B) $2,200
(C) $2,700
(D) $3,000
(E) $3,400

PS06937

9. If $x > y$ and $y > z$, which of the following represents the greatest number?

(A) $x - z$
(B) $x - y$
(C) $y - x$
(D) $z - y$
(E) $z - x$

PS12926

10. To order certain plants from a catalog, it costs $3.00 per plant, plus a 5 percent sales tax, plus $6.95 for shipping and handling regardless of the number of plants ordered. If Company C ordered these plants from the catalog at the total cost of $69.95, how many plants did Company C order?

(A) 22
(B) 21
(C) 20
(D) 19
(E) 18

PS00812

11. A rug manufacturer produces rugs at a cost of $75 per rug. What is the manufacturer's gross profit from the sale of 150 rugs if $\frac{2}{3}$ of the rugs are sold for $150 per rug and the rest are sold for $200 per rug?

(A) $10,350
(B) $11,250
(C) $13,750
(D) $16,250
(E) $17,800

PS07793

12. The value of Maureen's investment portfolio has decreased by 5.8 percent since her initial investment in the portfolio. If her initial investment was $16,800, what is the current value of the portfolio?

(A) $7,056.00
(B) $14,280.00
(C) $15,825.60
(D) $16,702.56
(E) $17,774.40

PS03036

13. Company C produces toy trucks at a cost of $5.00 each for the first 100 trucks and $3.50 for each additional truck. If 500 toy trucks were produced by Company C and sold for $10.00 each, what was Company C's gross profit?

(A) $2,250
(B) $2,500
(C) $3,100
(D) $3,250
(E) $3,500

PS07694

14. A group of store managers must assemble 280 displays for an upcoming sale. If they assemble 25 percent of the displays during the first hour and 40 percent of the remaining displays during the second hour, how many of the displays will <u>not</u> have been assembled by the end of the second hour?

(A) 70
(B) 98
(C) 126
(D) 168
(E) 182

Division	Profit or Loss (in millions of dollars)				
	1991	1992	1993	1994	1995
A	1.1	(3.4)	1.9	2.0	0.6
B	(2.3)	5.5	(4.5)	3.9	(2.9)
C	10.0	(6.6)	5.3	1.1	(3.0)

PS02019

15. The annual profit or loss for the three divisions of Company T for the years 1991 through 1995 are summarized in the table shown, where losses are enclosed in parentheses. For which division and which three consecutive years shown was the division's profit or loss for the three-year period closest to $0 ?

(A) Division A for 1991–1993
(B) Division A for 1992–1994
(C) Division B for 1991–1993
(D) Division B for 1993–1995
(E) Division C for 1992–1994

PS13583

16. Of the following, which is least?

(A) $\dfrac{0.03}{0.00071}$

(B) $\dfrac{0.03}{0.0071}$

(C) $\dfrac{0.03}{0.071}$

(D) $\dfrac{0.03}{0.71}$

(E) $\dfrac{0.03}{7.1}$

PS07385

17. The maximum recommended pulse rate R, when exercising, for a person who is x years of age is given by the equation $R = 176 - 0.8x$. What is the age, in years, of a person whose maximum recommended pulse rate when exercising is 140 ?

(A) 40
(B) 45
(C) 50
(D) 55
(E) 60

PS08011

18. If the average (arithmetic mean) of 5 numbers j, $j + 5$, $2j - 1$, $4j - 2$, and $5j - 1$ is 8, what is the value of j ?

(A) $\dfrac{1}{3}$

(B) $\dfrac{7}{13}$

(C) 1

(D) 3

(E) 8

PS14037

19. Guadalupe owns 2 rectangular tracts of land. One is 300 m by 500 m and the other is 250 m by 630 m. The combined area of these 2 tracts is how many square meters?

(A) 3,360
(B) 307,500
(C) 621,500
(D) 704,000
(E) 2,816,000

PS03918

20. There are five sales agents in a certain real estate office. One month Andy sold twice as many properties as Ellen, Bob sold 3 more than Ellen, Cary sold twice as many as Bob, and Dora sold as many as Bob and Ellen together. Who sold the most properties that month?

(A) Andy
(B) Bob
(C) Cary
(D) Dora
(E) Ellen

PS10862

21. In a field day at a school, each child who competed in *n* events and scored a total of *p* points was given an overall score of $\frac{p}{n} + n$. Andrew competed in 1 event and scored 9 points. Jason competed in 3 events and scored 5, 6, and 7 points, respectively. What was the ratio of Andrew's overall score to Jason's overall score?

(A) $\frac{10}{23}$

(B) $\frac{7}{10}$

(C) $\frac{4}{5}$

(D) $\frac{10}{9}$

(E) $\frac{12}{7}$

PS06719

22. A certain work plan for September requires that a work team, working every day, produce an average of 200 items per day. For the first half of the month, the team produced an average of 150 items per day. How many items per day must the team average during the second half of the month if it is to attain the average daily production rate required by the work plan?

(A) 225

(B) 250

(C) 275

(D) 300

(E) 350

PS01949

23. A company sells radios for $15.00 each. It costs the company $14.00 per radio to produce 1,000 radios and $13.50 per radio to produce 2,000 radios. How much greater will the company's gross profit be from the production and sale of 2,000 radios than from the production and sale of 1,000 radios?

(A) $500

(B) $1,000

(C) $1,500

(D) $2,000

(E) $2,500

PS06555

24. Which of the following represent positive numbers?

I. $-3 - (-5)$

II. $(-3)(-5)$

III. $-5 - (-3)$

(A) I only

(B) II only

(C) III only

(D) I and II

(E) II and III

PS02948

25. If $\frac{x}{4}$ is 2 more than $\frac{x}{8}$, then $x =$

(A) 4

(B) 8

(C) 16

(D) 32

(E) 64

PS09983

26. Point *X* lies on side *BC* of rectangle *ABCD*, which has length 12 and width 8. What is the area of triangular region *AXD* ?

(A) 96

(B) 48

(C) 32

(D) 24

(E) 20

PS07659

27. A grocer has 400 pounds of coffee in stock, 20 percent of which is decaffeinated. If the grocer buys another 100 pounds of coffee of which 60 percent is decaffeinated, what percent, by weight, of the grocer's stock of coffee is decaffeinated?

(A) 28%

(B) 30%

(C) 32%

(D) 34%

(E) 40%

PS05129

28. The toll T, in dollars, for a truck using a certain bridge is given by the formula $T = 1.50 + 0.50(x - 2)$, where x is the number of axles on the truck. What is the toll for an 18-wheel truck that has 2 wheels on its front axle and 4 wheels on each of its other axles?

(A) $2.50
(B) $3.00
(C) $3.50
(D) $4.00
(E) $5.00

PS13917

29. For what value of x between −4 and 4, inclusive, is the value of $x^2 - 10x + 16$ the greatest?

(A) −4
(B) −2
(C) 0
(D) 2
(E) 4

PS15994

30. If $x = -\dfrac{5}{8}$ and $y = -\dfrac{1}{2}$, what is the value of the expression $-2x - y^2$?

(A) $-\dfrac{3}{2}$

(B) -1

(C) 1

(D) $\dfrac{3}{2}$

(E) $\dfrac{7}{4}$

PS13686

31. If $x - y = R$ and $xy = S$, then $(x - 2)(y + 2) =$

(A) $R + S - 4$
(B) $R + 2S - 4$
(C) $2R - S - 4$
(D) $2R + S - 4$
(E) $2R + S$

PS01466

32. For positive integers a and b, the remainder when a is divided by b is equal to the remainder when b is divided by a. Which of the following could be a value of ab ?

I.   24
II. 30
III. 36

(A) II only
(B) III only
(C) I and II only
(D) II and III only
(E) I, II, and III

PS01867

33. List S consists of the positive integers that are multiples of 9 and are less than 100. What is the median of the integers in S ?

(A) 36
(B) 45
(C) 49
(D) 54
(E) 63

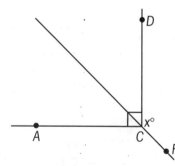

PS07397

34. In the figure above, if F is a point on the line that bisects angle ACD and the measure of angle DCF is $x°$, which of the following is true of x ?

(A) $90 \le x < 100$
(B) $100 \le x < 110$
(C) $110 \le x < 120$
(D) $120 \le x < 130$
(E) $130 \le x < 140$

PS07380

35. A rope 20.6 meters long is cut into two pieces. If the length of one piece of rope is 2.8 meters shorter than the length of the other, what is the length, in meters, of the longer piece of rope?

(A)   7.5
(B)   8.9
(C)   9.9
(D)   10.3
(E)   11.7

PS01120

36. If x and y are integers and $x - y$ is odd, which of the following must be true?

I. xy is even.
II. $x^2 + y^2$ is odd.
III. $(x + y)^2$ is even.

(A)   I only
(B)   II only
(C)   III only
(D)   I and II only
(E)   I, II, and III

PS00335

37. On Monday, the opening price of a certain stock was $100 per share and its closing price was $110 per share. On Tuesday the closing price of the stock was 10 percent less than its closing price on Monday, and on Wednesday the closing price of the stock was 4 percent greater than its closing price on Tuesday. What was the approximate percent change in the price of the stock from its opening price on Monday to its closing price on Wednesday?

(A)   A decrease of 6%
(B)   A decrease of 4%
(C)   A decrease of 1%
(D)   An increase of 3%
(E)   An increase of 4%

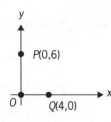

PS05109

38. In the rectangular coordinate system shown above, points O, P, and Q represent the sites of three proposed housing developments. If a fire station can be built at any point in the coordinate system, at which point would it be equidistant from all three developments?

(A)   (3,1)
(B)   (1,3)
(C)   (3,2)
(D)   (2,2)
(E)   (2,3)

PS05008

39. What is the perimeter, in meters, of a rectangular garden 6 meters wide that has the same area as a rectangular playground 16 meters long and 12 meters wide?

(A)   48
(B)   56
(C)   60
(D)   76
(E)   192

PS00918

40. $1 - 0.000001 =$

(A)   (1.01)(0.99)
(B)   (1.11)(0.99)
(C)   (1.001)(0.999)
(D)   (1.111)(0.999)
(E)   (1.0101)(0.0909)

PS04362

41. $|-4|(|-20|-|5|) =$

(A) −100
(B) −60
(C)   60
(D)   75
(E) 100

PS12934

42. Of the total amount that Jill spent on a shopping trip, excluding taxes, she spent 50 percent on clothing, 20 percent on food, and 30 percent on other items. If Jill paid a 4 percent tax on the clothing, no tax on the food, and an 8 percent tax on all other items, then the total tax that she paid was what percent of the total amount that she spent, excluding taxes?

(A) 2.8%
(B) 3.6%
(C) 4.4%
(D) 5.2%
(E) 6.0%

PS15469

43. How many integers x satisfy both $2 < x \le 4$ and $0 \le x \le 3$?

(A) 5
(B) 4
(C) 3
(D) 2
(E) 1

PS09322

44. At the opening of a trading day at a certain stock exchange, the price per share of stock K was $8. If the price per share of stock K was $9 at the closing of the day, what was the percent increase in the price per share of stock K for that day?

(A) 1.4%
(B) 5.9%
(C) 11.1%
(D) 12.5%
(E) 23.6%

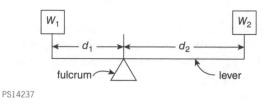

PS14237

45. As shown in the diagram above, a lever resting on a fulcrum has weights of w_1 pounds and w_2 pounds, located d_1 feet and d_2 feet from the fulcrum. The lever is balanced and $w_1 d_1 = w_2 d_2$. Suppose w_1 is 50 pounds and w_2 is 30 pounds. If d_1 is 4 feet less than d_2, what is d_2, in feet?

(A) 1.5
(B) 2.5
(C) 6
(D) 10
(E) 20

PS00037

46. The number of rooms at Hotel G is 10 less than twice the number of rooms at Hotel H. If the total number of rooms at Hotel G and Hotel H is 425, what is the number of rooms at Hotel G?

(A) 140
(B) 180
(C) 200
(D) 240
(E) 280

PS17036

47. $\dfrac{3}{100} + \dfrac{5}{1,000} + \dfrac{7}{100,000} =$

(A) 0.357
(B) 0.3507
(C) 0.35007
(D) 0.0357
(E) 0.03507

PS01650

48. If r and s are positive integers such that $(2^r)(4^s) = 16$, then $2r + s =$

(A) 2
(B) 3
(C) 4
(D) 5
(E) 6

PS06726

49. Three people each contributed x dollars toward the purchase of a car. They then bought the car for y dollars, an amount less than the total number of dollars contributed. If the excess amount is to be refunded to the three people in equal amounts, each person should receive a refund of how many dollars?

(A) $\dfrac{3x-y}{3}$

(B) $\dfrac{x-y}{3}$

(C) $\dfrac{x-3y}{3}$

(D) $\dfrac{y-3x}{3}$

(E) $3(x-y)$

$$2x + 2y = -4$$
$$4x + y = 1$$

PS07331

50. In the system of equations above, what is the value of x?

(A) -3

(B) -1

(C) $\dfrac{2}{5}$

(D) 1

(E) $1\dfrac{3}{4}$

PS07080

51. Last week Jack worked 70 hours and earned $1,260. If he earned his regular hourly wage for the first 40 hours worked, $1\dfrac{1}{2}$ times his regular hourly wage for the next 20 hours worked, and 2 times his regular hourly wage for the remaining 10 hours worked, what was his regular hourly wage?

(A) $7.00

(B) $14.00

(C) $18.00

(D) $22.00

(E) $31.50

PS02402

52. If Mel saved more than $10 by purchasing a sweater at a 15 percent discount, what is the smallest amount the original price of the sweater could be, to the nearest dollar?

(A) 45

(B) 67

(C) 75

(D) 83

(E) 150

PS13426

53. If a and b are positive integers and $(2^a)^b = 2^3$, what is the value of $2^a \, 2^b$?

(A) 6

(B) 8

(C) 16

(D) 32

(E) 64

PS03777

54. $\dfrac{1}{3 - \dfrac{1}{3 - \dfrac{1}{3-1}}} =$

(A) $\dfrac{7}{23}$

(B) $\dfrac{5}{13}$

(C) $\dfrac{2}{3}$

(D) $\dfrac{23}{7}$

(E) $\dfrac{13}{5}$

PS07386

55. After 4,000 gallons of water were added to a large water tank that was already filled to $\dfrac{3}{4}$ of its capacity, the tank was then at $\dfrac{4}{5}$ of its capacity. How many gallons of water does the tank hold when filled to capacity?

(A) 5,000

(B) 6,200

(C) 20,000

(D) 40,000

(E) 80,000

PS01099
56. Five machines at a certain factory operate at the same constant rate. If four of these machines, operating simultaneously, take 30 hours to fill a certain production order, how many <u>fewer</u> hours does it take all five machines, operating simultaneously, to fill the same production order?

(A)   3
(B)   5
(C)   6
(D)   16
(E)   24

PS01443
57. A certain toll station on a highway has 7 tollbooths, and each tollbooth collects $0.75 from each vehicle that passes it. From 6 o'clock yesterday morning to 12 o'clock midnight, vehicles passed each of the tollbooths at the average rate of 4 vehicles per minute. Approximately how much money did the toll station collect during that time period?

(A) $1,500
(B) $3,000
(C) $11,500
(D) $23,000
(E) $30,000

PS13829
58. How many integers between 1 and 16, inclusive, have exactly 3 different positive integer factors?
(Note: 6 is NOT such an integer because 6 has 4 different positive integer factors: 1, 2, 3, and 6.)

(A)   1
(B)   2
(C)   3
(D)   4
(E)   6

PS06288
59. If $d = 2.0453$ and d^* is the decimal obtained by rounding d to the nearest hundredth, what is the value of $d^* - d$?

(A)   −0.0053
(B)   −0.0003
(C)   0.0007
(D)   0.0047
(E)   0.0153

PS14063
60. Stephanie has $2\frac{1}{4}$ cups of milk on hand and makes 2 batches of cookies, using $\frac{2}{3}$ cup of milk for each batch of cookies. Which of the following describes the amount of milk remaining after she makes the cookies?

(A)   Less than $\frac{1}{2}$ cup

(B)   Between $\frac{1}{2}$ cup and $\frac{3}{4}$ cup

(C)   Between $\frac{3}{4}$ cup and 1 cup

(D)   Between 1 cup and $1\frac{1}{2}$ cups

(E)   More than $1\frac{1}{2}$ cups

PS01656
61. The expression $n!$ is defined as the product of the integers from 1 through n. If p is the product of the integers from 100 through 299 and q is the product of the integers from 200 through 299, which of the following is equal to $\frac{p}{q}$?

(A)   99!
(B)   199!
(C) $\frac{199!}{99!}$
(D) $\frac{299!}{99!}$
(E) $\frac{299!}{199!}$

PS15753
62. A school club plans to package and sell dried fruit to raise money. The club purchased 12 containers of dried fruit, each containing $16\frac{3}{4}$ pounds. What is the maximum number of individual bags of dried fruit, each containing $\frac{1}{4}$ pounds, that can be sold from the dried fruit the club purchased?

(A)   50
(B)   64
(C)   67
(D)   768
(E)   804

Height	Price
Less than 5 ft	$14.95
5 ft to 6 ft	$17.95
Over 6 ft	$21.95

PS02498

63. A nursery sells fruit trees priced as shown in the chart above. In its inventory 54 trees are less than 5 feet in height. If the expected revenue from the sale of its entire stock is estimated at $2,450, approximately how much of this will come from the sale of trees that are at least 5 feet tall?

(A) $1,730
(B) $1,640
(C) $1,410
(D) $1,080
(E) $810

PS10539

64. The sequence a_1, a_2, a_3, a_4, a_5 is such that $a_n = a_{n-1} + 5$ for $2 \leq n \leq 5$. If $a_5 = 31$, what is the value of a_1 ?

(A) 1
(B) 6
(C) 11
(D) 16
(E) 21

PS04971

65. A certain bridge is 4,024 feet long. Approximately how many minutes does it take to cross this bridge at a constant speed of 20 miles per hour? (1 mile = 5,280 feet)

(A) 1
(B) 2
(C) 4
(D) 6
(E) 7

PS04009

66. If $S = \{0, 4, 5, 2, 11, 8\}$, how much greater than the median of the numbers in S is the mean of the numbers in S ?

(A) 0.5
(B) 1.0
(C) 1.5
(D) 2.0
(E) 2.5

PS12657

67. The annual interest rate earned by an investment increased by 10 percent from last year to this year. If the annual interest rate earned by the investment this year was 11 percent, what was the annual interest rate last year?

(A) 1%
(B) 1.1%
(C) 9.1%
(D) 10%
(E) 10.8%

PS07394

68. A total of 5 liters of gasoline is to be poured into two empty containers with capacities of 2 liters and 6 liters, respectively, such that both containers will be filled to the same percent of their respective capacities. What amount of gasoline, in liters, must be poured into the 6-liter container?

(A) $4\frac{1}{2}$
(B) 4
(C) $3\frac{3}{4}$
(D) 3
(E) $1\frac{1}{4}$

PS02775

69. List S consists of 10 consecutive odd integers, and list T consists of 5 consecutive even integers. If the least integer in S is 7 more than the least integer in T, how much greater is the average (arithmetic mean) of the integers in S than the average of the integers in T ?

(A) 2
(B) 7
(C) 8
(D) 12
(E) 22

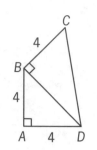

PS05616

70. In the figure above, what is the area of triangular region BCD ?

(A) $4\sqrt{2}$

(B) 8

(C) $8\sqrt{2}$

(D) 16

(E) $16\sqrt{2}$

PS13882

71. What is the larger of the 2 solutions of the equation $x^2 - 4x = 96$?

(A)   8

(B)   12

(C)   16

(D)   32

(E)   100

PS10493

72. Of the goose eggs laid at a certain pond, $\frac{2}{3}$ hatched, and $\frac{3}{4}$ of the geese that hatched from those eggs survived the first month. Of the geese that survived the first month, $\frac{3}{5}$ did not survive the first year. If 120 geese survived the first year and if no more than one goose hatched from each egg, how many goose eggs were laid at the pond?

(A)   280

(B)   400

(C)   540

(D)   600

(E)   840

PS09305

73. If $x^2 - 2x - 15 = 0$ and $x > 0$ which of the following must be equal to 0 ?

I. $x^2 - 6x + 9$

II. $x^2 - 7x + 10$

III. $x^2 - 10x + 25$

(A)   I only

(B)   II only

(C)   III only

(D)   II and III only

(E)   I, II, and III

PS10921

74. $\dfrac{(39,897)(0.0096)}{198.76}$ is approximately

(A)   0.02

(B)   0.2

(C)   2

(D)   20

(E)   200

PS13205

75. If a square region has area n, what is the length of the diagonal of the square in terms of n ?

(A) $\sqrt{2n}$

(B) $\sqrt{n}$

(C) $2\sqrt{n}$

(D) $2n$

(E) $2n^2$

PS00817

76. The "prime sum" of an integer n greater than 1 is the sum of all the prime factors of n, including repetitions. For example, the prime sum of 12 is 7, since $12 = 2 \times 2 \times 3$ and $2 + 2 + 3 = 7$. For which of the following integers is the prime sum greater than 35 ?

(A)   440

(B)   512

(C)   620

(D)   700

(E)   750

PS02256
77. Each machine at a toy factory assembles a certain kind of toy at a constant rate of one toy every 3 minutes. If 40 percent of the machines at the factory are to be replaced by new machines that assemble this kind of toy at a constant rate of one toy every 2 minutes, what will be the percent increase in the number of toys assembled in one hour by all the machines at the factory, working at their constant rates?

   (A)   20%
   (B)   25%
   (C)   30%
   (D)   40%
   (E)   50%

PS10339
78. When a subscription to a new magazine was purchased for m months, the publisher offered a discount of 75 percent off the regular monthly price of the magazine. If the total value of the discount was equivalent to buying the magazine at its regular monthly price for 27 months, what was the value of m?

   (A)   18
   (B)   24
   (C)   30
   (D)   36
   (E)   48

PS10422
79. At a garage sale, all of the prices of the items sold were different. If the price of a radio sold at the garage sale was both the 15th highest price and the 20th lowest price among the prices of the items sold, how many items were sold at the garage sale?

   (A)   33
   (B)   34
   (C)   35
   (D)   36
   (E)   37

PS11738
80. Half of a large pizza is cut into 4 equal-sized pieces, and the other half is cut into 6 equal-sized pieces. If a person were to eat 1 of the larger pieces and 2 of the smaller pieces, what fraction of the pizza would remain <u>uneaten</u>?

   (A) $\dfrac{5}{12}$

   (B) $\dfrac{13}{24}$

   (C) $\dfrac{7}{12}$

   (D) $\dfrac{2}{3}$

   (E) $\dfrac{17}{24}$

PS14293
81. If $a = 1 + \dfrac{1}{4} + \dfrac{1}{16} + \dfrac{1}{64}$ and $b = 1 + \dfrac{1}{4}a$, then what is the value of $a - b$?

   (A) $-\dfrac{85}{256}$

   (B) $-\dfrac{1}{256}$

   (C) $-\dfrac{1}{4}$

   (D) $\dfrac{125}{256}$

   (E) $\dfrac{169}{256}$

PS10174
82. In a certain learning experiment, each participant had three trials and was assigned, for each trial, a score of either -2, -1, 0, 1, or 2. The participant's final score consisted of the sum of the first trial score, 2 times the second trial score, and 3 times the third trial score. If Anne received scores of 1 and -1 for her first two trials, not necessarily in that order, which of the following could NOT be her final score?

   (A) -4
   (B) -2
   (C)   1
   (D)   5
   (E)   6

PS00111

83. For all positive integers m and v, the expression $m \ominus v$ represents the remainder when m is divided by v. What is the value of $((98 \ominus 33) \ominus 17) - (98 \ominus (33 \ominus 17))$?

    (A) −10
    (B) −2
    (C) 8
    (D) 13
    (E) 17

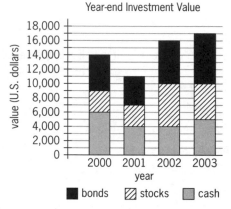

Year-end Investment Value

■ bonds ▨ stocks ▨ cash

PS13841

84. The chart above shows year-end values for Darnella's investments. For just the stocks, what was the increase in value from year-end 2000 to year-end 2003 ?

    (A) $1,000
    (B) $2,000
    (C) $3,000
    (D) $4,000
    (E) $5,000

PS05775

85. If the sum of the reciprocals of two consecutive odd integers is $\frac{12}{35}$, then the greater of the two integers is

    (A) 3
    (B) 5
    (C) 7
    (D) 9
    (E) 11

PS05916

86. What is the sum of the odd integers from 35 to 85, inclusive?

    (A) 1,560
    (B) 1,500
    (C) 1,240
    (D) 1,120
    (E) 1,100

PS00777

87. In a certain sequence, each term after the first term is one-half the previous term. If the tenth term of the sequence is between 0.0001 and 0.001, then the twelfth term of the sequence is between

    (A) 0.0025 and 0.025
    (B) 0.00025 and 0.0025
    (C) 0.000025 and 0.00025
    (D) 0.0000025 and 0.000025
    (E) 0.00000025 and 0.0000025

PS04765

88. A certain drive-in movie theater has a total of 17 rows of parking spaces. There are 20 parking spaces in the first row and 21 parking spaces in the second row. In each subsequent row there are 2 more parking spaces than in the previous row. What is the total number of parking spaces in the movie theater?

    (A) 412
    (B) 544
    (C) 596
    (D) 632
    (E) 692

PS10810

89. Ada and Paul received their scores on three tests. On the first test, Ada's score was 10 points higher than Paul's score. On the second test, Ada's score was 4 points higher than Paul's score. If Paul's average (arithmetic mean) score on the three tests was 3 points higher than Ada's average score on the three tests, then Paul's score on the third test was how many points higher than Ada's score?

    (A) 9
    (B) 14
    (C) 17
    (D) 23
    (E) 25

90. The price of a certain stock increased by 0.25 of 1 percent on a certain day. By what fraction did the price of the stock increase that day?

    (A) $\dfrac{1}{2,500}$

    (B) $\dfrac{1}{400}$

    (C) $\dfrac{1}{40}$

    (D) $\dfrac{1}{25}$

    (E) $\dfrac{1}{4}$

91. For each trip, a taxicab company charges $4.25 for the first mile and $2.65 for each additional mile or fraction thereof. If the total charge for a certain trip was $62.55, how many miles at most was the trip?

    (A) 21
    (B) 22
    (C) 23
    (D) 24
    (E) 25

92. When 24 is divided by the positive integer n, the remainder is 4. Which of the following statements about n must be true?

    I. n is even.
    II. n is a multiple of 5.
    III. n is a factor of 20.

    (A) III only
    (B) I and II only
    (C) I and III only
    (D) II and III only
    (E) I, II, and III

93. What is the thousandths digit in the decimal equivalent of $\dfrac{53}{5,000}$?

    (A) 0
    (B) 1
    (C) 3
    (D) 5
    (E) 6

94. The average (arithmetic mean) of the positive integers x, y, and z is 3. If $x < y < z$, what is the greatest possible value of z ?

    (A) 5
    (B) 6
    (C) 7
    (D) 8
    (E) 9

95. The product of 3,305 and the 1-digit integer x is a 5-digit integer. The units (ones) digit of the product is 5 and the hundreds digit is y. If A is the set of all possible values of x and B is the set of all possible values of y, then which of the following gives the members of A and B ?

	A	B
(A)	{1, 3, 5, 7, 9}	{0, 1, 2, 3, 4, 5, 6, 7, 8, 9}
(B)	{1, 3, 5, 7, 9}	{1, 3, 5, 7, 9}
(C)	{3, 5, 7, 9}	{1, 5, 7, 9}
(D)	{5, 7, 9}	{1, 5, 7}
(E)	{5, 7, 9}	{1, 5, 9}

96. What is the largest integer n such that $\dfrac{1}{2^n} > 0.01$?

    (A) 5
    (B) 6
    (C) 7
    (D) 10
    (E) 51

97. If x and y are integers such that $2 < x \le 8$ and $2 < y \le 9$, what is the maximum value of $\dfrac{1}{x} - \dfrac{x}{y}$?

    (A) $-3\dfrac{1}{8}$
    (B) 0
    (C) $\dfrac{1}{4}$
    (D) $\dfrac{5}{18}$
    (E) 2

PS01875
98. Items that are purchased together at a certain discount store are priced at $3 for the first item purchased and $1 for each additional item purchased. What is the maximum number of items that could be purchased together for a total price that is less than $30 ?

(A)   25
(B)   26
(C)   27
(D)   28
(E)   29

PS00774
99. What is the least integer z for which (0.000125)(0.0025)(0.00000125) × 10^z is an integer?

(A)   18
(B)   10
(C)   0
(D)   −10
(E)   −18

PS08407
100. The average (arithmetic mean) length per film for a group of 21 films is t minutes. If a film that runs for 66 minutes is removed from the group and replaced by one that runs for 52 minutes, what is the average length per film, in minutes, for the new group of films, in terms of t ?

(A) $t + \dfrac{2}{3}$

(B) $t - \dfrac{2}{3}$

(C) $21t + 14$

(D) $t + \dfrac{3}{2}$

(E) $t - \dfrac{3}{2}$

PS08051
101. An open box in the shape of a cube measuring 50 centimeters on each side is constructed from plywood. If the plywood weighs 1.5 grams per square centimeter, which of the following is closest to the total weight, in kilograms, of the plywood used for the box? (1 kilogram = 1,000 grams)

(A)   2
(B)   4
(C)   8
(D)   13
(E)   19

PS03614
102. A garden center sells a certain grass seed in 5-pound bags at $13.85 per bag, 10-pound bags at $20.43 per bag, and 25-pound bags at $32.25 per bag. If a customer is to buy at least 65 pounds of the grass seed, but no more than 80 pounds, what is the least possible cost of the grass seed that the customer will buy?

(A) $94.03
(B) $96.75
(C) $98.78
(D) $102.07
(E) $105.36

PS12785
103. If $x = -|w|$, which of the following must be true?

(A) $x = -w$
(B) $x = w$
(C) $x^2 = w$
(D) $x^2 = w^2$
(E) $x^3 = w^3$

PS05965
104. Which of the following lines in the xy-plane does not contain any point with integers as both coordinates?

(A) $y = x$

(B) $y = x + \dfrac{1}{2}$

(C) $y = x + 5$

(D) $y = \dfrac{1}{2}x$

(E) $y = \dfrac{1}{2}x + 5$

PS04160
105. A certain financial institution reported that its assets totaled $2,377,366.30 on a certain day. Of this amount, $31,724.54 was held in cash. Approximately what percent of the reported assets was held in cash on that day?

(A)   0.00013%
(B)   0.0013%
(C)   0.013%
(D)   0.13%
(E)   1.3%

$$AB$$
$$+\ BA$$
$$\overline{AAC}$$

PS09820

106. In the correctly worked addition problem shown, where the sum of the two-digit positive integers AB and BA is the three-digit integer AAC, and A, B, and C are different digits, what is the units digit of the integer AAC?

(A) 9
(B) 6
(C) 3
(D) 2
(E) 0

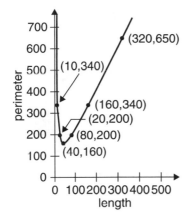

PS14060

107. Planning is in progress for a fenced, rectangular playground with an area of 1,600 square meters. The graph above shows the perimeter, in meters, as a function of the length of the playground. The length of the playground should be how many meters to minimize the perimeter and, therefore, the amount of fencing needed to enclose the playground?

(A) 10
(B) 40
(C) 60
(D) 160
(E) 340

$$3r \le 4s + 5$$
$$|s| \le 5$$

PS06913

108. Given the inequalities above, which of the following CANNOT be the value of r?

(A) −20
(B) −5
(C) 0
(D) 5
(E) 20

PS11647

109. If m is an even integer, v is an odd integer, and m > v > 0, which of the following represents the number of even integers less than m and greater than v?

(A) $\frac{m-v}{2} - 1$
(B) $\frac{m-v-1}{2}$
(C) $\frac{m-v}{2}$
(D) $m - v - 1$
(E) $m - v$

PS02378

110. A positive integer is divisible by 9 if and only if the sum of its digits is divisible by 9. If n is a positive integer, for which of the following values of k is $25 \times 10^n + k \times 10^{2n}$ divisible by 9?

(A) 9
(B) 16
(C) 23
(D) 35
(E) 47

PS17806

111. The perimeter of rectangle A is 200 meters. The length of rectangle B is 10 meters less than the length of rectangle A and the width of rectangle B is 10 meters more than the width of rectangle A. If rectangle B is a square, what is the width, in meters, of rectangle A?

(A) 10
(B) 20
(C) 40
(D) 50
(E) 60

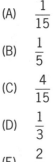

-9 -8 -7 -6 -5 -4 -3 -2 -1 0 1 2 3 4 5 6 7 8 9   x

PS08598

112. On the number line, the shaded interval is the graph of which of the following inequalities?

(A) $|x| \le 4$

(B) $|x| \le 8$

(C) $|x - 2| \le 4$

(D) $|x - 2| \le 6$

(E) $|x + 2| \le 6$

PS12450

113. Last year members of a certain professional organization for teachers consisted of teachers from 49 different school districts, with an average (arithmetic mean) of 9.8 schools per district. Last year the average number of teachers at these schools who were members of the organization was 22. Which of the following is closest to the total number of members of the organization last year?

(A) 10^7

(B) 10^6

(C) 10^5

(D) 10^4

(E) 10^3

PS09294

114. Of all the students in a certain dormitory, $\frac{1}{2}$ are first-year students and the rest are second-year students. If $\frac{4}{5}$ of the first-year students have not declared a major and if the fraction of second-year students who have declared a major is 3 times the fraction of first-year students who have declared a major, what fraction of all the students in the dormitory are second-year students who have not declared a major?

(A) $\frac{1}{15}$

(B) $\frac{1}{5}$

(C) $\frac{4}{15}$

(D) $\frac{1}{3}$

(E) $\frac{2}{5}$

PS09050

115. If the average (arithmetic mean) of x, y, and z is 7x and $x \ne 0$, what is the ratio of x to the sum of y and z ?

(A) 1:21

(B) 1:20

(C) 1:6

(D) 6:1

(E) 20:1

PS02352

116. In the coordinate plane, line k passes through the origin and has slope 2. If points (3,y) and (x,4) are on line k, then x + y =

(A) 3.5

(B) 7

(C) 8

(D) 10

(E) 14

PS08661

117. If a, b, and c are constants, a > b > c, and $x^3 - x = (x - a)(x - b)(x - c)$ for all numbers x, what is the value of b ?

(A) −3

(B) −1

(C) 0

(D) 1

(E) 3

PS06273

118. $17^3 + 17^4 =$

(A) 17^7

(B) $17^3(18)$

(C) $17^6(18)$

(D) $2(17^3) + 17$

(E) $2(17^3) - 17$

PS02934

119. Company K's earnings were $12 million last year. If this year's earnings are projected to be 150 percent greater than last year's earnings, what are Company K's projected earnings this year?

(A) $13.5 million

(B) $15 million

(C) $18 million

(D) $27 million

(E) $30 million

PS05413

120. Jonah drove the first half of a 100-mile trip in x hours and the second half in y hours. Which of the following is equal to Jonah's average speed, in miles per hour, for the entire trip?

(A) $\dfrac{50}{x+y}$

(B) $\dfrac{100}{x+y}$

(C) $\dfrac{25}{x}+\dfrac{25}{y}$

(D) $\dfrac{50}{x}+\dfrac{50}{y}$

(E) $\dfrac{100}{x}+\dfrac{100}{y}$

PS06135

121. What is the greatest number of identical bouquets that can be made out of 21 white and 91 red tulips if no flowers are to be left out? (Two bouquets are identical whenever the number of red tulips in the two bouquets is equal and the number of white tulips in the two bouquets is equal.)

(A) 3

(B) 4

(C) 5

(D) 6

(E) 7

PS11454

122. In the xy-plane, the points (c,d), $(c,-d)$, and $(-c,-d)$ are three vertices of a certain square. If $c < 0$ and $d > 0$, which of the following points is in the same quadrant as the fourth vertex of the square?

(A) $(-5,-3)$

(B) $(-5,3)$

(C) $(5,-3)$

(D) $(3,-5)$

(E) $(3,5)$

PS05470

123. If the amount of federal estate tax due on an estate valued at $1.35 million is $437,000 plus 43 percent of the value of the estate in excess of $1.25 million, then the federal tax due is approximately what percent of the value of the estate?

A. 30%

B. 35%

C. 40%

D. 45%

E. 50%

PS05924

124. If $\dfrac{3}{10^4} = x\%$, then $x =$

(A) 0.3

(B) 0.03

(C) 0.003

(D) 0.0003

(E) 0.00003

PS01285

125. What is the remainder when 3^{24} is divided by 5 ?

(A) 0

(B) 1

(C) 2

(D) 3

(E) 4

PS11692

126. In the figure shown, a square grid is superimposed on the map of a park, represented by the shaded region, in the middle of which is a pond, represented by the black region. If the area of the pond is 5,000 square yards, which of the following is closest to the area of the park, in square yards, including the area of the pond?

(A) 30,000

(B) 45,000

(C) 60,000

(D) 75,000

(E) 90,000

PS03623

127. If the volume of a ball is 32,490 cubic millimeters, what is the volume of the ball in cubic centimeters? (1 millimeter = 0.1 centimeter)

(A) 0.3249

(B) 3.249

(C) 32.49

(D) 324.9

(E) 3,249

PS07058

128. David used part of $100,000 to purchase a house. Of the remaining portion, he invested $\frac{1}{3}$ of it at 4 percent simple annual interest and $\frac{2}{3}$ of it at 6 percent simple annual interest. If after a year the income from the two investments totaled $320, what was the purchase price of the house?

(A) $96,000

(B) $94,000

(C) $88,000

(D) $75,000

(E) $40,000

PS11537

129. In the sequence x_0, x_1, x_2, ..., x_n, each term from x_1 to x_k is 3 greater than the previous term, and each term from x_{k+1} to x_n is 3 less than the previous term, where n and k are positive integers and $k < n$. If $x_0 = x_n = 0$ and if $x_k = 15$, what is the value of n?

(A) 5

(B) 6

(C) 9

(D) 10

(E) 15

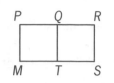

Note: Not drawn to scale.

PS11145

130. In the figure shown above, line segment QR has length 12, and rectangle $MPQT$ is a square. If the area of rectangular region $MPRS$ is 540, what is the area of rectangular region $TQRS$?

(A) 144

(B) 216

(C) 324

(D) 360

(E) 396

PS09439

131. A certain manufacturer sells its product to stores in 113 different regions worldwide, with an average (arithmetic mean) of 181 stores per region. If last year these stores sold an average of 51,752 units of the manufacturer's product per store, which of the following is closest to the total number of units of the manufacturer's product sold worldwide last year?

(A) 10^6

(B) 10^7

(C) 10^8

(D) 10^9

(E) 10^{10}

PS17708

132. Andrew started saving at the beginning of the year and had saved $240 by the end of the year. He continued to save and by the end of 2 years had saved a total of $540. Which of the following is closest to the percent increase in the amount Andrew saved during the second year compared to the amount he saved during the first year?

(A) 11%

(B) 25%

(C) 44%

(D) 56%

(E) 125%

PS19062

133. Two numbers differ by 2 and sum to S. Which of the following is the greater of the numbers in terms of S?

(A) $\dfrac{S}{2} - 1$

(B) $\dfrac{S}{2}$

(C) $\dfrac{S}{2} + \dfrac{1}{2}$

(D) $\dfrac{S}{2} + 1$

(E) $\dfrac{S}{2} + 2$

PS00904

134. The figure shown above consists of three identical circles that are tangent to each other. If the area of the shaded region is $64\sqrt{3} - 32\pi$, what is the radius of each circle?

(A) 4

(B) 8

(C) 16

(D) 24

(E) 32

PS02053

135. In a numerical table with 10 rows and 10 columns, each entry is either a 9 or a 10. If the number of 9s in the nth row is $n - 1$ for each n from 1 to 10, what is the average (arithmetic mean) of all the numbers in the table?

(A) 9.45

(B) 9.50

(C) 9.55

(D) 9.65

(E) 9.70

PS08485

136. A positive integer n is a perfect number provided that the sum of all the positive factors of n, including 1 and n, is equal to $2n$. What is the sum of the reciprocals of all the positive factors of the perfect number 28?

(A) $\dfrac{1}{4}$

(B) $\dfrac{56}{27}$

(C) 2

(D) 3

(E) 4

PS11430

137. The infinite sequence $a_1, a_2, \ldots, a_n, \ldots$ is such that $a_1 = 2$, $a_2 = -3$, $a_3 = 5$, $a_4 = -1$, and $a_n = a_{n-4}$ for $n > 4$. What is the sum of the first 97 terms of the sequence?

(A) 72

(B) 74

(C) 75

(D) 78

(E) 80

PS09901

138. The sequence $a_1, a_2, \ldots a_n, \ldots$ is such that $a_n = 2a_{n-1} - x$ for all positive integers $n \geq 2$ and for a certain number x. If $a_5 = 99$ and $a_3 = 27$, what is the value of x?

(A) 3

(B) 9

(C) 18

(D) 36

(E) 45

PS03779

139. A window is in the shape of a regular hexagon with each side of length 80 centimeters. If a diagonal through the center of the hexagon is w centimeters long, then $w =$

(A) 80

(B) 120

(C) 150

(D) 160

(E) 240

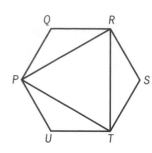

PS03695

140. In the figure shown, *PQRSTU* is a regular polygon with sides of length x. What is the perimeter of triangle *PRT* in terms of x ?

(A) $\dfrac{x\sqrt{3}}{2}$

(B) $x\sqrt{3}$

(C) $\dfrac{3x\sqrt{3}}{2}$

(D) $3x\sqrt{3}$

(E) $4x\sqrt{3}$

PS11755

141. In a certain medical survey, 45 percent of the people surveyed had the type A antigen in their blood and 3 percent had both the type A antigen and the type B antigen. Which of the following is closest to the percent of those with the type A antigen who also had the type B antigen?

(A)   1.35%

(B)   6.67%

(C)   13.50%

(D)   15.00%

(E)   42.00%

PS05146

142. On a certain transatlantic crossing, 20 percent of a ship's passengers held round-trip tickets and also took their cars aboard the ship. If 60 percent of the passengers with round-trip tickets did not take their cars aboard the ship, what percent of the ship's passengers held round-trip tickets?

(A) $33\dfrac{1}{3}\%$

(B)   40%

(C)   50%

(D)   60%

(E) $66\dfrac{2}{3}\%$

PS03696

143. If x and k are integers and $(12^x)(4^{2x+1}) = (2^k)(3^2)$, what is the value of k ?

(A)   5

(B)   7

(C)   10

(D)   12

(E)   14

PS11024

144. If *S* is the sum of the reciprocals of the 10 consecutive integers from 21 to 30, then *S* is between which of the following two fractions?

(A) $\dfrac{1}{3}$ and $\dfrac{1}{2}$

(B) $\dfrac{1}{4}$ and $\dfrac{1}{3}$

(C) $\dfrac{1}{5}$ and $\dfrac{1}{4}$

(D) $\dfrac{1}{6}$ and $\dfrac{1}{5}$

(E) $\dfrac{1}{7}$ and $\dfrac{1}{6}$

PS08729

145. For every even positive integer *m*, *f(m)* represents the product of all even integers from 2 to *m*, inclusive. For example, $f(12) = 2 \times 4 \times 6 \times 8 \times 10 \times 12$. What is the greatest prime factor of *f(24)* ?

(A)   23

(B)   19

(C)   17

(D)   13

(E)   11

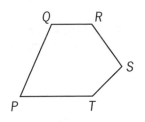

Note: Not drawn to scale.

PS08572

146. In pentagon *PQRST*, *PQ* = 3, *QR* = 2, *RS* = 4, and *ST* = 5. Which of the lengths 5, 10, and 15 could be the value of *PT* ?

    (A) 5 only
    (B) 15 only
    (C) 5 and 10 only
    (D) 10 and 15 only
    (E) 5, 10, and 15

3, *k*, 2, 8, *m*, 3

PS07771

147. The arithmetic mean of the list of numbers above is 4. If *k* and *m* are integers and *k* ≠ *m*, what is the median of the list?

    (A) 2
    (B) 2.5
    (C) 3
    (D) 3.5
    (E) 4

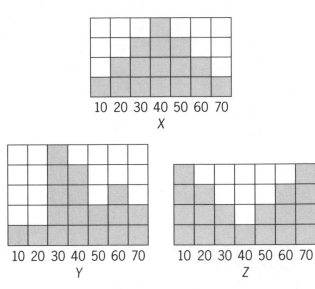

PS04987

148. If the variables, *X*, *Y*, and *Z* take on only the values 10, 20, 30, 40, 50, 60, or 70 with frequencies indicated by the shaded regions above, for which of the frequency distributions is the mean equal to the median?

    (A) *X* only
    (B) *Y* only
    (C) *Z* only
    (D) *X* and *Y*
    (E) *X* and *Z*

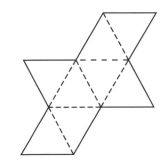

PS15538

149. When the figure above is cut along the solid lines, folded along the dashed lines, and taped along the solid lines, the result is a model of a geometric solid. This geometric solid consists of 2 pyramids, each with a square base that they share. What is the sum of the number of edges and the number of faces of this geometric solid?

    (A) 10
    (B) 18
    (C) 20
    (D) 24
    (E) 25

$$2x + y = 12$$
$$|y| \leq 12$$

PS03356

150. For how many ordered pairs (x,y) that are solutions of the system above are x and y both integers?

(A) 7

(B) 10

(C) 12

(D) 13

(E) 14

PS08859

151. The points R, T, and U lie on a circle that has radius 4. If the length of arc RTU is $\dfrac{4\pi}{3}$, what is the length of line segment RU?

(A) $\dfrac{4}{3}$

(B) $\dfrac{8}{3}$

(C) 3

(D) 4

(E) 6

PS02955

152. A certain university will select 1 of 7 candidates eligible to fill a position in the mathematics department and 2 of 10 candidates eligible to fill 2 identical positions in the computer science department. If none of the candidates is eligible for a position in both departments, how many different sets of 3 candidates are there to fill the 3 positions?

(A) 42

(B) 70

(C) 140

(D) 165

(E) 315

PS06189

153. A survey of employers found that during 1993 employment costs rose 3.5 percent, where employment costs consist of salary costs and fringe-benefit costs. If salary costs rose 3 percent and fringe-benefit costs rose 5.5 percent during 1993, then fringe-benefit costs represented what percent of employment costs at the beginning of 1993?

(A) 16.5%

(B) 20%

(C) 35%

(D) 55%

(E) 65%

PS02528

154. The subsets of the set $\{w, x, y\}$ are $\{w\}$, $\{x\}$, $\{y\}$, $\{w, x\}$, $\{w, y\}$, $\{x, y\}$, $\{w, x, y\}$, and $\{\ \}$ (the empty subset). How many subsets of the set $\{w, x, y, z\}$ contain w?

(A) Four

(B) Five

(C) Seven

(D) Eight

(E) Sixteen

PS10309

155. There are 5 cars to be displayed in 5 parking spaces, with all the cars facing the same direction. Of the 5 cars, 3 are red, 1 is blue, and 1 is yellow. If the cars are identical except for color, how many different display arrangements of the 5 cars are possible?

(A) 20

(B) 25

(C) 40

(D) 60

(E) 125

PS17461

156. The number $\sqrt{63 - 36\sqrt{3}}$ can be expressed as $x + y\sqrt{3}$ for some integers x and y. What is the value of xy?

(A) −18

(B) −6

(C) 6

(D) 18

(E) 27

PS01334

157. There are 10 books on a shelf, of which 4 are paperbacks and 6 are hardbacks. How many possible selections of 5 books from the shelf contain at least one paperback and at least one hardback?

(A) 75

(B) 120

(C) 210

(D) 246

(E) 252

PS03774

158. If x is to be chosen at random from the set $\{1, 2, 3, 4\}$ and y is to be chosen at random from the set $\{5, 6, 7\}$, what is the probability that xy will be even?

(A) $\dfrac{1}{6}$

(B) $\dfrac{1}{3}$

(C) $\dfrac{1}{2}$

(D) $\dfrac{2}{3}$

(E) $\dfrac{5}{6}$

PS04254

159. The function f is defined for each positive three-digit integer n by $f(n) = 2^x\, 3^y\, 5^z$, where x, y, and z are the hundreds, tens, and units digits of n, respectively. If m and v are three-digit positive integers such that $f(m) = 9f(v)$, then $m - v =$

(A) 8

(B) 9

(C) 18

(C) 20

(E) 80

PS06312

160. If $10^{50} - 74$ is written as an integer in base 10 notation, what is the sum of the digits in that integer?

(A) 424

(B) 433

(C) 440

(D) 449

(E) 467

PS09056

161. A certain company that sells only cars and trucks reported that revenues from car sales in 1997 were down 11 percent from 1996 and revenues from truck sales in 1997 were up 7 percent from 1996. If total revenues from car sales and truck sales in 1997 were up 1 percent from 1996, what is the ratio of revenue from car sales in 1996 to revenue from truck sales in 1996 ?

(A) 1:2

(B) 4:5

(C) 1:1

(D) 3:2

(E) 5:3

PS14267

162. Becky rented a power tool from a rental shop. The rent for the tool was $12 for the first hour and $3 for each additional hour. If Becky paid a total of $27, excluding sales tax, to rent the tool, for how many hours did she rent it?

(A) 5

(B) 6

(C) 9

(D) 10

(E) 12

PS06959

163. If $4 < \dfrac{7 - x}{3}$, which of the following must be true?

I. $5 < x$

II. $|x + 3| > 2$

III. $-(x + 5)$ is positive.

(A) II only

(B) III only

(C) I and II only

(D) II and III only

(E) I, II, and III

PS08654

164. A certain right triangle has sides of length x, y, and z, where $x < y < z$. If the area of this triangular region is 1, which of the following indicates all of the possible values of y ?

(A) $y > \sqrt{2}$

(B) $\dfrac{\sqrt{3}}{2} < y < \sqrt{2}$

(C) $\dfrac{\sqrt{2}}{3} < y < \dfrac{\sqrt{3}}{2}$

(D) $\dfrac{\sqrt{3}}{4} < y < \dfrac{\sqrt{2}}{3}$

(E) $y < \dfrac{\sqrt{3}}{4}$

PS14397
165. On a certain day, a bakery produced a batch of rolls at a total production cost of $300. On that day, $\frac{4}{5}$ of the rolls in the batch were sold, each at a price that was 50 percent greater than the average (arithmetic mean) production cost per roll. The remaining rolls in the batch were sold the next day, each at a price that was 20 percent less than the price of the day before. What was the bakery's profit on this batch of rolls?

(A) $150

(B) $144

(C) $132

(D) $108

(E) $90

PS05972
166. A set of numbers has the property that for any number t in the set, $t + 2$ is in the set. If -1 is in the set, which of the following must also be in the set?

I. -3

II. 1

III. 5

(A) I only

(B) II only

(C) I and II only

(D) II and III only

(E) I, II, and III

PS04780
167. A couple decides to have 4 children. If they succeed in having 4 children and each child is equally likely to be a boy or a girl, what is the probability that they will have exactly 2 girls and 2 boys?

(A) $\dfrac{3}{8}$

(B) $\dfrac{1}{4}$

(C) $\dfrac{3}{16}$

(D) $\dfrac{1}{8}$

(E) $\dfrac{1}{16}$

PS01564
168. The closing price of Stock X changed on each trading day last month. The percent change in the closing price of Stock X from the first trading day last month to each of the other trading days last month was less than 50 percent. If the closing price on the second trading day last month was $10.00, which of the following CANNOT be the closing price on the last trading day last month?

(A) $3.00

(B) $9.00

(C) $19.00

(D) $24.00

(E) $29.00

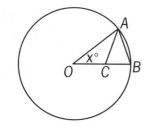

PS02389
169. In the figure above, point O is the center of the circle and $OC = AC = AB$. What is the value of x ?

(A) 40

(B) 36

(C) 34

(D) 32

(E) 30

PS16967
170. An airline passenger is planning a trip that involves three connecting flights that leave from Airports A, B, and C, respectively. The first flight leaves Airport A every hour, beginning at 8:00 a.m., and arrives at Airport B $2\frac{1}{2}$ hours later. The second flight leaves Airport B every 20 minutes, beginning at 8:00 a.m., and arrives at Airport C $1\frac{1}{6}$ hours later. The third flight leaves Airport C every hour, beginning at 8:45 a.m. What is the least total amount of time the passenger must spend between flights if all flights keep to their schedules?

(A) 25 min

(B) 1 hr 5 min

(C) 1 hr 15 min

(D) 2 hr 20 min

(E) 3 hr 40 min

PS07426
171. If n is a positive integer and n^2 is divisible by 72, then the largest positive integer that must divide n is

(A)   6

(B)   12

(C)   24

(D)   36

(E)   48

PS16977
172. A certain grocery purchased x pounds of produce for p dollars per pound. If y pounds of the produce had to be discarded due to spoilage and the grocery sold the rest for s dollars per pound, which of the following represents the gross profit on the sale of the produce?

(A) $(x - y)s - xp$

(B) $(x - y)p - ys$

(C) $(s - p)y - xp$

(D) $xp - ys$

(E) $(x - y)(s - p)$

PS16990
173. If x, y, and z are positive integers such that x is a factor of y, and x is a multiple of z, which of the following is NOT necessarily an integer?

(A) $\dfrac{x + z}{z}$

(B) $\dfrac{y + z}{x}$

(C) $\dfrac{x + y}{z}$

(D) $\dfrac{xy}{z}$

(E) $\dfrac{yz}{x}$

PS08416
174. Running at their respective constant rates, Machine X takes 2 days longer to produce w widgets than Machine Y. At these rates, if the two machines together produce $\dfrac{5}{4}w$ widgets in 3 days, how many days would it take Machine X alone to produce $2w$ widgets?

(A)   4

(B)   6

(C)   8

(D)   10

(E)   12

PS07117
175. A square wooden plaque has a square brass inlay in the center, leaving a wooden strip of uniform width around the brass square. If the ratio of the brass area to the wooden area is 25 to 39, which of the following could be the width, in inches, of the wooden strip?

I.   1

II.   3

III.   4

(A)   I only

(B)   II only

(C)   I and II only

(D)   I and III only

(E)   I, II, and III

PS16963
176. $\dfrac{2\frac{3}{5} - 1\frac{2}{3}}{\frac{2}{3} - \frac{3}{5}} =$

(A)   16

(B)   14

(C)   3

(D)   1

(E) -1

4.4 Answer Key

1.	A	33.	D	65.	B	97.	B
2.	D	34.	E	66.	A	98.	C
3.	A	35.	E	67.	D	99.	A
4.	B	36.	D	68.	C	100.	B
5.	D	37.	D	69.	D	101.	E
6.	E	38.	E	70.	C	102.	B
7.	C	39.	D	71.	B	103.	D
8.	E	40.	C	72.	D	104.	B
9.	A	41.	C	73.	D	105.	E
10.	C	42.	C	74.	C	106.	E
11.	C	43.	E	75.	A	107.	B
12.	C	44.	D	76.	C	108.	E
13.	C	45.	D	77.	A	109.	B
14.	C	46.	E	78.	D	110.	E
15.	E	47.	E	79.	B	111.	C
16.	E	48.	D	80.	E	112.	E
17.	B	49.	A	81.	B	113.	D
18.	D	50.	D	82.	E	114.	B
19.	B	51.	B	83.	D	115.	B
20.	C	52.	B	84.	B	116.	C
21.	D	53.	C	85.	C	117.	C
22.	B	54.	B	86.	A	118.	B
23.	D	55.	E	87.	C	119.	E
24.	D	56.	C	88.	C	120.	B
25.	C	57.	D	89.	D	121.	E
26.	B	58.	B	90.	B	122.	E
27.	A	59.	D	91.	C	123.	B
28.	B	60.	C	92.	D	124.	B
29.	A	61.	C	93.	A	125.	B
30.	C	62.	E	94.	B	126.	B
31.	D	63.	B	95.	D	127.	C
32.	B	64.	C	96.	B	128.	B

129.	D	141.	B	153.	B	165.	C
130.	B	142.	C	154.	D	166.	D
131.	D	143.	E	155.	A	167.	A
132.	B	144.	A	156.	A	168.	A
133.	D	145.	E	157.	D	169.	B
134.	B	146.	C	158.	D	170.	B
135.	C	147.	C	159.	D	171.	B
136.	C	148.	E	160.	C	172.	A
137.	B	149.	C	161.	A	173.	B
138.	A	150.	D	162.	B	174.	E
139.	D	151.	D	163.	D	175.	E
140.	D	152.	E	164.	A	176.	B

4.5 Answer Explanations

The following discussion is intended to familiarize you with the most efficient and effective approaches to the kinds of problems common to problem solving questions. The particular questions in this chapter are generally representative of the kinds of problem solving questions you will encounter on the GMAT. Remember that it is the problem solving strategy that is important, not the specific details of a particular question.

*PS03439

1. Working at a constant rate, a copy machine makes 20 copies of a one-page document per minute. If the machine works at this constant rate, how many hours does it take to make 4,800 copies of a one-page document?

   (A) 4
   (B) 5
   (C) 6
   (D) 7
   (E) 8

Arithmetic Rate

The copy machine produces 20 copies of the one-page document each minute. Because there are 60 minutes in an hour, the constant rate of 20 copies per minute is equal to $60 \times 20 = 1,200$ copies per hour. With the machine working at this rate, the amount of time that it takes to produce 4,800 copies of the document is

$$\frac{4800 \text{ copies}}{1200 \frac{\text{copies}}{\text{hour}}} = 4 \text{ hours.}$$

The correct answer is A.

PS11042

2. If $x + y = 2$ and $x^2 + y^2 = 2$, what is the value of xy?

   (A) −2
   (B) −1
   (C)   0
   (D)   1
   (E)   2

Algebra Second-degree equations

$x + y = 2$	given
$y = 2 - x$	subtract x from both sides
$x^2 + (2 - x)^2 = 2$	substitute $y = 2 - x$ into $x^2 + y^2 = 2$
$2x^2 - 4x + 4 = 2$	expand and combine like terms
$2x^2 - 4x + 2 = 0$	subtract 2 from both sides
$x^2 - 2x + 1 = 0$	divide both sides by 2
$(x - 1)(x - 1) = 0$	factor
$x = 1$	set each factor equal to 0
$y = 1$	use $x = 1$ and $y = 2 - x$
$xy = 1$	multiply 1 and 1

Alternatively, the value of xy can be found by first squaring both sides of the equation $x + y = 2$.

$x + y = 2$	given
$(x + y)^2 = 4$	square both sides
$x^2 + 2xy + y^2 = 4$	expand and combine like terms
$2 + 2xy = 4$	replace $x^2 + y^2$ with 2
$2xy = 2$	subtract 2 from both sides
$xy = 1$	divide both sides by 2

The correct answer is D.

PS02978

3. The sum S of the first n consecutive positive even integers is given by $S = n(n + 1)$. For what value of n is this sum equal to 110?

   (A) 10
   (B) 11
   (C) 12
   (D) 13
   (E) 14

---

*These numbers correlate with the online test bank question number. See the GMAT Quantitative Review Online Index in the back of this book.

Algebra Factoring

Given that the sum of the first n even numbers is $n(n + 1)$, the sum is equal to 110 when $110 = n(n + 1)$. To find the value of n in this case, we need to find the two consecutive integers whose product is 110. These integers are 10 and 11; $10 \times 11 = 110$. The smaller of these numbers is n.

The correct answer is A.

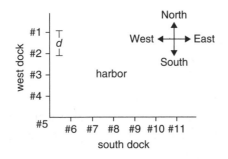

PS08375

4. A certain harbor has docking stations along its west and south docks, as shown in the figure; any two adjacent docking stations are separated by a uniform distance d. A certain boat left the west dock from docking station #2 and moved in a straight line diagonally until it reached the south dock. If the boat was at one time directly east of docking station #4 and directly north of docking station #7, at which docking station on the south dock did the boat arrive?

    (A)   #7
    (B)   #8
    (C)   #9
    (D)   #10
    (E)   #11

Geometry Coordinate geometry

The boat traveled in a straight line from docking station #2 on the west dock to one of the docking stations on the south dock, passing through a single point that is both due east of docking station #4 and due north of docking station #7. Call this point P. Having traveled to P, the boat was both $2d$ south of its starting point and $2d$ east of its starting point. Therefore, traveling in a straight line, the boat traveled one unit south for every one unit traveled east. And because at point P the boat was a distance d north of the south dock, the boat must have reached the south dock at a point which is a distance of d east of docking

station #7 (which is due south of point P). This point is the position of docking station #8. The boat therefore arrived at docking station #8.

The correct answer is B.

PS03887

5. $6(87.30 + 0.65) - 5(87.30) =$

    (A)   3.90
    (B)   39.00
    (C)   90.90
    (D)   91.20
    (E)   91.85

Arithmetic Factors, multiples, and divisibility

This question is most efficiently answered by distributing the 6 over 87.30 and 0.65, and then combining the terms that contain a factor of 87.30, as follows:

$6(87.30 + 0.65) - 5(87.30) = 6\,(87.30) + 6\,(0.65)$
$- 5\,(87.30) = (6 - 5)\,87.30 + 6(0.65) = 87.30 +$
$3.90 = 91.20$

The correct answer is D.

PS13800

6. Points A, B, C, and D, in that order, lie on a line. If $AB = 3$ cm, $AC = 4$ cm, and $BD = 6$ cm, what is CD, in centimeters?

    (A)   1
    (B)   2
    (C)   3
    (D)   4
    (E)   5

Geometry Lines and segments

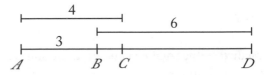

The figure shows points A, B, C, and D as well as the given measurements. Since $AC = AB + BC$, it follows that $4 = 3 + BC$, and so $BC = 1$. Then, since $BD = BC + CD$, it follows that $6 = 1 + CD$, and so $CD = 5$.

Alternately, $AD = AB + BD = 3 + 6 = 9$. Also, $AD = AC + CD$, so $9 = 4 + CD$ and $CD = 5$.

The correct answer is E.

PS05292

7. What is the value of $x^2yz - xyz^2$, if $x = -2$, $y = 1$, and $z = 3$?

(A) 20

(B) 24

(C) 30

(D) 32

(E) 48

Algebra Operations on integers

Given that $x = -2$, $y = 1$, and $z = 3$, it follows by substitution that

$$
\begin{aligned}
x^2yz - xyz^2 &= (-2)^2(1)(3) - (-2)(1)(3^2) \\
&= (4)(1)(3) - (-2)(1)(9) \\
&= 12 - (-18) \\
&= 12 + 18 \\
&= 30
\end{aligned}
$$

The correct answer is C.

PS11468

8. A souvenir vendor purchased 1,000 shirts for a special event at a price of $5 each. The vendor sold 600 of the shirts on the day of the event for $12 each and 300 of the shirts in the week following the event for $4 each. The vendor was unable to sell the remaining shirts. What was the vendor's gross profit on the sale of these shirts?

(A) $1,000

(B) $2,200

(C) $2,700

(D) $3,000

(E) $3,400

Arithmetic Applied problems

The vendor's gross profit on the sale of the shirts is equal to the total revenue from the shirts that were sold minus the total cost for all of the shirts. The total cost for all of the shirts is equal to the number of shirts the vendor purchased multiplied by the price paid by the vendor for each shirt: $1,000 \times \$5 = \$5,000$. The total revenue from the shirts that were sold is equal to the total revenue from the 600 shirts sold for $12 each plus the total revenue from the 300 shirts that were sold

for $4 each: $600 \times \$12 + 300 \times \$4 = \$7,200 + \$1,200 = \$8,400$. The gross profit is therefore $\$8,400 - \$5,000 = \$3,400$.

The correct answer is E.

PS06937

9. If $x > y$ and $y > z$, which of the following represents the greatest number?

(A) $x - z$

(B) $x - y$

(C) $y - x$

(D) $z - y$

(E) $z - x$

Algebra Inequalities

From $x > y$ and $y > z$, it follows that $x > z$. These inequalities imply the following about the differences that are given in the answer choices:

Answer choice	Difference	Algebraic sign	Reason
(A)	$x - z$	positive	$x > z$ implies $x - z > 0$
(B)	$x - y$	positive	$x > y$ implies $x - y > 0$
(C)	$y - x$	negative	$x - y > 0$ implies $y - x < 0$
(D)	$z - y$	negative	$y > z$ implies $0 > z - y$
(E)	$z - x$	negative	$x - z > 0$ implies $z - x < 0$

Since the expressions in A and B represent positive numbers and the expressions in C, D, and E represent negative numbers, the latter can be eliminated because every negative number is less than every positive number. To determine which of $x - z$ and $x - y$ is greater, consider the placement of points with coordinates x, y, and z on the number line.

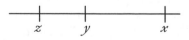

The distance between x and z (that is, $x - z$) is the sum of the distance between x and y (that is, $x - y$) and the distance between y and z (that is, $y - z$).

Therefore, $(x - z) > (x - y)$, which means that $x - z$ represents the greater of the numbers represented by $(x - z)$ and $(x - y)$. Thus, $x - z$ represents the greatest of the numbers represented by the answer choices.

Alternatively,

$$y > z \quad \text{given}$$
$$-y < -z \quad \text{multiply both sides by } -1$$
$$x - y < x - z \quad \text{add } x \text{ to both sides}$$

Thus, $x - z$ represents the greater of the numbers represented by $(x - z)$ and $(x - y)$. Therefore, $x - z$ represents the greatest of the numbers represented by the answer choices.

The correct answer is A.

PS12926

10. To order certain plants from a catalog, it costs $3.00 per plant, plus a 5 percent sales tax, plus $6.95 for shipping and handling regardless of the number of plants ordered. If Company C ordered these plants from the catalog at the total cost of $69.95, how many plants did Company C order?

(A) 22
(B) 21
(C) 20
(D) 19
(E) 18

Algebra First-degree equations

Letting x represent the number of plants Company C bought from the catalog, then, in dollars, $3.00x$ is the cost of the plants, $(0.05)(3.00x)$ is the sales tax, and 6.95 is the shipping and handling fee. It follows that

$$3.00x + (0.05)(3.00x) + 6.95 = 69.95 \quad \text{plants + tax + shipping = total}$$
$$(3.00x)(1.05) + 6.95 = 69.95 \quad \text{add like terms}$$
$$(3.00x)(1.05) = 63.00 \quad \text{subtract 6.95 from both sides}$$
$$x = 20 \quad \text{divide both sides by (3.00)(1.05)}$$

Therefore, Company C bought 20 plants from the catalog.

The correct answer is C.

PS00812

11. A rug manufacturer produces rugs at a cost of $75 per rug. What is the manufacturer's gross profit from the sale of 150 rugs if $\frac{2}{3}$ of the rugs are sold for $150 per rug and the rest are sold for $200 per rug?

(A) $10,350
(B) $11,250
(C) $13,750
(D) $16,250
(E) $17,800

Arithmetic Applied problems; Proportions

The gross profit from the sale of 150 rugs is equal to the revenue from the sale of the rugs minus the cost of producing them. For $\frac{2}{3}$ of the 150 rugs—100 of them—the gross profit per rug is $150 - $75 = 75. For the remaining 50 rugs, the gross profit per rug is $200 - $75 = 125. The gross profit from the sale of the 150 rugs is therefore $100 \times $75 + 50 \times $125 = $13,750$.

The correct answer is C.

PS07793

12. The value of Maureen's investment portfolio has decreased by 5.8 percent since her initial investment in the portfolio. If her initial investment was $16,800, what is the current value of the portfolio?

(A) $7,056.00
(B) $14,280.00
(C) $15,825.60
(D) $16,702.56
(E) $17,774.40

Arithmetic Percents

Maureen's initial investment was $16,800, and it has decreased by 5.8%. Its current value is therefore $(100\% - 5.8\%) = 94.2\%$ of $16,800, which is equal to $0.942 \times $16,800$. To make the multiplication simpler, this can be expressed as (942×16.8). Thus multiplying, we obtain the result of $15,825.60.

The correct answer is C.

PS03036

13. Company C produces toy trucks at a cost of $5.00 each for the first 100 trucks and $3.50 for each additional truck. If 500 toy trucks were produced by Company C and sold for $10.00 each, what was Company C's gross profit?

(A) $2,250
(B) $2,500
(C) $3,100
(D) $3,250
(E) $3,500

Arithmetic Applied problems

The company's gross profit on the 500 toy trucks is the company's revenue from selling the trucks minus the company's cost of producing the trucks. The revenue is $(500)(\$10.00) = \$5,000$. The cost for the first 100 trucks is $(100)(\$5.00) = \$500$, and the cost for the other 400 trucks is $(400)(\$3.50) = \$1,400$ for a total cost of $\$500 + \$1,400 = \$1,900$. Thus, the company's gross profit is $\$5,000 - \$1,900 = \$3,100$.

The correct answer is C.

PS07694

14. A group of store managers must assemble 280 displays for an upcoming sale. If they assemble 25 percent of the displays during the first hour and 40 percent of the remaining displays during the second hour, how many of the displays will not have been assembled by the end of the second hour?

(A) 70
(B) 98
(C) 126
(D) 168
(E) 182

Arithmetic Percents

If, during the first hour, 25 percent of the total displays were assembled, then $280(0.25) = 70$ displays were assembled, leaving $280 - 70 = 210$ displays remaining to be assembled. Since 40 percent of the remaining displays were assembled during the second hour, $0.40(210) = 84$ displays were assembled during the second hour. Thus, $70 + 84 = 154$ displays were assembled during the first two hours and $280 - 154 = 126$ displays had not been assembled by the end of the second hour.

The correct answer is C.

Division	Profit or Loss (in millions of dollars)				
	1991	1992	1993	1994	1995
A	1.1	(3.4)	1.9	2.0	0.6
B	(2.3)	5.5	(4.5)	3.9	(2.9)
C	10.0	(6.6)	5.3	1.1	(3.0)

PS02019

15. The annual profit or loss for the three divisions of Company T for the years 1991 through 1995 are summarized in the table shown, where losses are enclosed in parentheses. For which division and which three consecutive years shown was the division's profit or loss for the three-year period closest to $0 ?

(A) Division A for 1991–1993
(B) Division A for 1992–1994
(C) Division B for 1991–1993
(D) Division B for 1993–1995
(E) Division C for 1992–1994

Arithmetic Applied problems

For completeness, the table shows all 9 of the profit or loss amounts, in millions of dollars, for each of the 3 divisions and the 3 three-year periods.

	1991–1993	1992–1994	1993–1995
A	−0.4	0.5	4.5
B	−1.3	4.9	−3.5
C	8.7	**−0.2**	3.4

The correct answer is E.

PS13583

16. Of the following, which is least?

(A) $\dfrac{0.03}{0.00071}$

(B) $\dfrac{0.03}{0.0071}$

(C) $\dfrac{0.03}{0.071}$

(D) $\dfrac{0.03}{0.71}$

(E) $\dfrac{0.03}{7.1}$

Arithmetic Operations on rational numbers

Since the numerator of all of the fractions in the answer choices is 0.03, the least of the fractions will be the fraction with the greatest denominator. The greatest denominator is 7.1, and so the least of the fractions is $\dfrac{0.03}{7.1}$.

The correct answer is E.

PS07385

17. The maximum recommended pulse rate R, when exercising, for a person who is x years of age is given by the equation $R = 176 - 0.8x$. What is the age, in years, of a person whose maximum recommended pulse rate when exercising is 140 ?

(A) 40
(B) 45
(C) 50
(D) 55
(E) 60

Algebra Substitution; Operations with rational numbers

Substitute 140 for R in the given equation and solve for x.

$$140 = 176 - 0.8x$$
$$-36 = -0.8x$$
$$\frac{-36}{-0.8} = x$$
$$45 = x$$

The correct answer is B.

PS08011

18. If the average (arithmetic mean) of 5 numbers $j, j + 5, 2j - 1, 4j - 2,$ and $5j - 1$ is 8, what is the value of j ?

(A) $\dfrac{1}{3}$

(B) $\dfrac{7}{13}$

(C) 1

(D) 3

(E) 8

Algebra First-degree equations

$$\frac{j + (j + 5) + (2j - 1) + (4j - 2) + (5j - 1)}{5} = 8 \quad \text{given}$$

$$j + (j + 5) + (2j - 1) + (4j - 2) + (5j - 1) = 40 \quad \text{multiply both sides by 5}$$

$$13j + 1 = 40 \quad \text{combine like terms}$$

$$13j = 39 \quad \text{subtract 1 from both sides}$$

$$j = 3 \quad \text{divide both sides by 13}$$

The correct answer is D.

PS14037

19. Guadalupe owns 2 rectangular tracts of land. One is 300 m by 500 m and the other is 250 m by 630 m. The combined area of these 2 tracts is how many square meters?

(A) 3,360
(B) 307,500
(C) 621,500
(D) 704,000
(E) 2,816,000

Geometry Area

The area of a rectangle can be found by multiplying the length and width of the rectangle. Therefore, the combined area, in square meters, of the 2 rectangular tracts of land is $(300)(500) + (250)(630) = 150,000 + 157,500 = 307,500$.

The correct answer is B.

PS03918

20. There are five sales agents in a certain real estate office. One month Andy sold twice as many properties as Ellen, Bob sold 3 more than Ellen, Cary sold twice as many as Bob, and Dora sold as many as Bob and Ellen together. Who sold the most properties that month?

(A) Andy
(B) Bob
(C) Cary
(D) Dora
(E) Ellen

Algebra Order

Let x represent the number of properties that Ellen sold, where $x \geq 0$. Then, since Andy sold twice as many properties as Ellen, $2x$ represents the number of properties that Andy sold. Bob sold 3 more properties than Ellen, so $(x + 3)$ represents the number of properties that Bob sold. Cary sold twice as many properties as Bob, so $2(x + 3) = (2x + 6)$ represents the number of properties that Cary sold. Finally, Dora sold as many properties as Bob and Ellen combined, so $[(x + 3) + x] = (2x + 3)$ represents the number of properties that Dora sold. The following table summarizes these results.

Agent	Properties sold
Andy	$2x$
Bob	$x + 3$
Cary	$2x + 6$
Dora	$2x + 3$
Ellen	x

Since $x \geq 0$, clearly $2x + 6$ exceeds x, $x + 3$, $2x$, and $2x + 3$. Therefore, Cary sold the most properties.

The correct answer is C.

PS10862

21. In a field day at a school, each child who competed in n events and scored a total of p points was given an overall score of $\frac{p}{n} + n$. Andrew competed in 1 event and scored 9 points. Jason competed in 3 events and scored 5, 6, and 7 points, respectively. What was the ratio of Andrew's overall score to Jason's overall score?

(A) $\dfrac{10}{23}$

(B) $\dfrac{7}{10}$

(C) $\dfrac{4}{5}$

(D) $\dfrac{10}{9}$

(E) $\dfrac{12}{7}$

Algebra Applied problems; Substitution

Andrew participated in 1 event and scored 9 points, so his overall score was $\frac{9}{1} + 1 = 10$. Jason participated in 3 events and scored $5 + 6 + 7 = 18$ points, so his overall score was $\frac{18}{3} + 3 = 9$. The ratio of Andrew's overall score to Jason's overall score was $\frac{10}{9}$.

The correct answer is D.

PS06719

22. A certain work plan for September requires that a work team, working every day, produce an average of 200 items per day. For the first half of the month, the team produced an average of 150 items per day. How many items per day must the team average during the second half of the month if it is to attain the average daily production rate required by the work plan?

(A) 225
(B) 250
(C) 275
(D) 300
(E) 350

Arithmetic Rate problem

The work plan requires that the team produce an average of 200 items per day in September. Because the team has only produced an average of 150 items per day in the first half of September, it has a shortfall of $200 - 150 = 50$ items per day for the first half of the month. The team must make up for this shortfall in the second half of the month, which has an equal number of days as the first half of the month. The team must therefore produce in the second half of the month an average amount per day that is 50 items greater than the required average of 200 items per day for the entire month. This amount for the second half of September is 250 items per day.

The correct answer is B.

PS01949

23. A company sells radios for $15.00 each. It costs the company $14.00 per radio to produce 1,000 radios and $13.50 per radio to produce 2,000 radios. How much greater will the company's gross profit be from the production and sale of 2,000 radios than from the production and sale of 1,000 radios?

(A) $500
(B) $1,000
(C) $1,500
(D) $2,000
(E) $2,500

Arithmetic Applied problems

If the company produces and sells 1,000 radios, its gross profit from the sale of these radios is equal to the total revenue from the sale of these radios minus the total cost. The total cost is equal to the number of radios produced multiplied by the production cost per radio: 1,000 × $15.00. The total revenue is equal to the number of radios sold multiplied by the selling price: 1,000 × $14.00. The gross profit in this case is therefore 1,000 × $15.00 − 1,000 × $14.00 = 1,000 × ($15.00 − $14.00) = 1,000 ($1.00) = $1,000. If 2,000 radios are produced and sold, the total cost is equal to 2,000 × $13.50 and the total revenue is equal to 2,000 × $15.00. The gross profit in this case is therefore 2,000 × $15.00 − 2,000 × $13.50 = 2,000 × ($15.00 − $13.50) = 2,000 × ($1.50) = $3,000. This profit of $3,000 is $2,000 greater than the gross profit of $1,000 from producing and selling 1,000 radios.

The correct answer is D.

PS06555

24. Which of the following represent positive numbers?

I.   −3 − (−5)
II.   (−3)(−5)
III. −5 − (−3)

(A)   I only
(B)   II only
(C)   III only
(D)   I and II
(E)   II and III

Arithmetic Operations on integers

Find the value of each expression to determine if it is positive.

I. $-3 - (-5) = -3 + 5 = 2$, which is positive.

II. $(-3)(-5) = 15$, which is positive.

III. $-5 - (-3) = -5 + 3 = -2$, which is not positive.

The correct answer is D.

PS02948

25. If $\frac{x}{4}$ is 2 more than $\frac{x}{8}$, then $x =$

(A)   4
(B)   8
(C)   16
(D)   32
(E)   64

Algebra First-degree equations

Write an equation for the given information and solve for x.

$$\frac{x}{4} = 2 + \frac{x}{8}$$

$$(8)\left(\frac{x}{4}\right) = (8)\left(2 + \frac{x}{8}\right)$$

$$2x = 16 + x$$

$$x = 16$$

The correct answer is C.

PS09983

26. Point X lies on side BC of rectangle $ABCD$, which has length 12 and width 8. What is the area of triangular region AXD?

(A)   96
(B)   48
(C)   32
(D)   24
(E)   20

Geometry Area

Note that, in rectangle $ABCD$, the sides BC and AD do not share an endpoint and must therefore be on opposite sides of the rectangle. We thus see that the point X, which is both on triangle AXD and on side BC of the rectangle, lies on the side of the rectangle that is opposite the side AD of the rectangle. AD is also a side of the triangle. So if the rectangle is drawn with AD horizontal and on the bottom (see the diagram, which is not drawn to scale), the vertical height of the triangle from the base AD is equal to the length of the sides on the rectangle that are adjacent to AD. Given the formula for the area of a triangle, $\frac{1}{2} \times$ base $\times$ height, the area of the triangle AXD is thus $\frac{1}{2} \times AD \times AB$ (or equivalently $\frac{1}{2} \times AD \times CD$).

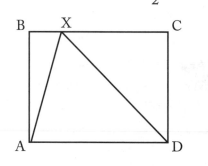

Now, AD may be either a length or a width of the rectangle—equal to 12 or equal to 8. If AD is equal to 12, then AB is a width and is equal to 8; the area of the triangle is thus $\frac{1}{2} \times 12 \times 8$. If AD is instead equal to 8, then AB is equal to 12, and the formula for the area of the triangle results in the expression $\frac{1}{2} \times 8 \times 12$. In both cases, the area of the triangle is equal to 48.

The correct answer is B.

PS07659

27. A grocer has 400 pounds of coffee in stock, 20 percent of which is decaffeinated. If the grocer buys another 100 pounds of coffee of which 60 percent is decaffeinated, what percent, by weight, of the grocer's stock of coffee is decaffeinated?

   (A) 28%
   (B) 30%
   (C) 32%
   (D) 34%
   (E) 40%

Arithmetic Percents

The grocer has 400 pounds of coffee in stock, of which (400)(20%) = 80 pounds is decaffeinated coffee. Therefore, if the grocer buys 100 pounds of coffee, of which (100)(60%) = 60 pounds is decaffeinated coffee, then the percent of the grocer's stock of coffee that is decaffeinated would be $\frac{80 + 60}{400 + 100} = \frac{140}{500} = \frac{28}{100} = 28\%$.

The correct answer is A.

PS05129

28. The toll T, in dollars, for a truck using a certain bridge is given by the formula $T = 1.50 + 0.50(x - 2)$, where x is the number of axles on the truck. What is the toll for an 18-wheel truck that has 2 wheels on its front axle and 4 wheels on each of its other axles?

   (A) $2.50
   (B) $3.00
   (C) $3.50
   (D) $4.00
   (E) $5.00

Algebra Operations on rational numbers

The 18-wheel truck has 2 wheels on its front axle and 4 wheels on each of its other axles, and so if A represents the number of axles on the truck in addition to the front axle, then $2 + 4A = 18$, from which it follows that $4A = 16$ and $A = 4$. Therefore, the total number of axles on the truck is $1 + A = 1 + 4 = 5$. Then, using $T = 1.50 + 0.50(x - 2)$, where x is the number of axles on the truck and $x = 5$, it follows that $T = 1.50 + 0.50(5 - 2) = 1.50 + 1.50 = 3.00$. Therefore, the toll for the truck is $3.00.

The correct answer is B.

PS13917

29. For what value of x between −4 and 4, inclusive, is the value of $x^2 - 10x + 16$ the greatest?

   (A) −4
   (B) −2
   (C) 0
   (D) 2
   (E) 4

Algebra Second-degree equations

Given the expression $x^2 - 10x + 16$, a table of values can be created for the corresponding function $f(x) = x^2 - 10x + 16$ and the graph in the standard (x,y) coordinate plane can be sketched by plotting selected points:

x	$f(x)$
-4	72
-3	55
-2	40
-1	27
0	16
1	7
2	0
3	-5
4	-8
5	-9
6	-8
7	-5
8	0
9	7

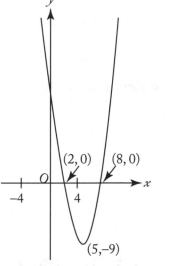

It is clear from both the table of values and the sketch of the graph that as the value of x increases from -4 to 4, the values of $x^2 - 10x + 16$ decrease. Therefore, the value of $x^2 - 10x + 16$ is greatest when $x = -4$.

Alternatively, the given expression, $x^2 - 10x + 16$, has the form $ax^2 + bx + c$, where $a = 1$, $b = -10$, and $c = 16$. The graph in the standard (x,y) coordinate plane of the corresponding function $f(x) = ax^2 + bx + c$ is a parabola with vertex at

$x = -\dfrac{b}{2a}$, and so the vertex of the graph of $f(x) = x^2 - 10x + 16$ is at

$$x = -\left(\dfrac{-10}{2(1)}\right) = 5.$$

Because $a = 1$ and 1 is positive, this parabola opens upward and values of $x^2 - 10x + 16$ decrease as x increases from -4 to 4. Therefore, the greatest value of $x^2 - 10x + 16$ for all values of x between -4 and 4, inclusive, is at $x = -4$.

The correct answer is A.

PS15994

30. If $x = -\dfrac{5}{8}$ and $y = -\dfrac{1}{2}$, what is the value of the expression $-2x - y^2$?

(A) $-\dfrac{3}{2}$

(B) -1

(C) 1

(D) $\dfrac{3}{2}$

(E) $\dfrac{7}{4}$

Algebra Fractions

If $x = -\dfrac{5}{8}$ and $y = -\dfrac{1}{2}$, then

$$-2x - y^2 = -2\left(-\dfrac{5}{8}\right) - \left(-\dfrac{1}{2}\right)^2 = \dfrac{5}{4} - \dfrac{1}{4} = \dfrac{4}{4} = 1.$$

The correct answer is C.

PS13686

31. If $x - y = R$ and $xy = S$, then $(x - 2)(y + 2) =$

(A) $R + S - 4$

(B) $R + 2S - 4$

(C) $2R - S - 4$

(D) $2R + S - 4$

(E) $2R + S$

Algebra Simplifying algebraic expressions; Substitution

$(x - 2)(y + 2) = xy + 2x - 2y - 4$ multiply binomials

$\quad = xy + 2(x - y) - 4$ distributive principle

$\quad = S + 2R - 4$ substitution

$\quad = 2R + S - 4$ commutative principle

The correct answer is D.

PS01466

32. For positive integers *a* and *b*, the remainder when *a* is divided by *b* is equal to the remainder when *b* is divided by *a*. Which of the following could be a value of *ab* ?

  I.   24

  II.   30

  III. 36

(A) II only

(B) III only

(C) I and II only

(D) II and III only

(E) I, II, and III

Arithmetic Properties of integers

We are given that the remainder when *a* is divided by *b* is equal to the remainder when *b* is divided by *a*, and asked about possible values of *ab*. We thus need to find what our given condition implies about *a* and *b*.

We consider two cases: *a* = *b* and *a* ≠ *b*.

If *a* = *b*, then our given condition is trivially satisfied: the remainder when *a* is divided by *a* is equal to the remainder when *a* is divided by *b*. The condition thus allows that *a* be equal to *b*.

Now consider the case of *a* ≠ *b*. Either a < b or *b* < *a*. Supposing that *a* < *b*, the remainder when *a* is divided by *b* is simply *a*. (For example, if 7 is divided by 10, then the remainder is 7.) However, according to our given condition, this remainder, *a*, is also the remainder when *b* is divided by *a*, which is impossible. If *b* is divided by *a*, then the remainder must be less than *a*. (For example, for any number that is divided by 10, the remainder cannot be 10 or greater.) Similar reasoning applies if we suppose that *b* < *a*. This is also impossible.

We thus see that *a* must be equal to *b*, and consider the statements I, II, and III.

  I. Factored in terms of prime numbers, 24 = 3 × 2 × 2 × 2. Because "3" occurs only once in the factorization, we see that there is no integer *a* such that *a* × *a* = 24. Based on the reasoning above, we see that 24 cannot be a value of *ab*.

  II. Factored in terms of prime numbers, 30 = 5 × 3 × 2. Because there is no integer *a* such that *a* × *a* = 30, we see that 30 cannot be a value of *ab*.

  III. Because 36 = 6 × 6, we see that 36 is a possible value of *ab* (with *a* = *b*).

The correct answer is B.

PS01867

33. List *S* consists of the positive integers that are multiples of 9 and are less than 100. What is the median of the integers in *S* ?

(A) 36

(B) 45

(C) 49

(D) 54

(E) 63

Arithmetic Series and sequences

In the set of positive integers less than 100, the greatest multiple of 9 is 99 (9 × 11) and the least multiple of 9 is 9 (9 × 1). The sequence of positive multiples of 9 that are less than 100 is therefore the sequence of numbers 9 × *k*, where *k* ranges from 1 through 11. The median of the numbers *k* from 1 through 11 is 6. Therefore the median of the numbers 9 × *k*, where *k* ranges from 1 through 11, is 9 × 6 = 54.

The correct answer is D.

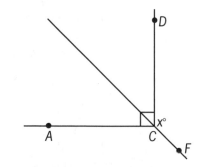

PS07397

34. In the figure above, if *F* is a point on the line that bisects angle *ACD* and the measure of angle *DCF* is *x*°, which of the following is true of *x* ?

(A)   90 ≤ x < 100

(B) 100 ≤ x < 110

(C) 110 ≤ x < 120

(D) 120 ≤ x < 130

(E) 130 ≤ x < 140

Geometry Angles

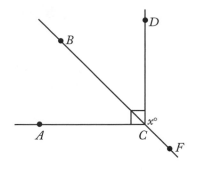

As shown in the figure above, if B is on the line that bisects $\angle ACD$ then the degree measure of $\angle DCB$ is $\dfrac{90}{2} = 45$. Then because B, C, and F are collinear, the sum of the degree measures of $\angle BCD$ and $\angle DCF$ is 180. Therefore, $x = 180 - 45 = 135$ and $130 \le 135 < 140$.

The correct answer is E.

PS07380
35. A rope 20.6 meters long is cut into two pieces. If the length of one piece of rope is 2.8 meters shorter than the length of the other, what is the length, in meters, of the longer piece of rope?

(A) 7.5
(B) 8.9
(C) 9.9
(D) 10.3
(E) 11.7

Algebra First-degree equations

If x represents the length of the longer piece of rope, then $x - 2.8$ represents the length of the shorter piece, where both lengths are in meters. The total length of the two pieces of rope is 20.6 meters so,

$$
\begin{aligned}
x + (x - 2.8) &= 20.6 \quad \text{given} \\
2x - 2.8 &= 20.6 \quad \text{add like terms} \\
2x &= 23.4 \quad \text{add 2.8 to both sides} \\
x &= 11.7 \quad \text{divide both sides by 2}
\end{aligned}
$$

Thus, the length of the longer piece of rope is 11.7 meters.

The correct answer is E.

PS01120
36. If x and y are integers and x − y is odd, which of the following must be true?

I. xy is even.
II. $x^2 + y^2$ is odd.
III. $(x + y)^2$ is even.

(A) I only
(B) II only
(C) III only
(D) I and II only
(E) I, II, and III

Arithmetic Properties of numbers

We are given that x and y are integers and that $x - y$ is odd, and then asked, for various operations on x and y, whether the results of the operations are odd or even. It is therefore useful to determine, given that $x - y$ is odd, whether x and y are odd or even. If both x and y are even—that is, divisible by 2—then $x - y = 2m - 2n = 2(m - n)$ for integers m and n. We thus see if both x and y are even then $x - y$ cannot be odd. And because $x - y$ *is* odd, we see that x and y cannot both be even. Similarly, if both x and y are odd, then, for integers j and k, $x = 2j + 1$ and $y = 2k + 1$. Therefore, $x - y = (2j + 1) - (2k + 1)$. The ones cancel, and we are left with $x - y = 2j - 2k = 2(j - k)$. Because $2(j - k)$ would be even, x and y cannot both be odd if $x - y$ is odd. It follows from all of this that one of x or y must be even and the other odd.

Now consider the statements I through III.

I.   If one of x or y is even, then one of x or y is divisible by 2. It follows that xy is divisible by 2 and that xy is even.

II. Given that a number x or y is odd—not divisible by 2—we know that its product with itself is not divisible by 2 and is therefore odd. On the other hand, given that a number x or y is even, we know that its product with itself *is* divisible by 2 and is therefore even. The sum $x^2 + y^2$ is therefore the sum of an even number and an odd number. In such a case, the sum can be written as $(2m) + (2n + 1) = 2(m + n) + 1$, with m and n integers. It follows that $x^2 + y^2$ is not divisible by 2 and is therefore odd.

III. We know that one of x or y is even and the other is odd. We can therefore see from the discussion of statement II that $x + y$ is odd, and then also see, from the discussion of statement II, that the product of $x + y$ with itself, $(x + y)^2$, is odd.

The correct answer is D.

PS00335

37. On Monday, the opening price of a certain stock was $100 per share and its closing price was $110 per share. On Tuesday the closing price of the stock was 10 percent less than its closing price on Monday, and on Wednesday the closing price of the stock was 4 percent greater than its closing price on Tuesday. What was the approximate percent change in the price of the stock from its opening price on Monday to its closing price on Wednesday?

(A) A decrease of 6%

(B) A decrease of 4%

(C) A decrease of 1%

(D) An increase of 3%

(E) An increase of 4%

Arithmetic Percents

The closing share price on Tuesday was 10% less than the closing price on Monday, $110. 10% of $110 is equal to $0.1 \times \$110 = \$11$, so the closing price on Tuesday was $110 - \$11 = \$99$. The closing price on Wednesday was 4% greater than this: $\$99 + (0.04 \times \$99) = \$99 + \$3.96 = \$102.96$. This value, $102.96, is 2.96% greater than $100, the opening price on Monday. The percentage change from the opening share price on Monday is therefore an increase of approximately 3%, which is the closest of the available answers to an increase of 2.96%.

The correct answer is D.

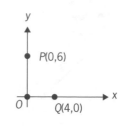

PS05109

38. In the rectangular coordinate system shown above, points O, P, and Q represent the sites of three proposed housing developments. If a fire station can be built at any point in the coordinate system, at which point would it be equidistant from all three developments?

(A) (3,1)

(B) (1,3)

(C) (3,2)

(D) (2,2)

(E) (2,3)

Geometry Coordinate geometry

Any point equidistant from the points $(0,0)$ and $(4,0)$ must lie on the perpendicular bisector of the segment with endpoints $(0,0)$ and $(4,0)$, which is the line with equation $x = 2$. Any point equidistant from the points $(0,0)$ and $(0,6)$ must lie on the perpendicular bisector of the segment with endpoints $(0,0)$ and $(0,6)$, which is the line with equation $y = 3$. Therefore, the point that is equidistant from $(0,0)$, $(4,0)$, and $(0,6)$ must lie on both of the lines $x = 2$ and $y = 3$, which is the point $(2,3)$.

Alternatively, let (x,y) be the point equidistant from $(0,0)$, $(4,0)$, and $(0,6)$. Since the distance between (x,y) and $(0,0)$ is equal to the distance between (x,y) and $(4,0)$, it follows from the distance formula that $\sqrt{x^2 + y^2} = \sqrt{(x-4)^2 + y^2}$. Squaring both sides gives $x^2 + y^2 = (x - 4)^2 + y^2$. Subtracting y^2 from both sides of the last equation and then expanding the right side gives $x^2 = x^2 - 8x + 16$, or $0 = -8x + 16$, or $x = 2$. Also, since the distance between (x,y) and $(0,0)$ is equal to the distance between (x,y) and $(0,6)$, it follows from the distance formula that $\sqrt{x^2 + y^2} = \sqrt{x^2 + (y-6)^2}$.

Squaring both sides of the last equation gives $x^2 + y^2 = x^2 + (y - 6)^2$. Subtracting x^2 from both sides and then expanding the right side gives $y^2 = y^2 - 12y + 36$, or $0 = -12y + 36$, or $y = 3$.

The correct answer is E.

PS05008

39. What is the perimeter, in meters, of a rectangular garden 6 meters wide that has the same area as a rectangular playground 16 meters long and 12 meters wide?

(A) 48
(B) 56
(C) 60
(D) 76
(E) 192

Geometry Perimeter and area

Let L represent the length, in meters, of the rectangular garden. It is given that the width of the garden is 6 meters and the area of the garden is the same as the area of a rectangular playground that is 16 meters long and 12 meters wide. It follows that $6L = (16)(12)$, and so $L = 32$. The perimeter of the garden is, then, $2(32 + 6) = 2(38) = 76$ meters.

The correct answer is D.

PS00918

40. $1 - 0.000001 =$

(A) $(1.01)(0.99)$
(B) $(1.11)(0.99)$
(C) $(1.001)(0.999)$
(D) $(1.111)(0.999)$
(E) $(1.0101)(0.0909)$

Arithmetic Place value

The task in this question is to find among the available answers the expression that is equal to $1 - 0.000001 = 0.999999$. In the case of option C, the first of the two factors, (1.001), is equal to $1 + 0.001$. One may therefore observe that $(1.001)(0.999) = (1 + 0.001)(0.999) = 0.999 + 0.000999 = 0.999999$. Option C is therefore a correct answer.

For option A, $(1.01)(0.99) = (1 + 0.01)(0.99) = 0.9999$. This option is therefore incorrect. For option B, $(1.11)(0.99) = (1 + 0.1 + 0.01)(0.99) = 0.99 + 0.099 + 0.0099 = 1.0989$. This option is therefore incorrect. For option D, $(1.111)(0.999) = 0.999 + 0.0999 + 0.00999 + 0.000999 = 1.109889$. This option is therefore incorrect. For option E, $(1.0101)(0.909) = 0.909 + 0.00909 + 0.0000909 = 0.9181809$. This option is therefore incorrect.

The correct answer is C.

PS04362

41. $|-4|(|-20|-|5|) =$

(A) -100
(B) -60
(C) 60
(D) 75
(E) 100

Arithmetic Absolute value

$|-4|(|-20|-|5|) = 4(20 - 5) = 4 \times 15 = 60$

The correct answer is C.

PS12934

42. Of the total amount that Jill spent on a shopping trip, excluding taxes, she spent 50 percent on clothing, 20 percent on food, and 30 percent on other items. If Jill paid a 4 percent tax on the clothing, no tax on the food, and an 8 percent tax on all other items, then the total tax that she paid was what percent of the total amount that she spent, excluding taxes?

(A) 2.8%
(B) 3.6%
(C) 4.4%
(D) 5.2%
(E) 6.0%

Arithmetic Applied problems

Let T represent the total amount Jill spent, excluding taxes. Jill paid a 4% tax on the clothing she bought, which accounted for 50% of the total amount she spent, and so the tax she paid on the clothing was $(0.04)(0.5T)$. Jill paid an 8% tax on the other items she bought, which accounted for 30% of the total amount she spent, and so the tax she paid on the other items was $(0.08)(0.3T)$. Therefore, the total amount of tax Jill paid was $(0.04)(0.5T) + (0.08)(0.3T) = 0.02T + 0.024T = 0.044T$. The tax as a percent of the total amount Jill spent, excluding taxes, was

$$\left(\frac{0.044T}{T} \times 100\right)\% = 4.4\%.$$

The correct answer is C.

PS15469

43. How many integers *x* satisfy both $2 < x \le 4$ and $0 \le x \le 3$?

(A)   5
(B)   4
(C)   3
(D)   2
(E)   1

Arithmetic Inequalities

The integers that satisfy $2 < x \le 4$ are 3 and 4. The integers that satisfy $0 \le x \le 3$ are 0, 1, 2, and 3. The only integer that satisfies both $2 < x \le 4$ and $0 \le x \le 3$ is 3, and so there is only one integer that satisfies both $2 < x \le 4$ and $0 \le x \le 3$.

The correct answer is E.

PS09322

44. At the opening of a trading day at a certain stock exchange, the price per share of stock K was $8. If the price per share of stock K was $9 at the closing of the day, what was the percent increase in the price per share of stock K for that day?

(A)   1.4%
(B)   5.9%
(C)   11.1%
(D)   12.5%
(E)   23.6%

Arithmetic Percents

An increase from $8 to $9 represents an increase of $\left(\dfrac{9-8}{8} \times 100 \right)\% = \dfrac{100}{8}\% = 12.5\%$.

The correct answer is D.

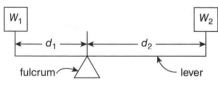

PS14237

45. As shown in the diagram above, a lever resting on a fulcrum has weights of w_1 pounds and w_2 pounds, located d_1 feet and d_2 feet from the fulcrum. The lever is balanced and $w_1 d_1 = w_2 d_2$. Suppose w_1 is 50 pounds and w_2 is 30 pounds. If d_1 is 4 feet less than d_2, what is d_2, in feet?

(A)   1.5
(B)   2.5
(C)   6
(D)   10
(E)   20

Algebra First-degree equations; Substitution

Given $w_1 d_1 = w_2 d_2$, $w_1 = 50$, $w_2 = 30$, and $d_1 = d_2 - 4$, it follows that $50(d_2 - 4) = 30 d_2$, and so

$50(d_2 - 4) = 30 d_2$ given
$50 d_2 - 200 = 30 d_2$ distributive principle
$20 d_2 = 200$ add $200 - 30 d_2$ to both sides
$d_2 = 10$ divide both sides by 20

The correct answer is D.

PS00037

46. The number of rooms at Hotel G is 10 less than twice the number of rooms at Hotel H. If the total number of rooms at Hotel G and Hotel H is 425, what is the number of rooms at Hotel G?

(A)   140
(B)   180
(C)   200
(D)   240
(E)   280

Algebra Simultaneous equations

Let *G* be the number of rooms in Hotel G and let *H* be the number of rooms in Hotel H. Expressed in symbols, the given information is the following system of equations

$$\begin{cases} G = 2H - 10 \\ 425 = G + H \end{cases}$$

Solving the second equation for H gives $H = 425 - G$. Then, substituting $425 - G$ for H in the first equation gives

$$G = 2(425 - G) - 10$$
$$G = 850 - 2G - 10$$
$$G = 840 - 2G$$
$$3G = 840$$
$$G = 280$$

The correct answer is E.

PS17036
47. $\dfrac{3}{100} + \dfrac{5}{1,000} + \dfrac{7}{100,000} =$

(A) 0.357
(B) 0.3507
(C) 0.35007
(D) 0.0357
(E) 0.03507

Arithmetic Operations on rational numbers

If each fraction is written in decimal form, the sum to be found is

$$
\begin{array}{r}
0.03 \\
0.005 \\
+ 0.00007 \\
\hline
0.03507
\end{array}
$$

The correct answer is E.

PS01650
48. If r and s are positive integers such that $(2^r)(4^s) = 16$, then $2r + s =$

(A) 2
(B) 3
(C) 4
(D) 5
(E) 6

Algebra Exponents

Using the rules of exponents,

$(2^r)(4^s) = 16$ given
$(2^r)(2^{2s}) = 2^4$ $4^s = (2^2)^s = 2^{2s}, 16 = 2^4$
$2^{r+2s} = 2^4$ addition property of exponents

Thus, $r + 2s = 4$. However, the problem asks for the value of $2r + s$. Since r and s are positive integers, $s < 2$; otherwise, r would not be positive. Therefore, $s = 1$, and it follows that $r + (2)(1) = 4$, or $r = 2$. The value of $2r + s$ is $(2)(2) + 1 = 5$.

Alternatively, since $(2^r)(4^s) = 16$ and both r and s are positive, it follows that $s < 2$; otherwise, $4^s \geq 16$ and r would not be positive. Therefore, $s = 1$ and $(2^r)(4) = 16$. It follows that $2^r = 4$ and $r = 2$. The value of $2r + s$ is $(2)(2) + 1 = 5$.

The correct answer is D.

PS06726
49. Three people each contributed x dollars toward the purchase of a car. They then bought the car for y dollars, an amount less than the total number of dollars contributed. If the excess amount is to be refunded to the three people in equal amounts, each person should receive a refund of how many dollars?

(A) $\dfrac{3x - y}{3}$

(B) $\dfrac{x - y}{3}$

(C) $\dfrac{x - 3y}{3}$

(D) $\dfrac{y - 3x}{3}$

(E) $3(x - y)$

Algebra Applied problems

The total to be refunded is equal to the total contributed minus the amount paid, or $3x - y$. If $3x - y$ is divided into three equal amounts, then each amount will be $\dfrac{3x - y}{3}$.

The correct answer is A.

$$2x + 2y = -4$$
$$4x + y = 1$$

PS07331
50. In the system of equations above, what is the value of x ?

(A) −3
(B) −1
(C) $\dfrac{2}{5}$
(D) 1
(E) $1\dfrac{3}{4}$

Algebra Simultaneous equations

Solving the second equation for y gives $y = 1 - 4x$. Then, substituting $1 - 4x$ for y in the first equation gives

$$2x + 2(1 - 4x) = -4$$
$$2x + 2 - 8x = -4$$
$$-6x + 2 = -4$$
$$-6x = -6$$
$$x = 1$$

The correct answer is D.

PS07080

51. Last week Jack worked 70 hours and earned $1,260. If he earned his regular hourly wage for the first 40 hours worked, $1\frac{1}{2}$ times his regular hourly wage for the next 20 hours worked, and 2 times his regular hourly wage for the remaining 10 hours worked, what was his regular hourly wage?

   (A) $7.00
   (B) $14.00
   (C) $18.00
   (D) $22.00
   (E) $31.50

Algebra First-degree equations

If w represents Jack's regular hourly wage, then Jack's earnings for the week can be represented by the sum of the following amounts, in dollars: $40w$ (his earnings for the first 40 hours he worked), $(20)(1.5w)$ (his earnings for the next 20 hours he worked), and $(10)(2w)$ (his earnings for the last 10 hours he worked). Therefore,

$$40w + (20)(1.5w) + (10)(2w) = 1,260 \quad \text{given}$$
$$90w = 1,260 \quad \text{add like terms}$$
$$w = 14 \quad \text{divide both sides by 90}$$

Jack's regular hourly wage was $14.00.

The correct answer is B.

PS02402

52. If Mel saved more than $10 by purchasing a sweater at a 15 percent discount, what is the smallest amount the original price of the sweater could be, to the nearest dollar?

   (A)   45
   (B)   67
   (C)   75
   (D)   83
   (E)   150

Arithmetic; Algebra Percents; Inequalities; Applied problems

Letting P be the original price of the sweater in dollars, the given information can be expressed as $(0.15)P > 10$. Solving for P gives

$$(0.15)P > 10$$
$$P > \frac{10}{0.15} = \frac{1,000}{15} = \frac{200}{3}$$
$$P > 66\frac{2}{3}$$

Thus, to the nearest dollar, the smallest amount P could have been is $67.

The correct answer is B.

PS13426

53. If a and b are positive integers and $(2^a)^b = 2^3$, what is the value of $2^a \, 2^b$?

   (A)   6
   (B)   8
   (C)   16
   (D)   32
   (E)   64

Algebra Exponents

It is given that $(2^a)^b = 2^3$, or $2^{ab} = 2^3$. Therefore, $ab = 3$. Since a and b are positive integers, it follows that either $a = 1$ and $b = 3$, or $a = 3$ and $b = 1$. In either case $a + b = 4$, and so $2^a 2^b = 2^{a+b} = 2^4 = 16$.

The correct answer is C.

54.

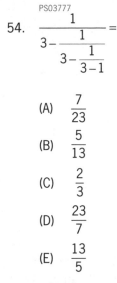

$$\frac{1}{3-\dfrac{1}{3-\dfrac{1}{3-1}}} =$$

(A) $\dfrac{7}{23}$

(B) $\dfrac{5}{13}$

(C) $\dfrac{2}{3}$

(D) $\dfrac{23}{7}$

(E) $\dfrac{13}{5}$

Arithmetic Operations with rational numbers

Perform each subtraction beginning at the lowest level in the fraction and proceeding upward.

$$\frac{1}{3-\dfrac{1}{3-\dfrac{1}{3-1}}} = \frac{1}{3-\dfrac{1}{3-\dfrac{1}{2}}}$$

$$= \frac{1}{3-\dfrac{1}{\dfrac{6}{2}-\dfrac{1}{2}}}$$

$$= \frac{1}{3-\dfrac{1}{\dfrac{5}{2}}}$$

$$= \frac{1}{3-\dfrac{2}{5}}$$

$$= \frac{1}{\dfrac{15}{5}-\dfrac{2}{5}}$$

$$= \frac{1}{\dfrac{13}{5}}$$

$$= \frac{5}{13}$$

The correct answer is B.

55. After 4,000 gallons of water were added to a large water tank that was already filled to $\dfrac{3}{4}$ of its capacity, the tank was then at $\dfrac{4}{5}$ of its capacity. How many gallons of water does the tank hold when filled to capacity?

(A) 5,000
(B) 6,200
(C) 20,000
(D) 40,000
(E) 80,000

Algebra First-degree equations

Let C be the capacity of the tank. In symbols, the given information is $4,000 + \dfrac{3}{4}C = \dfrac{4}{5}C$. Solve for C.

$$4,000 + \frac{3}{4}C = \frac{4}{5}C$$

$$4,000 = \left(\frac{4}{5} - \frac{3}{4}\right)C$$

$$4,000 = \frac{16-15}{20}C$$

$$4,000 = \frac{1}{20}C$$

$$20(4,000) = C$$

$$80,000 = C$$

The correct answer is E.

56. Five machines at a certain factory operate at the same constant rate. If four of these machines, operating simultaneously, take 30 hours to fill a certain production order, how many fewer hours does it take all five machines, operating simultaneously, to fill the same production order?

(A) 3
(B) 5
(C) 6
(D) 16
(E) 24

Arithmetic Applied problems

If 4 machines, working simultaneously, each work for 30 hours to fill a production order, it takes $(4)(30)$ machine hours to fill the order. If 5 machines are working simultaneously, it will take $\dfrac{(4)(30)}{5} = 24$ hours. Thus, 5 machines working simultaneously will take $30 - 24 = 6$ fewer hours to fill the production order than 4 machines working simultaneously.

The correct answer is C.

PS01443

57. A certain toll station on a highway has 7 tollbooths, and each tollbooth collects $0.75 from each vehicle that passes it. From 6 o'clock yesterday morning to 12 o'clock midnight, vehicles passed each of the tollbooths at the average rate of 4 vehicles per minute. Approximately how much money did the toll station collect during that time period?

(A) $1,500
(B) $3,000
(C) $11,500
(D) $23,000
(E) $30,000

Arithmetic Rate problem

On average, 4 vehicles pass each tollbooth every minute. There are 7 tollbooths at the station, and each passing vehicle pays $0.75. Therefore, the average rate, per minute, at which money is collected by the toll station is $ $(7 \times 4 \times 0.75) =$ $ $(7 \times 4 \times \dfrac{3}{4}) = $ $(7 \times 3) = \$21$. From 6 a.m. through midnight there are 18 hours. And because 18 hours is equal to 18×60 minutes, from 6 a.m. through midnight there are 1,080 minutes. The total amount of money collected by the toll station during this period is therefore $1,080 \times \$21 = \$22,680$, which is approximately $23,000.

The correct answer is D.

PS13829

58. How many integers between 1 and 16, inclusive, have exactly 3 different positive integer factors? (Note: 6 is NOT such an integer because 6 has 4 different positive integer factors: 1, 2, 3, and 6.)

(A) 1
(B) 2
(C) 3
(D) 4
(E) 6

Arithmetic Properties of numbers

Using the process of elimination to eliminate integers that do NOT have exactly 3 different positive integer factors, the integer 1 can be eliminated since 1 has only 1 positive integer factor, namely 1 itself. Because each prime number has exactly 2 positive factors, each prime number between 1 and 16, inclusive, (namely, 2, 3, 5, 7, 11, and 13) can be eliminated. The integer 6 can also be eliminated since it was used as an example of an integer with exactly 4 positive integer factors. Check the positive integer factors of each of the remaining integers.

Integer	Positive integer factors	Number of factors
4	1, 2, 4	3
8	1, 2, 4, 8	4
9	1, 3, 9	3
10	1, 2, 5, 10	4
12	1, 2, 3, 4, 6, 12	6
14	1, 2, 7, 14	4
15	1, 3, 5, 15	4
16	1, 2, 4, 8, 16	5

Just the integers 4 and 9 have exactly 3 positive integer factors.

Alternatively, if the integer n, where $n > 1$, has exactly 3 positive integer factors, which include 1 and n, then n has exactly one other positive integer factor, say p. Since any factor of p would also be a factor of n, then p is prime, and so p is the only prime factor of n. It follows that $n = p^k$ for some integer $k > 1$. But if $k \geq 3$, then p^2 is a factor of n in addition to 1, p, and n, which contradicts the fact that n has exactly 3 positive integer factors. Therefore, $k = 2$ and $n = p^2$, which means that n is the square of a prime number. Of the integers between 1 and 16, inclusive, only 4 and 9 are the squares of prime numbers.

The correct answer is B.

PS06288

59. If $d = 2.0453$ and d^* is the decimal obtained by rounding d to the nearest hundredth, what is the value of $d^* - d$?

(A) −0.0053

(B) −0.0003

(C) 0.0007

(D) 0.0047

(E) 0.0153

Arithmetic Operations on rational numbers

Since $d = 2.0453$ rounded to the nearest hundredth is 2.05, $d^* = 2.05$; therefore, $d^* - d = 2.05 - 2.0453 = 0.0047$.

The correct answer is D.

PS14063

60. Stephanie has $2\frac{1}{4}$ cups of milk on hand and makes 2 batches of cookies, using $\frac{2}{3}$ cup of milk for each batch of cookies. Which of the following describes the amount of milk remaining after she makes the cookies?

(A) Less than $\frac{1}{2}$ cup

(B) Between $\frac{1}{2}$ cup and $\frac{3}{4}$ cup

(C) Between $\frac{3}{4}$ cup and 1 cup

(D) Between 1 cup and $1\frac{1}{2}$ cups

(E) More than $1\frac{1}{2}$ cups

Arithmetic Applied problems

In cups, the amount of milk remaining is

$2\frac{1}{4} - 2\left(\frac{2}{3}\right) = \frac{9}{4} - \frac{4}{3} = \frac{27-16}{12} = \frac{11}{12}$, which is

greater than $\frac{3}{4} = \frac{9}{12}$ and less than 1.

The correct answer is C.

PS01656

61. The expression $n!$ is defined as the product of the integers from 1 through n. If p is the product of the integers from 100 through 299 and q is the product of the integers from 200 through 299, which of the following is equal to $\frac{p}{q}$?

(A) $99!$

(B) $199!$

(C) $\dfrac{199!}{99!}$

(D) $\dfrac{299!}{99!}$

(E) $\dfrac{299!}{199!}$

Arithmetic Series and sequences

The number p is equal to $100 \times 101 \times 102 \times \ldots \times 299$ and the number q is equal to $200 \times 201 \times 202 \times \ldots \times 299$. The number $\frac{p}{q}$ is thus equal to $\dfrac{100 \times 101 \times 102 \times \ldots \times 299}{200 \times 201 \times 202 \times \ldots \times 299} =$

$\dfrac{100 \times 101 \times 102 \times \ldots \times 199 \times 200 \times 201 \times 202 \times \ldots \times 299}{200 \times 201 \times 202 \times \ldots \times 299}.$

Canceling $200 \times 201 \times 202 \times \ldots \times 299$ from the numerator and the denominator, we see that $\frac{p}{q} = 100 \times 101 \times 102 \times \ldots \times 199$. Note that the multiplication in this expression for $\frac{p}{q}$ begins with 100 (the smallest of the numbers being multiplied), whereas the multiplication in $n! = 1 \times 2 \times 3 \times \ldots \times n$ begins with 1. Starting with $199!$ as our numerator, we thus need to find a denominator that will cancel the undesired elements of the multiplication (in $199!$). This number is $1 \times 2 \times 3 \times \ldots \times 99 = 99!$ That is, $\frac{p}{q} = 100 \times 101 \times 102 \times \ldots \times 199 =$

$\dfrac{1 \times 2 \times 3 \times \ldots \times 99 \times 100 \times 101 \times 102 \times \ldots \times 199}{1 \times 2 \times 3 \times \ldots \times 99} = \dfrac{199!}{99!}.$

The correct answer is C.

PS15753
62. A school club plans to package and sell dried fruit to raise money. The club purchased 12 containers of dried fruit, each containing $16\frac{3}{4}$ pounds. What is the maximum number of individual bags of dried fruit, each containing $\frac{1}{4}$ pounds, that can be sold from the dried fruit the club purchased?

(A)   50

(B)   64

(C)   67

(D)   768

(E)   804

Arithmetic Applied problems; Operations with fractions

The 12 containers, each containing $16\frac{3}{4}$ pounds of dried fruit, contain a total of $(12)\left(16\frac{3}{4}\right) =$ $(12)\left(\frac{67}{4}\right) = (3)(67) = 201$ pounds of dried fruit, which will make $\frac{201}{\frac{1}{4}} = (201)(4) = 804$ individual bags that can be sold.

The correct answer is E.

Height	Price
Less than 5 ft	$14.95
5 ft to 6 ft	$17.95
Over 6 ft	$21.95

PS02498
63. A nursery sells fruit trees priced as shown in the chart above. In its inventory 54 trees are less than 5 feet in height. If the expected revenue from the sale of its entire stock is estimated at $2,450, approximately how much of this will come from the sale of trees that are at least 5 feet tall?

(A) $1,730

(B) $1,640

(C) $1,410

(D) $1,080

(E) $810

Arithmetic Applied problems

If the nursery sells its entire stock of trees, it will sell the 54 trees that are less than 5 feet in height at the price per tree of $14.95 shown in the chart. The expected revenue from the sale of the trees that are less than 5 feet tall is therefore $54 \times \$14.95 = \$807.30$. The revenue from the sale of the trees that are at least 5 feet tall is thus equal to the total revenue from the sale of the entire stock of trees minus $807.30. The revenue from the sale of the entire stock of trees is estimated at $2,450. Based on this estimate, the revenue from the sale of the trees that are at least 5 feet tall will be $2,450 - \$807.30 = \$1,642.70$, which is approximately $1,640.

The correct answer is B.

PS10539
64. The sequence a_1, a_2, a_3, a_4, a_5 is such that $a_n = a_{n-1} + 5$ for $2 \le n \le 5$. If $a_5 = 31$, what is the value of a_1 ?

(A)   1

(B)   6

(C)   11

(D)   16

(E)   21

Algebra Sequences

Since $a_n = a_{n-1} + 5$, then $a_n - a_{n-1} = 5$. So,

$a_5 - a_4 = 5$
$a_4 - a_3 = 5$
$a_3 - a_2 = 5$
$a_2 - a_1 = 5$

Adding the equations gives

$a_5 - a_4 + a_4 - a_3 + a_3 - a_2 + a_2 - a_1 = 5 + 5 + 5 + 5$

$$a_5 - a_1 = 20$$

and substituting 31 for a_5 gives

$31 - a_1 = 20$

$$a_1 = 11.$$

The correct answer is C.

PS04971

65. A certain bridge is 4,024 feet long. Approximately how many minutes does it take to cross this bridge at a constant speed of 20 miles per hour? (1 mile = 5,280 feet)

    (A) 1
    (B) 2
    (C) 4
    (D) 6
    (E) 7

Arithmetic Applied problems

First, convert 4,024 feet to miles since the speed is given in miles per hour:

$$4{,}024 \ \cancel{ft} \times \frac{1 \text{ mi}}{5{,}280 \ \cancel{ft}} = \frac{4{,}024}{5{,}280} \text{ mi.}$$

Now, divide by 20 mph: $\dfrac{4{,}024}{5{,}280}$ mi $\div \dfrac{20 \text{ mi}}{1 \text{ hr}}$

$$= \frac{4{,}024 \ \cancel{mi}}{5{,}280} \times \frac{1 \text{ hr}}{20 \ \cancel{mi}} = \frac{4{,}024 \text{ hr}}{(5{,}280)(20)}.$$

Last, convert $\dfrac{4{,}024 \text{ hr}}{(5{,}280)(20)}$ to minutes:

$$\frac{4{,}024 \ \cancel{hr}}{(5{,}280)(20)} \times \frac{60 \text{ min}}{1 \ \cancel{hr}} = \frac{(4{,}024)(60) \text{ min}}{(5{,}280)(20)} \approx$$

$$\frac{4{,}000}{5{,}000} \times \frac{60}{20} \text{ min. Then,} \frac{4{,}000}{5{,}000} \times \frac{60}{20} \text{ min} =$$

$= 0.8 \times 3 \text{ min} \approx 2 \text{ min}$. Thus, at a constant speed of 20 miles per hour, it takes approximately 2 minutes to cross the bridge.

The correct answer is B.

PS04009

66. If $S = \{0, 4, 5, 2, 11, 8\}$, how much greater than the median of the numbers in S is the mean of the numbers in S?

    (A) 0.5
    (B) 1.0
    (C) 1.5
    (D) 2.0
    (E) 2.5

Arithmetic; Algebra Statistics; Concepts of sets

The median of S is found by ordering the values according to size (0, 2, 4, 5, 8, 11) and taking the average of the two middle numbers: $\dfrac{4+5}{2} = 4.5$.

The mean is $\dfrac{\text{sum of } n \text{ values}}{n} =$

$$\frac{0+4+5+2+11+8}{6} = 5.$$

The difference between the mean and the median is $5 - 4.5 = 0.5$.

The correct answer is A.

PS12657

67. The annual interest rate earned by an investment increased by 10 percent from last year to this year. If the annual interest rate earned by the investment this year was 11 percent, what was the annual interest rate last year?

    (A) 1%
    (B) 1.1%
    (C) 9.1%
    (D) 10%
    (E) 10.8%

Arithmetic Percents

If L is the annual interest rate last year, then the annual interest rate this year is 10% greater than L, or $1.1L$. It is given that $1.1L = 11\%$. Therefore, $L = \dfrac{11\%}{1.1} = 10\%$. (Note that if the given information had been that the investment increased by *10 percentage points*, then the equation would have been $L + 10\% = 11\%$.)

The correct answer is D.

PS07394

68. A total of 5 liters of gasoline is to be poured into two empty containers with capacities of 2 liters and 6 liters, respectively, such that both containers will be filled to the same percent of their respective capacities. What amount of gasoline, in liters, must be poured into the 6-liter container?

    (A) $4\dfrac{1}{2}$
    (B) 4
    (C) $3\dfrac{3}{4}$
    (D) 3
    (E) $1\dfrac{1}{4}$

Algebra Ratio and proportion

If x represents the amount, in liters, of gasoline poured into the 6-liter container, then $5 - x$ represents the amount, in liters, of gasoline poured into the 2-liter container. After the gasoline is poured into the containers, the 6-liter container will be filled to $\left(\dfrac{x}{6} \times 100\right)$% of its capacity and the 2-liter container will be filled to $\left(\dfrac{5-x}{2} \times 100\right)$% of its capacity. Because these two percents are equal,

$$\dfrac{x}{6} = \dfrac{5-x}{2} \qquad \text{given}$$
$$2x = 6(5 - x) \qquad \text{multiply both sides by 12}$$
$$2x = 30 - 6x \qquad \text{use distributive property}$$
$$8x = 30 \qquad \text{add } 6x \text{ to both sides}$$
$$x = 3\dfrac{3}{4} \qquad \text{divide both sides by 8}$$

Therefore, $3\dfrac{3}{4}$ liters of gasoline must be poured into the 6-liter container.

The correct answer is C.

PS02775

69. List S consists of 10 consecutive odd integers, and list T consists of 5 consecutive even integers. If the least integer in S is 7 more than the least integer in T, how much greater is the average (arithmetic mean) of the integers in S than the average of the integers in T?

(A)   2
(B)   7
(C)   8
(D)   12
(E)   22

Arithmetic Statistics

Let the integers in S be $s, s + 2, s + 4, \ldots, s + 18$, where s is odd. Let the integers in T be $t, t + 2, t + 4, t + 6, t + 8$, where t is even. Given that $s = t + 7$, it follows that $s - t = 7$. The average of the integers in S is $\dfrac{10s + 90}{10} = s + 9$, and, similarly, the average of the integers in T is $\dfrac{5t + 20}{5} = t + 4$. The difference in these averages is $(s + 9) - (t + 4) = (s - t) + (9 - 4) = 7 + 5 = 12$.

Thus, the average of the integers in S is 12 greater than the average of the integers in T.

The correct answer is D.

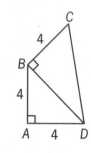

PS05616

70. In the figure above, what is the area of triangular region *BCD* ?

(A) $4\sqrt{2}$
(B)   8
(C) $8\sqrt{2}$
(D)   16
(E) $16\sqrt{2}$

Geometry Triangles; Area

By the Pythagorean theorem, $BD = \sqrt{4^2 + 4^2} = 4\sqrt{2}$. Then the area of $\triangle BCD$ is $\dfrac{1}{2}\left(4\sqrt{2}\right)(4) = 8\sqrt{2}$.

The correct answer is C.

PS13882

71. What is the larger of the 2 solutions of the equation $x^2 - 4x = 96$?

(A)   8
(B)   12
(C)   16
(D)   32
(E)   100

Algebra Second-degree equations

It is given that $x^2 - 4x = 96$, or $x^2 - 4x - 96 = 0$, or $(x - 12)(x + 8) = 0$. Therefore, $x = 12$ or $x = -8$, and the larger of these two numbers is 12.

Alternatively, from $x^2 - 4x = 96$ it follows that $x(x - 4) = 96$. By inspection, the left side is either the product of 12 and 8, where the value of x is 12, or the product of -8 and -12, where the value of x is -8, and the larger of these two values of x is 12.

The correct answer is B.

PS10493

72. Of the goose eggs laid at a certain pond, $\frac{2}{3}$ hatched, and $\frac{3}{4}$ of the geese that hatched from those eggs survived the first month. Of the geese that survived the first month, $\frac{3}{5}$ did <u>not</u> survive the first year. If 120 geese survived the first year and if no more than one goose hatched from each egg, how many goose eggs were laid at the pond?

(A)   280

(B)   400

(C)   540

(D)   600

(E)   840

Arithmetic Operations with rational numbers

Let N represent the number of eggs laid at the pond. Then $\frac{2}{3}N$ eggs hatched and $\frac{3}{4}\left(\frac{2}{3}N\right)$ goslings (baby geese) survived the first month. Since $\frac{3}{5}$ of these goslings did not survive the first year, then $\frac{2}{5}$ did survive the first year. This means that $\frac{2}{5}\left(\frac{3}{4}\left(\frac{2}{3}N\right)\right)$ goslings survived the first year. But this number is 120 and so, $\frac{2}{5}\left(\frac{3}{4}\left(\frac{2}{3}N\right)\right)=120$, $\frac{1}{5}N=120$ and $N=5(120)=600$.

The correct answer is D.

PS09305

73. If $x^2-2x-15=0$ and $x>0$, which of the following must be equal to 0 ?

I. x^2-6x+9

II. $x^2-7x+10$

III. $x^2-10x+25$

(A)   I only

(B)   II only

(C)   III only

(D)   II and III only

(E)   I, II, and III

Algebra Second-degree equations

Since $x^2-2x-15=0$, then $(x-5)(x+3)=0$, so $x=5$ or $x=-3$. Since $x>0$, then $x=5$.

I. $5^2-6(5)+9=25-30+9=4\neq0$

II. $5^2-7(5)+10=25-35+10=0$

III. $5^2-10(5)+25=25-50+25=0$

The correct answer is D.

PS10921

74. $\dfrac{(39,897)(0.0096)}{198.76}$ is approximately

(A)   0.02

(B)   0.2

(C)   2

(D)   20

(E)   200

Arithmetic Estimation

$$\frac{(39,897)(0.0096)}{198.76}\approx\frac{(40,000)(0.01)}{200}=(200)(0.01)=2$$

The correct answer is C.

PS13205

75. If a square region has area n, what is the length of the diagonal of the square in terms of n ?

(A) $\sqrt{2n}$

(B) $\sqrt{n}$

(C) $2\sqrt{n}$

(D) $2n$

(E) $2n^2$

Geometry Area; Pythagorean theorem

If s represents the side length of the square, then $n=s^2$. By the Pythagorean theorem, the length of the diagonal of the square is $\sqrt{s^2+s^2}=\sqrt{n+n}=\sqrt{2n}.$

The correct answer is A.

PS00817

76. The "prime sum" of an integer n greater than 1 is the sum of all the prime factors of n, including repetitions. For example, the prime sum of 12 is 7, since $12=2\times2\times3$ and $2+2+3=7$. For which of the following integers is the prime sum greater than 35 ?

(A)   440

(B)   512

(C)   620

(D)   700

(E)   750

Arithmetic Properties of numbers

A   Since $440 = 2 \times 2 \times 2 \times 5 \times 11$, the prime sum of 440 is $2 + 2 + 2 + 5 + 11 = 22$, which is not greater than 35.

B   Since $512 = 2^9$, the prime sum of 512 is $9(2) = 18$, which is not greater than 35.

C   Since $620 = 2 \times 2 \times 5 \times 31$, the prime sum of 620 is $2 + 2 + 5 + 31 = 40$, which is greater than 35.

Because there can be only one correct answer, D and E need not be checked. However, for completeness,

D   Since $700 = 2 \times 2 \times 5 \times 5 \times 7$, the prime sum of 700 is $2 + 2 + 5 + 5 + 7 = 21$, which is not greater than 35.

E   Since $750 = 2 \times 3 \times 5 \times 5 \times 5$, the prime sum of 750 is $2 + 3 + 5 + 5 + 5 = 20$, which is not greater than 35.

The correct answer is C.

PS02256

77.   Each machine at a toy factory assembles a certain kind of toy at a constant rate of one toy every 3 minutes. If 40 percent of the machines at the factory are to be replaced by new machines that assemble this kind of toy at a constant rate of one toy every 2 minutes, what will be the percent increase in the number of toys assembled in one hour by all the machines at the factory, working at their constant rates?

(A)   20%

(B)   25%

(C)   30%

(D)   40%

(E)   50%

Arithmetic Applied problems; Percents

Let n be the total number of machines working. Currently, it takes each machine 3 minutes to assemble 1 toy, so each machine assembles 20 toys in 1 hour and the total number of toys assembled in 1 hour by all the current machines is $20n$. It takes each new machine 2 minutes to assemble 1 toy, so each new machine assembles 30 toys in 1 hour. If 60% of the machines assemble 20 toys each hour and 40% assemble 30 toys each hour, then the total number of toys produced by the machines each hour is $(0.60n)(20) + (0.40n)(30) = 24n$.

The percent increase in hourly production is $\dfrac{24n - 20n}{20n} = \dfrac{1}{5}$ or 20%.

The correct answer is A.

PS10339

78.   When a subscription to a new magazine was purchased for m months, the publisher offered a discount of 75 percent off the regular monthly price of the magazine. If the total value of the discount was equivalent to buying the magazine at its regular monthly price for 27 months, what was the value of m?

(A)   18

(B)   24

(C)   30

(D)   36

(E)   48

Algebra Percents

Let P represent the regular monthly price of the magazine. The discounted monthly price is then $0.75P$. Paying this price for m months is equivalent to paying the regular price for 27 months. Therefore, $0.75mP = 27P$, and so $0.75m = 27$. It follows that $m = \dfrac{27}{0.75} = 36$.

The correct answer is D.

PS10422

79.   At a garage sale, all of the prices of the items sold were different. If the price of a radio sold at the garage sale was both the 15th highest price and the 20th lowest price among the prices of the items sold, how many items were sold at the garage sale?

(A)   33

(B)   34

(C)   35

(D)   36

(E)   37

Arithmetic Operations with integers

If the price of the radio was the 15th highest price, there were 14 items that sold for prices higher than the price of the radio. If the price of the radio was the 20th lowest price, there were 19 items that sold for prices lower than the price of the radio. Therefore, the total number of items sold is $14 + 1 + 19 = 34$.

The correct answer is B.

PS11738

80. Half of a large pizza is cut into 4 equal-sized pieces, and the other half is cut into 6 equal-sized pieces. If a person were to eat 1 of the larger pieces and 2 of the smaller pieces, what fraction of the pizza would remain <u>uneaten</u>?

(A) $\dfrac{5}{12}$

(B) $\dfrac{13}{24}$

(C) $\dfrac{7}{12}$

(D) $\dfrac{2}{3}$

(E) $\dfrac{17}{24}$

Arithmetic Operations with fractions

Each of the 4 equal-sized pieces represents $\dfrac{1}{8}$ of the whole pizza since each slice is $\dfrac{1}{4}$ of $\dfrac{1}{2}$ of the pizza. Each of the 6 equal-sized pieces represents $\dfrac{1}{12}$ of the whole pizza since each slice is $\dfrac{1}{6}$ of $\dfrac{1}{2}$ of the pizza. The fraction of the pizza remaining after a person eats one of the larger pieces and

2 of the smaller pieces is $1 - \left[\dfrac{1}{8} + 2\left(\dfrac{1}{12}\right) \right] =$

$1 - \left(\dfrac{1}{8} + \dfrac{1}{6}\right) = 1 - \dfrac{6+8}{48} = 1 - \dfrac{7}{24} = \dfrac{17}{24}.$

The correct answer is E.

PS14293

81. If $a = 1 + \dfrac{1}{4} + \dfrac{1}{16} + \dfrac{1}{64}$ and $b = 1 + \dfrac{1}{4}a$, then what is the value of $a - b$?

(A) $-\dfrac{85}{256}$

(B) $-\dfrac{1}{256}$

(C) $-\dfrac{1}{4}$

(D) $\dfrac{125}{256}$

(E) $\dfrac{169}{256}$

Arithmetic Operations with fractions

Given that $a = 1 + \dfrac{1}{4} + \dfrac{1}{16} + \dfrac{1}{64}$, it follows that $\dfrac{1}{4}a = \dfrac{1}{4} + \dfrac{1}{16} + \dfrac{1}{64} + \dfrac{1}{256}$ and so $b = 1 + \dfrac{1}{4} + \dfrac{1}{16} + \dfrac{1}{64} + \dfrac{1}{256}$. Then $a - b =$

$\left(1 + \dfrac{1}{4} + \dfrac{1}{16} + \dfrac{1}{64}\right) - \left(1 + \dfrac{1}{4} + \dfrac{1}{16} + \dfrac{1}{64} + \dfrac{1}{256}\right) =$

$-\dfrac{1}{256}.$

The correct answer is B.

PS10174

82. In a certain learning experiment, each participant had three trials and was assigned, for each trial, a score of either −2, −1, 0, 1, or 2. The participant's final score consisted of the sum of the first trial score, 2 times the second trial score, and 3 times the third trial score. If Anne received scores of 1 and −1 for her first two trials, not necessarily in that order, which of the following could NOT be her final score?

(A) −4

(B) −2

(C) 1

(D) 5

(E) 6

Arithmetic Applied problems

If x represents Anne's score on the third trial, then Anne's final score is either $1 + 2(-1) + 3x = 3x - 1$ or $-1 + 2(1) + 3x = 3x + 1$, where x can have the value −2, −1, 0, 1, or 2. The following table shows Anne's final score for each possible value of x.

x	$3x - 1$	$3x + 1$
−2	−7	−5
−1	−4	−2
0	−1	1
1	2	4
2	5	7

Among the answer choices, the only one not found in the table is 6.

The correct answer is E.

PS00111
83. For all positive integers m and v, the expression $m \ominus v$ represents the remainder when m is divided by v. What is the value of $((98 \ominus 33) \ominus 17) - (98 \ominus (33 \ominus 17))$?

(A)   −10
(B)   −2
(C)   8
(D)   13
(E)   17

Arithmetic Operations with integers

First, for $((98 \ominus 33) \ominus 17)$, determine $98 \ominus 33$, which equals 32, since 32 is the remainder when 98 is divided by 33 $(98 = 2(33) + 32)$. Then, determine $32 \ominus 17$, which equals 15, since 15 is the remainder when 32 is divided by 17 $(32 = 1(17) + 15)$. Thus, $((98 \ominus 33) \ominus 17) = 15$.

Next, for $(98 \ominus (33 \ominus 17))$, determine $33 \ominus 17$, which equals 16, since 16 is the remainder when 33 is divided by 17 $(33 = 1(17) + 16)$. Then, determine $98 \ominus 16$, which equals 2, since 2 is the remainder when 98 is divided by 16 $(98 = 6(16) + 2)$. Thus, $(98 \ominus (33 \ominus 17)) = 2$.

Finally, $((98 \ominus 33) \ominus 17 - (98 \ominus (33 \ominus 17)) = 15 - 2 = 13$.

The correct answer is D.

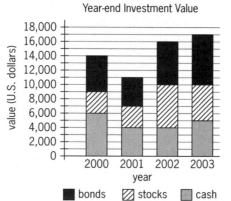

Year-end Investment Value

■ bonds   ▨ stocks   ▨ cash

PS13841
84. The chart above shows year-end values for Darnella's investments. For just the stocks, what was the increase in value from year-end 2000 to year-end 2003 ?

(A) $1,000
(B) $2,000
(C) $3,000
(D) $4,000
(E) $5,000

Arithmetic Interpretation of graphs

From the graph, the year-end 2000 value for stocks is $9,000 − 6,000 = 3,000$ and the year-end 2003 value for stocks is $10,000 − 5,000 = 5,000$. Therefore, for just the stocks, the increase in value from year-end 2000 to year-end 2003 is $5,000 − 3,000 = 2,000$.

The correct answer is B.

PS05775
85. If the sum of the reciprocals of two consecutive odd integers is $\frac{12}{35}$, then the greater of the two integers is

(A)   3
(B)   5
(C)   7
(D)   9
(E)   11

Arithmetic Operations with fractions

The sum of the reciprocals of 2 integers, a and b, is $\frac{1}{a} + \frac{1}{b} = \frac{a+b}{ab}$. Therefore, since $\frac{12}{35}$ is the sum of the reciprocals of 2 consecutive odd integers, the integers must be such that their sum is a multiple of 12 and their product is the same multiple of 35 so that the fraction reduces to $\frac{12}{35}$. Considering the simplest case where $a + b = 12$ and $ab = 35$, it is easy to see that the integers are 5 and 7 since 5 and 7 are the only factors of 35 that are consecutive odd integers. The larger of these is 7.

Algebraically, if a is the greater of the two integers, then $b = a - 2$ and

$$\frac{a + (a - 2)}{a(a - 2)} = \frac{12}{35}$$

$$\frac{2a - 2}{a(a - 2)} = \frac{12}{35}$$

$$35(2a - 2) = 12a(a - 2)$$
$$70a - 70 = 12a^2 - 24a$$
$$0 = 12a^2 - 94a + 70$$
$$0 = 2(6a - 5)(a - 7)$$

Thus, $6a - 5 = 0$, so $a = \frac{5}{6}$, or $a - 7 = 0$, so $a = 7$.

Since a must be an integer, it follows that $a = 7$.

The correct answer is C.

PS05916

86. What is the sum of the odd integers from 35 to 85, inclusive?

(A) 1,560
(B) 1,500
(C) 1,240
(D) 1,120
(E) 1,100

Arithmetic Operations on integers

The odd integers from 35 through 85 form an arithmetic sequence with first term 35 and each subsequent term 2 more than the preceding term. Thus the sum $35 + 37 + 39 + \ldots + 85$ can be found as follows:

1st term	35	= 35		
2nd term	37	= 35	+	1(2)
3rd term	39	= 35	+	2(2)
4th term	41	= 35	+	3(2)
...	...	... ...		... ...
26th term	85	= 35	+	25(2)

$$\text{Sum} = 35(26) + (1 + 2 + 3 + \ldots + 25)(2)$$
$$= 35(26) + \frac{(25)(26)}{2}(2)$$

See note below

$$= 910 + 650$$
$$= 1{,}560$$

Note that if $s = 1 + 2 + 3 + \ldots + 25$, then $2s = (1 + 2 + 3 + \ldots + 25) + (25 + 24 + 23 + \ldots + 1)$, and so $2s = (1 + 25) + (2 + 24) + (3 + 23) + \ldots + (25 + 1) = (25)(26)$. Therefore, $s = \frac{(25)(26)}{2}$.

Alternatively, to determine the number of odd integers from 35 to 85, inclusive, consider that 3 of them (35, 37, and 39) have tens digit 3. Half of the integers with tens digit 4 are odd, so 5 of the odd integers between 35 and 85, inclusive, have tens digit 4. Similarly, 5 of the odd integers between 35 and 85, inclusive, have tens digit 5; 5 have tens digit 6; and 5 have tens digit 7. Finally, 3 have tens digit 8 (81, 83, and 85), and so the number of odd integers between 35

and 85, inclusive, is $3 + 5 + 5 + 5 + 5 + 3 = 26$. Now, let $S = 35 + 37 + 39 + \ldots + 85$. Then, $S = 85 + 83 + 81 + \ldots + 35$, and it follows that $2S = (35 + 85) + (37 + 83) + (39 + 81) + \ldots + (85 + 35) = (120)(26)$. Thus, $S = 35 + 37 + 39 + \ldots + 85 = \frac{(120)(26)}{2} = 1{,}560$.

The correct answer is A.

PS00777

87. In a certain sequence, each term after the first term is one-half the previous term. If the tenth term of the sequence is between 0.0001 and 0.001, then the twelfth term of the sequence is between

(A) 0.0025 and 0.025
(B) 0.00025 and 0.0025
(C) 0.000025 and 0.00025
(D) 0.0000025 and 0.000025
(E) 0.00000025 and 0.0000025

Arithmetic Sequences

Let a_n represent the nth term of the sequence. It is given that each term after the first term is $\frac{1}{2}$ the previous term and that $0.0001 < a_{10} < 0.001$.

Then for a_{11}, $\frac{0.0001}{2} < a_{11} < \frac{0.001}{2}$, or $0.00005 < a_{11} < 0.0005$. For a_{12}, $\frac{0.00005}{2} < a_{12} < \frac{0.0005}{2}$, or $0.000025 < a_{12} < 0.00025$. Thus, the twelfth term of the sequence is between 0.000025 and 0.00025.

The correct answer is C.

PS04765

88. A certain drive-in movie theater has a total of 17 rows of parking spaces. There are 20 parking spaces in the first row and 21 parking spaces in the second row. In each subsequent row there are 2 more parking spaces than in the previous row. What is the total number of parking spaces in the movie theater?

(A) 412
(B) 544
(C) 596
(D) 632
(E) 692

Arithmetic Operations on integers

Row	Number of parking spaces
1st row	20
2nd row	21
3rd row	21 + 1(2)
4th row	21 + 2(2)
...	... ...
17th row	21 + 15(2)

Then, letting S represent the total number of parking spaces in the theater,

$$S = 20 + (16)(21) + (1 + 2 + 3 + \ldots + 15)(2)$$

$$= 20 + 336 + \frac{(15)(16)}{2}(2)$$

See note below

$$= 356 + 240$$

$$= 596$$

Note that if $s = 1 + 2 + 3 + \ldots + 15$, then $2s = (1 + 2 + 3 + \ldots + 15) + (15 + 14 + 13 + \ldots + 1)$, and so $2s = (1 + 15) + (2 + 14) + (3 + 13) + \ldots + (15 + 1) = (15)(16)$. Therefore, $s = \frac{(15)(16)}{2}$.

The correct answer is C.

PS10810

89. Ada and Paul received their scores on three tests. On the first test, Ada's score was 10 points higher than Paul's score. On the second test, Ada's score was 4 points higher than Paul's score. If Paul's average (arithmetic mean) score on the three tests was 3 points higher than Ada's average score on the three tests, then Paul's score on the third test was how many points higher than Ada's score?

(A) 9
(B) 14
(C) 17
(D) 23
(E) 25

Algebra Statistics

Let a_1, a_2, and a_3 be Ada's scores on the first, second, and third tests, respectively, and let p_1, p_2, and p_3 be Paul's scores on the first, second, and third tests, respectively. Then, Ada's average score is $\frac{a_1 + a_2 + a_3}{3}$ and Paul's average score is $\frac{p_1 + p_2 + p_3}{3}$. But, Paul's average score is 3 points higher than Ada's average score, so $\frac{p_1 + p_2 + p_3}{3} = \frac{a_1 + a_2 + a_3}{3} + 3$. Also, it is given that $a_1 = p_1 + 10$ and $a_2 = p_2 + 4$, so by substitution, $\frac{p_1 + p_2 + p_3}{3} = \frac{(p_1 + 10) + (p_2 + 4) + a_3}{3} + 3$. Then, $p_1 + p_2 + p_3 = (p_1 + 10) + (p_2 + 4) + a_3 + 9$ and so $p_3 = a_3 + 23$. On the third test, Paul's score was 23 points higher than Ada's score.

The correct answer is D.

PS06180

90. The price of a certain stock increased by 0.25 of 1 percent on a certain day. By what fraction did the price of the stock increase that day?

(A) $\dfrac{1}{2,500}$

(B) $\dfrac{1}{400}$

(C) $\dfrac{1}{40}$

(D) $\dfrac{1}{25}$

(E) $\dfrac{1}{4}$

Arithmetic Percents

It is given that the price of a certain stock increased by 0.25 of 1 percent on a certain day. This is equivalent to an increase of $\frac{1}{4}$ of $\frac{1}{100}$, which is $\left(\frac{1}{4}\right)\left(\frac{1}{100}\right)$, and $\left(\frac{1}{4}\right)\left(\frac{1}{100}\right) = \frac{1}{400}$.

The correct answer is B.

PS03831
91. For each trip, a taxicab company charges $4.25 for the first mile and $2.65 for each additional mile or fraction thereof. If the total charge for a certain trip was $62.55, how many miles at most was the trip?

    (A)   21
    (B)   22
    (C)   23
    (D)   24
    (E)   25

Arithmetic Applied problems

Subtracting the charge for the first mile leaves a charge of $62.55 − $4.25 = $58.30 for the miles after the first mile. Divide this amount by $2.65 to find the number of miles to which $58.30 corresponds: $\frac{58.30}{2.65} = 22$ miles. Therefore, the total number of miles is at most 1 (the first mile) added to 22 (the number of miles after the first mile), which equals 23.

The correct answer is C.

PS12857
92. When 24 is divided by the positive integer n, the remainder is 4. Which of the following statements about n must be true?

    I. n is even.
    II. n is a multiple of 5.
    III. n is a factor of 20.

    (A)   III only
    (B)   I and II only
    (C)   I and III only
    (D)   II and III only
    (E)   I, II, and III

Arithmetic Properties of numbers

Since the remainder is 4 when 24 is divided by the positive integer n and the remainder must be less than the divisor, it follows that $24 = qn + 4$ for some positive integer q and $4 < n$, or $qn = 20$ and $n > 4$. It follows that $n = 5$, or $n = 10$, or $n = 20$ since these are the only factors of 20 that exceed 4.

   I. n is not necessarily even. For example, n could be 5.

   II. n is necessarily a multiple of 5 since the value of n is either 5, 10, or 20.
   III. n is a factor of 20 since $20 = qn$ for some positive integer q.

The correct answer is D.

PS12759
93. What is the thousandths digit in the decimal equivalent of $\frac{53}{5,000}$?

    (A)   0
    (B)   1
    (C)   3
    (D)   5
    (E)   6

Arithmetic Place value

$\frac{53}{5,000} = \frac{106}{10,000} = 0.0106$ and the thousandths digit is 0.

The correct answer is A.

PS00986
94. The average (arithmetic mean) of the positive integers x, y, and z is 3. If $x < y < z$, what is the greatest possible value of z ?

    (A)   5
    (B)   6
    (C)   7
    (D)   8
    (E)   9

Algebra Inequalities

It is given that $\frac{x+y+z}{3} = 3$, or $x + y + z = 9$, or $z = 9 + (-x - y)$. It follows that the greatest possible value of z occurs when $-x - y = -(x + y)$ has the greatest possible value, which occurs when $x + y$ has the least possible value. Because x and y are different positive integers, the least possible value of $x + y$ occurs when $x = 1$ and $y = 2$. Therefore, the greatest possible value of z is $9 - 1 - 2 = 6$.

The correct answer is B.

PS14087
95. The product of 3,305 and the 1-digit integer x is a 5-digit integer. The units (ones) digit of the product is 5 and the hundreds digit is y. If A is the set of all possible values of x and B is the set of all possible values of y, then which of the following gives the members of A and B?

	A	B
(A)	{1, 3, 5, 7, 9}	{0, 1, 2, 3, 4, 5, 6, 7, 8, 9}
(B)	{1, 3, 5, 7, 9}	{1, 3, 5, 7, 9}
(C)	{3, 5, 7, 9}	{1, 5, 7, 9}
(D)	{5, 7, 9}	{1, 5, 7}
(E)	{5, 7, 9}	{1, 5, 9}

Arithmetic Properties of numbers

Since the products of 3,305 and 1, 3,305 and 2, and 3,305 and 3 are the 4-digit integers 3,305, 6,610, and 9,915, respectively, it follows that x must be among the 1-digit integers 4, 5, 6, 7, 8, and 9. Also, since the units digit of the product of 3,305 and x is 5, it follows that x cannot be 4 (product has units digit 0), 6 (product has units digit 0), or 8 (product has units digit 0). Therefore, $A = \{5, 7, 9\}$. The possibilities for y will be the hundreds digits of the products $(3,305)(5) = 16,525$, $(3,305)(7) = 23,135$, and $(3,305)(9) = 29,745$. Thus, y can be 5, 1, or 7, and so $B = \{1, 5, 7\}$.

The correct answer is D.

PS05083
96. What is the largest integer n such that $\frac{1}{2^n} > 0.01$?

(A) 5
(B) 6
(C) 7
(D) 10
(E) 51

Arithmetic Exponents; Operations with rational numbers

Since $\frac{1}{2^n} > 0.01$ is equivalent to $2^n < 100$, find the largest integer n such that $2^n < 100$. Using trial and error, $2^6 = 64$ and $64 < 100$, but $2^7 = 128$ and $128 > 100$. Therefore, 6 is the largest integer such that $\frac{1}{2^n} > 0.01$.

The correct answer is B.

PS07001
97. If x and y are integers such that $2 < x \le 8$ and $2 < y \le 9$, what is the maximum value of $\frac{1}{x} - \frac{x}{y}$?

(A) $-3\frac{1}{8}$

(B) 0

(C) $\frac{1}{4}$

(D) $\frac{5}{18}$

(E) 2

Algebra Inequalities

Because x and y are both positive, the maximum value of $\frac{1}{x} - \frac{x}{y}$ will occur when the value of $\frac{1}{x}$ is maximum and the value of $\frac{x}{y}$ is minimum. The value of $\frac{1}{x}$ is maximum when the value of x is minimum or when $x = 3$. The value of $\frac{x}{y}$ is minimum when the value of x is minimum (or when $x = 3$) and the value of y is maximum (or when $y = 9$). Thus, the maximum value of $\frac{1}{x} - \frac{x}{y}$ is $\frac{1}{3} - \frac{3}{9} = 0$.

The correct answer is B.

PS01875
98. Items that are purchased together at a certain discount store are priced at $3 for the first item purchased and $1 for each additional item purchased. What is the maximum number of items that could be purchased together for a total price that is less than $30?

(A) 25
(B) 26
(C) 27
(D) 28
(E) 29

Arithmetic Applied problems

After the first item is purchased, $29.99 − $3.00 = $26.99 remains to purchase the additional items. Since the price for each of the additional items is $1.00, a maximum of 26 additional items could be purchased. Therefore, a maximum of $1 + 26 = 27$ items could be purchased for less than $30.00.

The correct answer is C.

PS00774

99. What is the least integer z for which (0.000125) $(0.0025)(0.00000125) \times 10^z$ is an integer?

(A)   18
(B)   10
(C)   0
(D)   −10
(E)   −18

Arithmetic Decimals

Considering each of the three decimal numbers in parentheses separately, we know that 0.000125×10^6 is the integer 125, 0.0025×10^4 is the integer 25, and 0.00000125×10^8 is the integer 125. We thus know that $(0.000125) \times 10^6 \times (0.0025) \times 10^4 \times (0.00000125) \times 10^8 = (0.000125)(0.0025)(0.00000125) \times 10^6 \times 10^4 \times 10^8 = (0.000125)(0.0025)(0.00000125) \times 10^{6+4+8} = (0.000125)(0.0025)(0.00000125) \times 10^{18}$ is the integer $125 \times 25 \times 125$. We therefore know that if $z = 18$, then $(0.000125)(0.0025)$ $(0.00000125) \times 10^z$ is an integer.

Now, if the product $125 \times 25 \times 125$ were divisible by 10, then for at least one integer z less than 18, $(0.000125)(0.0025)(0.00000125) \times 10^z$ would be an integer. However, each of the three numbers being multiplied in the product $125 \times 25 \times 125$ is odd (not divisible by 2). We thus know that $125 \times 25 \times 125$ is not divisible by 2 and is therefore odd. Because only even numbers are divisible by 10, we know that $125 \times 25 \times 125$ is not divisible by 10. We thus know that 18 is the *least* integer z such that $(0.000125)(0.0025)$ $(0.00000125) \times 10^z$ is an integer.

Note that it is not necessary to perform the multiplication $125 \times 25 \times 125$.

The correct answer is A.

PS08407

100. The average (arithmetic mean) length per film for a group of 21 films is t minutes. If a film that runs for 66 minutes is removed from the group and replaced by one that runs for 52 minutes, what is the average length per film, in minutes, for the new group of films, in terms of t?

(A) $t + \dfrac{2}{3}$

(B) $t - \dfrac{2}{3}$

(C) $21t + 14$

(D) $t + \dfrac{3}{2}$

(E) $t - \dfrac{3}{2}$

Arithmetic Statistics

Let S denote the sum of the lengths, in minutes, of the 21 films in the original group. Since the average length is t minutes, it follows that $\dfrac{S}{21} = t$.

If a 66-minute film is replaced by a 52-minute film, then the sum of the lengths of the 21 films in the resulting group is $S - 66 + 52 = S - 14$. Therefore, the average length of the resulting 21 films is $\dfrac{S - 14}{21} = \dfrac{S}{21} - \dfrac{14}{21} = t - \dfrac{2}{3}$.

The correct answer is B.

PS08051

101. An open box in the shape of a cube measuring 50 centimeters on each side is constructed from plywood. If the plywood weighs 1.5 grams per square centimeter, which of the following is closest to the total weight, in kilograms, of the plywood used for the box? (1 kilogram = 1,000 grams)

(A)   2
(B)   4
(C)   8
(D)   13
(E)   19

Geometry Surface area

The total weight of the box is the sum of the weights of the 4 lateral sides of the box and the bottom of the box. Since the sides of the box all have the same area and the same density throughout, the total weight of the box is 5 times the weight of a side of the box. In grams, the weight of a side of the box is $(A \text{ cm}^2)\left(1.5 \ \dfrac{g}{\text{cm}^2}\right)$, where A is the area of a side of the box in square centimeters. Since $A = (50 \text{ cm})(50 \text{ cm}) = 2{,}500 \text{ cm}^2$, the weight of a side of the box is $(2{,}500)(1.5) = 3{,}750$ grams $= 3.75$ kilograms. Therefore, the total weight of the box is $5(3.75) = 18.75$ kilograms.

The correct answer is E.

PS03614

102. A garden center sells a certain grass seed in 5-pound bags at $13.85 per bag, 10-pound bags at $20.43 per bag, and 25-pound bags at $32.25 per bag. If a customer is to buy at least 65 pounds of the grass seed, but no more than 80 pounds, what is the least possible cost of the grass seed that the customer will buy?

    (A) $94.03
    (B) $96.75
    (C) $98.78
    (D) $102.07
    (E) $105.36

Arithmetic Applied problems

Let x represent the amount of grass seed, in pounds, the customer is to buy. It follows that $65 \le x \le 80$. Since the grass seed is available in only 5-pound, 10-pound, and 25-pound bags, then the customer must buy either 65, 70, 75, or 80 pounds of grass seed. Because the seed is more expensive per pound for smaller bags, the customer should minimize the number of the smaller bags and maximize the number of 25-pound bags to incur the least possible cost for the grass seed. The possible purchases are given in the table below.

x	Number of 25-pound bags	Number of 10-pound bags	Number of 5-pound bags	Total cost
65	2	1	1	$98.78
70	2	2	0	$105.36
75	3	0	0	$96.75
80	3	0	1	$110.60

The least possible cost is then $3(\$32.25) = \$96.75$.

The correct answer is B.

PS12785

103. If $x = -|w|$, which of the following must be true?

    (A) $x = -w$
    (B) $x = w$
    (C) $x^2 = w$
    (D) $x^2 = w^2$
    (E) $x^3 = w^3$

Algebra Absolute value

Squaring both sides of $x = -|w|$ gives $x^2 = (-|w|)^2$, or $x^2 = |w|^2 = w^2$.

Alternatively, if (x, w) is equal to either of the pairs $(-1,1)$ or $(-1,-1)$, then $x = -|w|$ is true. However, each of the answer choices except $x^2 = w^2$ is false for at least one of these two pairs.

The correct answer is D.

PS05965

104. Which of the following lines in the xy-plane does <u>not</u> contain any point with integers as both coordinates?

    (A) $y = x$
    (B) $y = x + \dfrac{1}{2}$
    (C) $y = x + 5$
    (D) $y = \dfrac{1}{2}x$
    (E) $y = \dfrac{1}{2}x + 5$

Algebra; Arithmetic Substitution; Operations with rational numbers

A   If x is an integer, y is an integer since $y = x$. Thus, the line given by $y = x$ contains points with integers as both coordinates.

B   If x is an integer, then if y were an integer, then $y - x$ would be an integer. But, $y - x = \frac{1}{2}$ and $\frac{1}{2}$ is NOT an integer. Since assuming that y is an integer leads to a contradiction, then y cannot be an integer and the line given by $y = x + \frac{1}{2}$ does NOT contain any points with integers as both coordinates.

Since there can be only one correct answer, the lines in C, D, and E need not be checked, but for completeness,

C   If x is an integer, $x + 5$ is an integer and so y is an integer since $y = x + 5$. Thus, the line given by $y = x + 5$ contains points with integers as both coordinates.

D   If x is an even integer, $\frac{1}{2}x$ is an integer and so y is an integer since $y = \frac{1}{2}x$. Thus, the line given by $y = \frac{1}{2}x$ contains points with integers as both coordinates.

E   If x is an even integer, $\frac{1}{2}x$ is an integer and $\frac{1}{2}x + 5$ is also an integer so y is an integer since $y = \frac{1}{2}x + 5$. Thus, the line given by $y = \frac{1}{2}x + 5$ contains points with integers as both coordinates.

The correct answer is B.

PS04160

105. A certain financial institution reported that its assets totaled $2,377,366.30 on a certain day. Of this amount, $31,724.54 was held in cash. Approximately what percent of the reported assets was held in cash on that day?

(A)   0.00013%

(B)   0.0013%

(C)   0.013%

(D)   0.13%

(E)   1.3%

Arithmetic Percents; Estimation

The requested percent can be estimated by converting the values into scientific notation.

$$\frac{31,724.54}{2,377,366.30} \qquad \text{value as fraction}$$

$$= \frac{3.172454 \times 10^4}{2.37736630 \times 10^6} \qquad \begin{array}{l}\text{convert to scientific} \\ \text{notation}\end{array}$$

$$= \frac{3.172454}{2.37736630} \times \frac{10^4}{10^6} \qquad \begin{array}{l}\text{arithmetic property of} \\ \text{fractions}\end{array}$$

$$= \frac{3.172454}{2.37736630} \times 10^{-2} \qquad \text{subtract exponents}$$

$$\approx \frac{3}{2} \times 10^{-2} \qquad \text{approximate}$$

$$= 1.5 \times 10^{-2} \qquad \text{convert to decimal fraction}$$

$$= 0.015 \qquad \text{multiply}$$

$$= 1.5\% \qquad \text{convert to percent}$$

A more detailed computation would show that 1.3% is a better approximation. However, in order to select the best value from the values given as answer choices, the above computation is sufficient.

The correct answer is E.

$$\begin{array}{r} AB \\ + \ BA \\ \hline AAC \end{array}$$

PS09820

106. In the correctly worked addition problem shown, where the sum of the two-digit positive integers AB and BA is the three-digit integer AAC, and A, B, and C are different digits, what is the units digit of the integer AAC?

(A)   9

(B)   6

(C)   3

(D)   2

(E)   0

Arithmetic Place value

Determine the value of C.

It is given that $(10A + B) + (10B + A) = 100A + 10A + C$ or $11A + 11B = 110A + C$. Thus, $11B - 99A = C$, or $11(B - 9A) = C$. Therefore, C is divisible by 11, and 0 is the only digit that is divisible by 11.

The correct answer is E.

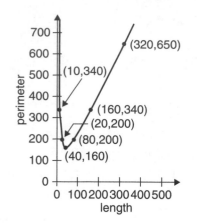

PS14060

107. Planning is in progress for a fenced, rectangular playground with an area of 1,600 square meters. The graph above shows the perimeter, in meters, as a function of the length of the playground. The length of the playground should be how many meters to minimize the perimeter and, therefore, the amount of fencing needed to enclose the playground?

(A)   10
(B)   40
(C)   60
(D)   160
(E)   340

Geometry Simple coordinate geometry

Since values of the perimeter are represented on the vertical axis, the point on the graph that corresponds to the minimum perimeter is the point on the graph that has the least y-coordinate, which is (40,160). This point corresponds to a length of 40 meters, which is what the question asked, and a perimeter of 160 meters.

The correct answer is B.

$$3r \leq 4s + 5$$
$$|s| \leq 5$$

PS06913

108. Given the inequalities above, which of the following CANNOT be the value of r?

(A)   −20
(B)   −5
(C)   0
(D)   5
(E)   20

Algebra Inequalities

Since $|s| \leq 5$, it follows that $-5 \leq s \leq 5$. Therefore, $-20 \leq 4s \leq 20$, and hence $-15 \leq 4s + 5 \leq 25$. Since $3r \leq 4s + 5$ (given) and $4s + 5 \leq 25$ (end of previous sentence), it follows that $3r \leq 25$. Among the answer choices, $3r \leq 25$ is false only for $r = 20$.

The correct answer is E.

PS11647

109. If m is an even integer, v is an odd integer, and $m > v > 0$, which of the following represents the number of even integers less than m and greater than v?

(A) $\dfrac{m-v}{2} - 1$

(B) $\dfrac{m-v-1}{2}$

(C) $\dfrac{m-v}{2}$

(D) $m - v - 1$

(E) $m - v$

Arithmetic Properties of numbers

Since there is only one correct answer, one method of solving the problem is to choose values for m and v and determine which of the expressions gives the correct number for these values. For example, if $m = 6$ and $v = 1$, then there are 2 even integers less than 6 and greater than 1, namely the even integers 2 and 4. As the table below shows, $\dfrac{m-v-1}{2}$ is the only expression given that equals 2.

$$\frac{m - v}{2} - 1 = 1.5$$

$$\frac{m - v - 1}{2} = 2$$

$$\frac{m - v}{2} = 2.5$$

$$m - v - 1 = 4$$

$$m - v = 5$$

To solve this problem it is not necessary to show that $\frac{m - v - 1}{2}$ always gives the correct number of even integers. However, one way this can be done is by the following method, first shown for a specific example and then shown in general. For the specific example, suppose $v = 15$ and $m = 144$. Then a list—call it the first list—of the even integers greater than v and less than m is 16, 18, 20, ..., 140, 142. Now subtract 14 (chosen so that the second list will begin with 2) from each of the integers in the first list to form a second list, which has the same number of integers as the first list: 2, 4, 6, ..., 128. Finally, divide each of the integers in the second list (all of which are even) by 2 to form a third list, which also has the same number of integers as the first list: 1, 2, 3, ..., 64. Since the number of integers in the third list is 64, it follows that the number of integers in the first list is 64. For the general situation, the first list is the following list of even integers: $v + 1$, $v + 3$, $v + 5$, ..., $m - 4$, $m - 2$. Now subtract the even integer $v - 1$ from (i.e., add $-v + 1$ to) each of the integers in the first list to obtain the second list: 2, 4, 6, ..., $m - v - 3$, $m - v - 1$. (Note, for example, that $m - 4 - (v - 1) = m - v - 3$.) Finally, divide each of the integers (all of which are even) in the second list by 2 to obtain the third list: 1, 2, 3, ..., $\frac{m - v - 3}{2}$, $\frac{m - v - 1}{2}$. Since the number of integers in the third list is $\frac{m - v - 1}{2}$, it follows that the number of integers in the first list is $\frac{m - v - 1}{2}$.

The correct answer is B.

PS02378
110. A positive integer is divisible by 9 if and only if the sum of its digits is divisible by 9. If n is a positive integer, for which of the following values of k is $25 \times 10^n + k \times 10^{2n}$ divisible by 9 ?

(A)   9

(B)   16

(C)   23

(D)   35

(E)   47

Arithmetic Properties of numbers

Since n can be any positive integer, let $n = 2$. Then $25 \times 10^n = 2{,}500$, so its digits consist of the digits 2 and 5 followed by two digits of 0. Also, $k \times 10^{2n} = k \times 10{,}000$, so its digits consist of the digits of k followed by four digits of 0. Therefore, the digits of $(25 \times 10^n) + (k \times 10^{2n})$ consist of the digits of k followed by the digits 2 and 5, followed by two digits of 0. The table below shows this for $n = 2$ and $k = 35$:

$$25 \times 10^n = \quad 2{,}500$$
$$35 \times 10^{2n} = 350{,}000$$
$$(25 \times 10^n) + (35 \times 10^{2n}) = 352{,}500$$

Thus, when $n = 2$, the sum of the digits of $(25 \times 10^n) + (k \times 10^{2n})$ will be $2 + 5 = 7$ plus the sum of the digits of k. Of the answer choices, this sum of digits is divisible by 9 only for $k = 47$, which gives $2 + 5 + 4 + 7 = 18$. It can also be verified that, for each positive integer n, the only such answer choice is $k = 47$, although this additional verification is not necessary to obtain the correct answer.

The correct answer is E.

PS17806
111. The perimeter of rectangle A is 200 meters. The length of rectangle B is 10 meters less than the length of rectangle A and the width of rectangle B is 10 meters more than the width of rectangle A. If rectangle B is a square, what is the width, in meters, of rectangle A ?

(A)   10

(B)   20

(C)   40

(D)   50

(E)   60

Geometry Rectangles; Perimeter

Let L meters and W meters be the length and width, respectively, of rectangle A. Then $(L - 10)$ meters and $(W + 10)$ meters are the length and width, respectively, of rectangle B. Since the perimeter of rectangle A is 200 meters, it follows that $2L + 2W = 200$, or $L + W = 100$. Since rectangle B is a square, it follows that $L - 10 = W + 10$, or $L - W = 20$. Adding the equations $L + W = 100$ and $L - W = 20$ gives $2L = 120$, or $L = 60$. From $L - W = 20$ and $L = 60$, it follows that $W = 40$, and so the width of rectangle A is 40 meters.

The correct answer is C.

PS08598

112. On the number line, the shaded interval is the graph of which of the following inequalities?

(A) $|x| \leq 4$

(B) $|x| \leq 8$

(C) $|x - 2| \leq 4$

(D) $|x - 2| \leq 6$

(E) $|x + 2| \leq 6$

Algebra Inequalities; Absolute value

The midpoint of the interval from –8 to 4, inclusive, is $\dfrac{-8 + 4}{2} = -2$ and the length of the interval from –8 to 4, inclusive, is $4 - (-8) = 12$, so the interval consists of all numbers within a distance of $\dfrac{12}{2} = 6$ from –2. Using an inequality involving absolute values, this can be described by $|x - (-2)| \leq 6$, or $|x + 2| \leq 6$.

Alternatively, the inequality $-8 \leq x \leq 4$ can be written as the conjunction $-8 \leq x$ and $x \leq 4$. Rewrite this conjunction so that the lower value, –8, and the upper value, 4, are shifted to values that have the same magnitude. This can be done by adding 2 to each side of each inequality, which gives $-6 \leq x + 2$ and $x + 2 \leq 6$. Thus, $x + 2$ lies between –6 and 6, inclusive, and it follows that $|x + 2| \leq 6$.

The correct answer is E.

PS12450

113. Last year members of a certain professional organization for teachers consisted of teachers from 49 different school districts, with an average (arithmetic mean) of 9.8 schools per district. Last year the average number of teachers at these schools who were members of the organization was 22. Which of the following is closest to the total number of members of the organization last year?

(A) 10^7

(B) 10^6

(C) 10^5

(D) 10^4

(E) 10^3

Arithmetic Statistics

There are 49 school districts and an average of 9.8 schools per district, so the number of schools is $(49)(9.8) \approx (50)(10) = 500$. There are approximately 500 schools and an average of 22 teachers at each school, so the number of teachers is approximately $(500)(22) \approx (500)(20) = 10{,}000 = 10^4$.

The correct answer is D.

PS09294

114. Of all the students in a certain dormitory, $\dfrac{1}{2}$ are first-year students and the rest are second-year students. If $\dfrac{4}{5}$ of the first-year students have not declared a major and if the fraction of second-year students who have declared a major is 3 times the fraction of first-year students who have declared a major, what fraction of all the students in the dormitory are second-year students who have not declared a major?

(A) $\dfrac{1}{15}$

(B) $\dfrac{1}{5}$

(C) $\dfrac{4}{15}$

(D) $\dfrac{1}{3}$

(E) $\dfrac{2}{5}$

Arithmetic Applied problems

Consider the table below in which T represents the total number of students in the dormitory. Since $\frac{1}{2}$ of the students are first-year students and the rest are second-year students, it follows that $\frac{1}{2}$ of the students are second-year students, and so the totals for the first-year and second-year columns are both $0.5T$. Since $\frac{4}{5}$ of the first-year students have not declared a major, it follows that the middle entry in the first-year column is $\frac{4}{5}(0.5T) = 0.4T$ and the first entry in the first-year column is $0.5T - 0.4T = 0.1T$. Since the fraction of second-year students who have declared a major is 3 times the fraction of first-year students who have declared a major, it follows that the first entry in the second-year column is $3(0.1T) = 0.3T$ and the second entry in the second-year column is $0.5T - 0.3T = 0.2T$. Thus, the fraction of students that are second-year students who have not declared a major is $\frac{0.2T}{T} = 0.2 = \frac{1}{5}$.

	First-year	Second-year	Total
Declared major	$0.1T$	$0.3T$	$0.4T$
Not declared major	$0.4T$	$0.2T$	$0.6T$
Total	$0.5T$	$0.5T$	T

The correct answer is B.

PS09050

115. If the average (arithmetic mean) of x, y, and z is 7x and x ≠ 0, what is the ratio of x to the sum of y and z?

(A)   1:21
(B)   1:20
(C)   1:6
(D)   6:1
(E)   20:1

Algebra Ratio and proportion

Given that the average of x, y, and z is $7x$, it follows that $\frac{x + y + z}{3} = 7x$, or $x + y + z = 21x$, or $y + z = 20x$. Dividing both sides of the last equation by $20(y + z)$ gives $\frac{1}{20} = \frac{x}{y+z}$, so the ratio of x to the sum of y and z is 1:20.

The correct answer is B.

PS02352

116. In the coordinate plane, line k passes through the origin and has slope 2. If points (3,y) and (x,4) are on line k, then x + y =

(A)   3.5
(B)   7
(C)   8
(D)   10
(E)   14

Algebra Simple coordinate geometry

Since line k has slope 2 and passes through the origin, the equation of line k is $y = 2x$. If the point $(3,y)$ is on line k, then $y = 2(3) = 6$. If the point $(x,4)$ is on line k, then $4 = 2x$ and so $x = 2$. Therefore, $x + y = 6 + 2 = 8$.

The correct answer is C.

PS08661

117. If a, b, and c are constants, a > b > c, and $x^3 - x = (x - a)(x - b)(x - c)$ for all numbers x, what is the value of b?

(A)   −3
(B)   −1
(C)   0
(D)   1
(E)   3

Algebra Simplifying algebraic expressions

Since $(x - a)(x - b)(x - c) = x^3 - x = x(x^2 - 1) = x(x + 1)(x - 1) = (x - 0)(x - 1)(x + 1)$ then a, b, and c are 0, 1, and −1 in some order. Since $a > b > c$, it follows that $a = 1$, $b = 0$, and $c = -1$.

The correct answer is C.

PS06273
118. $17^3 + 17^4 =$

(A) 17^7

(B) $17^3(18)$

(C) $17^6(18)$

(D) $2(17^3) + 17$

(E) $2(17^3) - 17$

Arithmetic Exponents

Since $17^3 = 17^3 \times 1$ and $17^4 = 17^3 \times 17$, then 17^3 may be factored out of each term. It follows that $17^3 + 17^4 = 17^3(1 + 17) = 17^3(18)$.

The correct answer is B.

PS02934
119. Company K's earnings were $12 million last year. If this year's earnings are projected to be 150 percent greater than last year's earnings, what are Company K's projected earnings this year?

(A) $13.5 million

(B) $15 million

(C) $18 million

(D) $27 million

(E) $30 million

Arithmetic Percents

If one quantity x is p percent greater than another quantity y, then $x = y + \left(\dfrac{p}{100}\right)y$. Let y represent last year's earnings and x represent this year's earnings, which are projected to be 150 percent greater than last year's earnings. Then, $x = y + \left(\dfrac{150}{100}\right)y = y + 1.5\,y = 2.5\,y$. Since last year's earnings were $12 million, this year's earnings are projected to be 2.5($12 million) = $30 million.

The correct answer is E.

PS05413
120. Jonah drove the first half of a 100-mile trip in x hours and the second half in y hours. Which of the following is equal to Jonah's average speed, in miles per hour, for the entire trip?

(A) $\dfrac{50}{x + y}$

(B) $\dfrac{100}{x + y}$

(C) $\dfrac{25}{x} + \dfrac{25}{y}$

(D) $\dfrac{50}{x} + \dfrac{50}{y}$

(E) $\dfrac{100}{x} + \dfrac{100}{y}$

Algebra Applied problems

Using average speed $= \dfrac{\text{total distance}}{\text{total time}}$, it follows that Jonah's average speed for his entire 100-mile trip is $\dfrac{100}{x + y}$.

The correct answer is B.

PS06135
121. What is the greatest number of identical bouquets that can be made out of 21 white and 91 red tulips if no flowers are to be left out? (Two bouquets are identical whenever the number of red tulips in the two bouquets is equal and the number of white tulips in the two bouquets is equal.)

(A) 3

(B) 4

(C) 5

(D) 6

(E) 7

Arithmetic Properties of numbers

Since the question asks for the greatest number of bouquets that can be made using all of the flowers, the number of bouquets will need to be the greatest common factor of 21 and 91. Since $21 = (3)(7)$ and $91 = (7)(13)$, the greatest common factor of 21 and 91 is 7. Therefore, 7 bouquets can be made, each with 3 white tulips and 13 red tulips.

The correct answer is E.

PS11454

122. In the *xy*-plane, the points (*c,d*), (*c,–d*), and (*–c,–d*) are three vertices of a certain square. If *c* < 0 and *d* > 0, which of the following points is in the same quadrant as the fourth vertex of the square?

(A) (–5,–3)

(B) (–5,3)

(C) (5,–3)

(D) (3,–5)

(E) (3,5)

Geometry Coordinate geometry

Because the points (*c,d*) and (*c,–d*) lie on the same vertical line (the line with equation *x = c*), one side of the square has length 2*d* and is vertical. Therefore, the side of the square opposite this side has length 2*d*, is vertical, and contains the vertex (*–c,–d*). From this it follows that the remaining vertex is (*–c,d*), because (*–c,d*) lies on the same vertical line as (*–c,–d*) (the line with equation *x = –c*) and these two vertices are a distance 2*d* apart. Because *c* < 0 and *d* > 0, the point (*–c,d*) has positive *x*-coordinate and positive *y*-coordinate. Thus, the point (*–c,d*) is in Quadrant I. Of the answer choices, only (3,5) is in Quadrant I.

The correct answer is E.

PS05470

123. If the amount of federal estate tax due on an estate valued at $1.35 million is $437,000 plus 43 percent of the value of the estate in excess of $1.25 million, then the federal tax due is approximately what percent of the value of the estate?

A. 30%

B. 35%

C. 40%

D. 45%

E. 50%

Arithmetic Percents; Estimation

The amount of tax divided by the value of the estate is

$$\frac{[0.437 + (0.43)(1.35 - 1.25)]\ \cancel{\text{million}}}{1.35\ \cancel{\text{million}}} \quad \text{value as fraction}$$

$$= \quad \frac{0.437 + (0.43)(0.1)}{1.35} \quad \text{arithmetic}$$

$$= \quad \frac{0.48}{1.35} = \frac{48}{135} \quad \text{arithmetic}$$

By long division, $\frac{48}{135}$ is approximately 35.6, so the closest answer choice is 35%.

Alternatively, $\frac{48}{135}$ can be estimated by

$\frac{48}{136} = \frac{6}{17} \approx \frac{6}{18} = \frac{1}{3} \approx 33\%$, so the closest answer choice is 35%. Note that $\frac{48}{135}$ is greater than $\frac{48}{136}$, and $\frac{6}{17}$ is greater than $\frac{6}{18}$, so the correct value is greater than 33%, which rules out 30% being the closest.

The correct answer is B.

PS05924

124. If $\frac{3}{10^4} = x\%$, then *x* =

(A) 0.3

(B) 0.03

(C) 0.003

(D) 0.0003

(E) 0.00003

Arithmetic Percents

Given that $\frac{3}{10^4} = x\%$, and writing *x*% as $\frac{x}{100}$, it follows that $\frac{3}{10^4} = \frac{x}{100}$. Multiplying both sides by 100 gives $x = \frac{300}{10^4} = \frac{300}{10,000} = \frac{3}{100} = 0.03$.

The correct answer is B.

PS01285

125. What is the remainder when 3^{24} is divided by 5 ?

(A) 0

(B) 1

(C) 2

(D) 3

(E) 4

Arithmetic Properties of numbers

A pattern in the units digits of the numbers $3, 3^2 = 9, 3^3 = 27, 3^4 = 81, 3^5 = 243$, etc., can be found by observing that the units digit of a product of two integers is the same as the units digit of the product of the units digit of the two integers. For example, the units digit of $3^5 = 3 \times 3^4 = 3 \times 81$ is 3 since the units digit of 3×1 is 3, and the units digit of $3^6 = 3 \times 3^5 = 3 \times 243$ is 9 since the units digit of 3×3 is 9. From this it follows that the units digit of the powers of 3 follow the pattern 3, 9, 7, 1, 3, 9, 7, 1, etc., with a units digit of 1 for $3^4, 3^8, 3^{12}, \dots$, $3^{24}, \dots$. Therefore, the units digit of 3^{24} is 1. Thus, 3^{24} is 1 more than a multiple of 10, and hence 3^{24} is 1 more than a multiple of 5, and so the remainder when 3^{24} is divided by 5 is 1.

The correct answer is B.

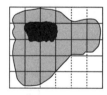

PS11692

126. In the figure shown, a square grid is superimposed on the map of a park, represented by the shaded region, in the middle of which is a pond, represented by the black region. If the area of the pond is 5,000 square yards, which of the following is closest to the area of the park, in square yards, including the area of the pond?

(A) 30,000

(B) 45,000

(C) 60,000

(D) 75,000

(E) 90,000

Geometry Estimation; Area

Let s be the side length, in yards, represented by each of the squares that form the square grid. By inspection, the map of the pond fills approximately 2 squares, so the area of the pond is approximately $2s^2$ yd². Since it is given that the area of the pond is 5,000 yd², it follows that $2s^2 = 5,000$, or $s^2 = 2,500$, or $s = 50$. The entire rectangular figure has a horizontal length of 6 squares, which represents $6(50 \text{ yd}) = 300 \text{ yd}$, and a vertical length of 5 squares, which represents $5(50 \text{ yd}) = 250 \text{ yd}$, so the area of the entire rectangular figure represents $(300 \text{ yd})(250 \text{ yd}) = 75,000 \text{ yd}^2$.

In the rectangular figure, less area is not shaded than is shaded, so to estimate the area represented by the shaded portion it will be easier to estimate the area represented by the portion that is not shaded and subtract this estimate from 75,000 yd², the area represented by the entire rectangular figure. By inspection, the area not shaded in the upper right corner represents approximately 2 squares, the area not shaded in the lower right corner represents approximately 6 squares, and the area not shaded on the left side represents approximately 2 squares. Thus, the area not shaded represents approximately $(2 + 6 + 2)$ squares, or approximately 10 squares, or approximately $10(2,500 \text{ yd}^2) = 25,000 \text{ yd}^2$. Therefore, the area of the park is approximately $75,000 \text{ yd}^2 - 25,000 \text{ yd}^2 = 50,000 \text{ yd}^2$, and of the values available, 45,000 is the closest.

The correct answer is B.

PS03623

127. If the volume of a ball is 32,490 cubic millimeters, what is the volume of the ball in cubic centimeters? (1 millimeter = 0.1 centimeter)

(A) 0.3249

(B) 3.249

(C) 32.49

(D) 324.9

(E) 3,249

Arithmetic Measurement conversion

Since 1 mm = 0.1 cm, it follows that $1 \text{ mm}^3 = (0.1)^3 \text{ cm}^3 = 0.001 \text{ cm}^3$. Therefore, $32,490 \text{ mm}^3 = (32,490)(0.001) \text{ cm}^3 = 32.49 \text{ cm}^3$.

The correct answer is C.

PS07058
128. David used part of $100,000 to purchase a house. Of the remaining portion, he invested $\frac{1}{3}$ of it at 4 percent simple annual interest and $\frac{2}{3}$ of it at 6 percent simple annual interest. If after a year the income from the two investments totaled $320, what was the purchase price of the house?

(A) $96,000
(B) $94,000
(C) $88,000
(D) $75,000
(E) $40,000

Algebra Applied problems; Percents

Let x be the amount, in dollars, that David used to purchase the house. Then David invested $(100,000 - x)$ dollars, $\frac{1}{3}$ at 4% simple annual interest and $\frac{2}{3}$ at 6% simple annual interest. After one year the total interest, in dollars, on this investment was $\frac{1}{3}(100,000 - x)(0.04) + \frac{2}{3}(100,000 - x)(0.06) = 320$. Solve this equation to find the value of x.

$$\frac{1}{3}(100,000 - x)(0.04) +$$

$\frac{2}{3}(100,000 - x)(0.06) = 320$ given

$(100,000 - x)(0.04) +$
$2(100,000 - x)(0.06) = 960$ multiply both sides by 3

$4,000 - 0.04x +$
$12,000 - 0.12x = 960$ distributive property

$16,000 - 0.16x = 960$ combine like terms

$16,000 - 960 = 0.16x$ add $0.16x - 960$ to both sides

$100,000 - 6,000 = x$ divide both sides by 0.16

$94,000 = x$

Therefore, the purchase price of the house was $94,000.

The correct answer is B.

PS11537
129. In the sequence $x_0, x_1, x_2, ..., x_n$, each term from x_1 to x_k is 3 greater than the previous term, and each term from x_{k+1} to x_n is 3 less than the previous term, where n and k are positive integers and $k < n$. If $x_0 = x_n = 0$ and if $x_k = 15$, what is the value of n?

(A) 5
(B) 6
(C) 9
(D) 10
(E) 15

Algebra Sequences

Since $x_0 = 0$ and each term from x_1 to x_k is 3 greater than the previous term, then $x_k = 0 + (k)(3)$. Since $x_k = 15$, then $15 = 3k$ and $k = 5$. Since each term from x_{k+1} to x_n is 3 less than the previous term, then $x_n = x_k - (n - k)(3)$. Substituting the known values for x_k, x_n, and k gives $0 = 15 - (n - 5)(3)$, from which it follows that $3n = 30$ and $n = 10$.

The correct answer is D.

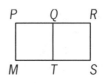

Note: Not drawn to scale.

PS11145
130. In the figure shown above, line segment QR has length 12, and rectangle $MPQT$ is a square. If the area of rectangular region $MPRS$ is 540, what is the area of rectangular region $TQRS$?

(A) 144
(B) 216
(C) 324
(D) 360
(E) 396

Geometry; Algebra Area; Second-degree equations

Since $MPQT$ is a square, let $MP = PQ = x$. Then $PR = PQ + QR = x + 12$. The area of $MPRS$ can be expressed as $x(x + 12)$. Since the area of $MPRS$ is given to be 540,

$$x(x+12) = 540$$
$$x^2 + 12x = 540$$
$$x^2 + 12x - 540 = 0$$
$$(x-18)(x+30) = 0$$
$$x = 18 \text{ or } x = -30$$

Since x represents a length and must be positive, $x = 18$. The area of $TQRS$ is then $(12)(18) = 216$.

As an alternative to solving the quadratic equation, look for a pair of positive numbers such that their product is 540 and one is 12 greater than the other. The pair is 18 and 30, so $x = 18$ and the area of $TQRS$ is then $(12)(18) = 216$.

The correct answer is B.

PS09439

131. A certain manufacturer sells its product to stores in 113 different regions worldwide, with an average (arithmetic mean) of 181 stores per region. If last year these stores sold an average of 51,752 units of the manufacturer's product per store, which of the following is closest to the total number of units of the manufacturer's product sold worldwide last year?

(A) 10^6
(B) 10^7
(C) 10^8
(D) 10^9
(E) 10^{10}

Arithmetic Estimation

$$(113)(181)(51,752) \approx (100)(200)(50,000)$$
$$= 10^2 \times (2 \times 10^2) \times (5 \times 10^4)$$
$$= (2 \times 5) \times 10^{2+2+4}$$
$$= 10^1 \times 10^8 = 10^9$$

The correct answer is D.

PS17708

132. Andrew started saving at the beginning of the year and had saved $240 by the end of the year. He continued to save and by the end of 2 years had saved a total of $540. Which of the following is closest to the percent increase in the amount Andrew saved during the second year compared to the amount he saved during the first year?

(A) 11%
(B) 25%
(C) 44%
(D) 56%
(E) 125%

Arithmetic Percents

Andrew saved $240 in the first year and $540 − $240 = $300 in the second year. The percent increase in the amount Andrew saved in the second year compared to the amount he saved in the first year is $\left(\dfrac{300 - 240}{240} \times 100 \right)\% =$ $\left(\dfrac{60}{240} \times 100 \right)\% = \left(\dfrac{1}{4} \times 100 \right)\% = 25\%$.

The correct answer is B.

PS19062

133. Two numbers differ by 2 and sum to S. Which of the following is the greater of the numbers in terms of S?

(A) $\dfrac{S}{2} - 1$

(B) $\dfrac{S}{2}$

(C) $\dfrac{S}{2} + \dfrac{1}{2}$

(D) $\dfrac{S}{2} + 1$

(E) $\dfrac{S}{2} + 2$

Algebra First-degree equations

Let x represent the greater of the two numbers that differ by 2. Then, $x - 2$ represents the lesser of the two numbers. The two numbers sum to S, so $x + (x - 2) = S$. It follows that $2x - 2 = S$, or $2x = S + 2$, or $x = \dfrac{S}{2} + 1$.

The correct answer is D.

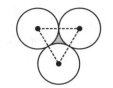

PS00904

134. The figure shown above consists of three identical circles that are tangent to each other. If the area of the shaded region is $64\sqrt{3} - 32\pi$, what is the radius of each circle?

(A)   4

(B)   8

(C)   16

(D)   24

(E)   32

Geometry Circles; Triangles; Area

Let r represent the radius of each circle. Then the triangle shown dashed in the figure is equilateral with sides $2r$ units long. The interior of the triangle is comprised of the shaded region and three circular sectors. The area of the shaded region can be found as the area of the triangle minus the sum of the areas of the three sectors. Since the triangle is equilateral, its side lengths are in the proportions as shown in the diagram below. The area of the interior of the triangle is

$$\frac{1}{2}(2r)\left(r\sqrt{3}\right) = r^2\sqrt{3}.$$

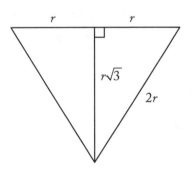

Each of the three sectors has a central angle of 60° because the central angle is an angle of the equilateral triangle. Therefore, the area of each sector is $\dfrac{60}{360} = \dfrac{1}{6}$ of the area of the circle. The sum of the areas of the three sectors is then

$3\left(\dfrac{1}{6}\pi r^2\right) = \dfrac{1}{2}\pi r^2$. Thus, the area of the shaded

region is $r^2\sqrt{3} - \dfrac{1}{2}\pi r^2 = r^2\left(\sqrt{3} - \dfrac{1}{2}\pi\right)$. But, this

area is given as $64\sqrt{3} - 32\pi = 64\left(\sqrt{3} - \dfrac{1}{2}\pi\right)$.

Thus $r^2 = 64$, and $r = 8$.

The correct answer is B.

PS02053

135. In a numerical table with 10 rows and 10 columns, each entry is either a 9 or a 10. If the number of 9s in the nth row is $n - 1$ for each n from 1 to 10, what is the average (arithmetic mean) of all the numbers in the table?

(A)   9.45

(B)   9.50

(C)   9.55

(D)   9.65

(E)   9.70

Arithmetic Operations with integers

There are $(10)(10) = 100$ entries in the table. In rows $1, 2, 3, \ldots, 10$, the number of 9s is $0, 1, 2, \ldots, 9$, respectively, giving a total of $0 + 1 + 2 + \ldots + 9 = 45$ entries with a 9. This leaves a total of $100 - 45 = 55$ entries with a 10. Therefore, the sum of the 100 entries is $45(9) + 55(10) = 405 + 550 = 955$, and the average of the 100 entries is $\dfrac{955}{100} = 9.55$

The correct answer is C.

PS08485

136. A positive integer n is a perfect number provided that the sum of all the positive factors of n, including 1 and n, is equal to $2n$. What is the sum of the reciprocals of all the positive factors of the perfect number 28 ?

(A) $\dfrac{1}{4}$

(B) $\dfrac{56}{27}$

(C)   2

(D)   3

(E)   4

Arithmetic Properties of numbers

The factors of 28 are 1, 2, 4, 7, 14, and 28. Therefore, the sum of the reciprocals of the factors of 28 is $\dfrac{1}{1} + \dfrac{1}{2} + \dfrac{1}{4} + \dfrac{1}{7} + \dfrac{1}{14} + \dfrac{1}{28} =$

$\dfrac{28}{28} + \dfrac{14}{28} + \dfrac{7}{28} + \dfrac{4}{28} + \dfrac{2}{28} + \dfrac{1}{28} =$

$\dfrac{28 + 14 + 7 + 4 + 2 + 1}{28} = \dfrac{56}{28} = 2.$

The correct answer is C.

PS11430

137. The infinite sequence $a_1, a_2, \ldots, a_n, \ldots$ is such that $a_1 = 2$, $a_2 = -3$, $a_3 = 5$, $a_4 = -1$, and $a_n = a_{n-4}$ for $n > 4$. What is the sum of the first 97 terms of the sequence?

(A) 72
(B) 74
(C) 75
(D) 78
(E) 80

Arithmetic Sequences and series

Because $a_n = a_{n-4}$ for $n > 4$, it follows that the terms of the sequence repeat in groups of 4 terms:

Values for n	Values for a_n
1, 2, 3, 4	2, −3, 5, −1
5, 6, 7, 8	2, −3, 5, −1
9, 10, 11, 12	2, −3, 5, −1
13, 14, 15, 16	2, −3, 5, −1

Thus, since $97 = 24(4) + 1$, the sum of the first 97 terms can be grouped into 24 groups of 4 terms each, with one remaining term, which allows the sum to be easily found:

$(a_1 + a_2 + a_3 + a_4) + (a_5 + a_6 + a_7 + a_8) + \ldots + (a_{93} + a_{94} + a_{95} + a_{96}) + a_{97}$

$= (2 - 3 + 5 - 1) + (2 - 3 + 5 - 1) + \ldots + (2 - 3 + 5 - 1) + 2$

$= 24(2 - 3 + 5 - 1) + 2 = 24(3) + 2 = 74$

The correct answer is B.

PS09901

138. The sequence $a_1, a_2, \ldots, a_n, \ldots$ is such that $a_n = 2a_{n-1} - x$ for all positive integers $n \geq 2$ and for a certain number x. If $a_5 = 99$ and $a_3 = 27$, what is the value of x?

(A) 3
(B) 9
(C) 18
(D) 36
(E) 45

Algebra Sequences and series

An expression for a_5 that involves x can be obtained using $a_3 = 27$ and applying the equation $a_n = 2a_{n-1} - x$ twice, once for $n = 4$ and once for $n = 5$.

$a_4 = 2a_3 - x$	using $a_n = 2a_{n-1} - x$ for $n = 4$
$\quad = 2(27) - x$	using $a_3 = 27$
$a_5 = 2a_4 - x$	using $a_n = 2a_{n-1} - x$ for $n = 5$
$\quad = 2[2(27) - x] - x$	using $a_4 = 2(27) - x$
$\quad = 4(27) - 3x$	combine like terms

Therefore, using $a_5 = 99$, we have

$99 = 4(27) - 3x$	given
$3x = 4(27) - 99$	adding $(3x - 99)$ to both sides
$x = 4(9) - 33$	dividing both sides by 3
$x = 3$	arithmetic

The correct answer is A.

PS03779

139. A window is in the shape of a regular hexagon with each side of length 80 centimeters. If a diagonal through the center of the hexagon is w centimeters long, then $w =$

(A) 80
(B) 120
(C) 150
(D) 160
(E) 240

Geometry Polygons

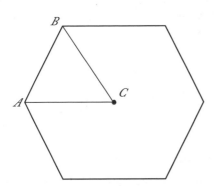

Let A and B be the endpoints of one of the sides of the hexagon and let C be the center of the hexagon. Then the degree measure of $\angle ACB$ is $\frac{360}{6} = 60$ and the sum of the degree measures of $\angle ABC$ and $\angle BAC$ is $180 - 60 = 120$. Also, since $AC = BC$, the degree measures of $\angle ABC$ and $\angle BAC$ are equal. Therefore, the degree measure of each of $\angle ABC$ and $\angle BAC$ is 60. Thus, $\triangle ABC$ is an equilateral triangle with side length $AB = 80$. It follows that the length of a diagonal through the center of the hexagon is $2(AC) = 2(80) = 160$.

The correct answer is D.

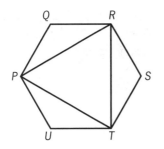

PS03695

140. In the figure shown, $PQRSTU$ is a regular polygon with sides of length x. What is the perimeter of triangle PRT in terms of x ?

(A) $\dfrac{x\sqrt{3}}{2}$

(B) $x\sqrt{3}$

(C) $\dfrac{3x\sqrt{3}}{2}$

(D) $3x\sqrt{3}$

(E) $4x\sqrt{3}$

Geometry Polygons

Since $PQRSTU$ is a regular hexagon, $\triangle PQR$, $\triangle RST$, and $\triangle TUP$ are the same size and shape, so $PR = RT = TP$ and the perimeter of $\triangle PRT$ is $3(PR)$. Note that in the figure above, $PQRSTU$ is partitioned into four triangles. The sum of the degree measures of the interior angles of each triangle is 180°. The total of the degree measures of the interior angles of these four triangles is equal to the sum of the degree measures of the six interior angles of $PQRSTU$. Since $PQRSTU$ is a regular hexagon, each of $\angle UPQ$, $\angle PQR$, $\angle QRS$, $\angle RST$, $\angle STU$, and $\angle TUP$ has the same measure, which is $\dfrac{(4)(180°)}{6} = 120°$.

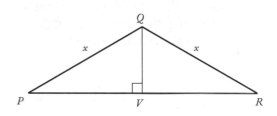

In the figure above, $\triangle PQR$ is isosceles with $PQ = QR = x$. The measure of $\angle PQR$ is 120°, and the measure of $\angle P =$ the measure of $\angle R = \dfrac{180° - 120°}{2} = 30°$. $\overline{QV}$ is perpendicular to $\overline{PR}$ and $PV = VR$. Since $\triangle PVQ$ is a 30°–60°–90° triangle, its side lengths are in the ratio $1{:}\sqrt{3}{:}2$, and so $PV = \dfrac{x\sqrt{3}}{2}$ and $PR = x\sqrt{3}$. Therefore, the perimeter of $\triangle PRT$ is $3(x\sqrt{3}) = 3x\sqrt{3}$.

The correct answer is D.

PS11755

141. In a certain medical survey, 45 percent of the people surveyed had the type A antigen in their blood and 3 percent had both the type A antigen and the type B antigen. Which of the following is closest to the percent of those with the type A antigen who also had the type B antigen?

(A) 1.35%

(B) 6.67%

(C) 13.50%

(D) 15.00%

(E) 42.00%

Arithmetic Applied problems; Percents

Let n be the total number of people surveyed. Then, the proportion of the people who had type A who also had type B is $\dfrac{(3\%)n}{(45\%)n} = \dfrac{3}{45} = \dfrac{1}{15}$, which as a percent is approximately 6.67%. Note that by using $\dfrac{1}{15} = \dfrac{1}{3} \times \dfrac{1}{5}$, which equals $\dfrac{1}{3}$ of 20%, we can avoid dividing by a 2-digit integer.

The correct answer is B.

PS05146

142. On a certain transatlantic crossing, 20 percent of a ship's passengers held round-trip tickets and also took their cars aboard the ship. If 60 percent of the passengers with round-trip tickets did <u>not</u> take their cars aboard the ship, what percent of the ship's passengers held round-trip tickets?

(A) $33\dfrac{1}{3}\%$

(B) 40%

(C) 50%

(D) 60%

(E) $66\dfrac{2}{3}\%$

Arithmetic Percents

Since the number of passengers on the ship is immaterial, let the number of passengers on the ship be 100 for convenience. Let x be the number of passengers that held round-trip tickets. Then, since 20 percent of the passengers held a round-trip ticket and took their cars aboard the ship, $0.20(100) = 20$ passengers held round-trip tickets and took their cars aboard the ship. The remaining passengers with round-trip tickets did not take their cars aboard, and they represent $0.6x$ (that is, 60 percent of the passengers with round-trip tickets). Thus $0.6x + 20 = x$, from which it follows that $20 = 0.4x$, and so $x = 50$. The percent of passengers with round-trip tickets is, then, $\dfrac{50}{100} = 50\%$.

The correct answer is C.

PS03696

143. If x and k are integers and $(12^x)(4^{2x+1}) = (2^k)(3^2)$, what is the value of k?

(A) 5

(B) 7

(C) 10

(D) 12

(E) 14

Arithmetic Exponents

Rewrite the expression on the left so that it is a product of powers of 2 and 3.

$$(12^x)(4^{2x+1}) = [(3 \cdot 2^2)^x][(2^2)^{2x+1}]$$
$$= (3^x)[(2^2)^x][2^{2(2x+1)}]$$
$$= (3^x)(2^{2x})(2^{4x+2})$$
$$= (3^x)(2^{6x+2})$$

Then, since $(12^x)(4^{2x+1}) = (2^k)(3^2)$, it follows that $(3^x)(2^{6x+2}) = (2^k)(3^2) = (3^2)(2^k)$, so $x = 2$ and $k = 6x + 2$. Substituting 2 for x gives $k = 6(2) + 2 = 14$.

The correct answer is E.

PS11024

144. If S is the sum of the reciprocals of the 10 consecutive integers from 21 to 30, then S is between which of the following two fractions?

(A) $\dfrac{1}{3}$ and $\dfrac{1}{2}$

(B) $\dfrac{1}{4}$ and $\dfrac{1}{3}$

(C) $\dfrac{1}{5}$ and $\dfrac{1}{4}$

(D) $\dfrac{1}{6}$ and $\dfrac{1}{5}$

(E) $\dfrac{1}{7}$ and $\dfrac{1}{6}$

Arithmetic Estimation

The value of $\dfrac{1}{21} + \dfrac{1}{22} + \dfrac{1}{23} + \ldots + \dfrac{1}{30}$ is LESS than $\dfrac{1}{20} + \dfrac{1}{20} + \dfrac{1}{20} + \ldots + \dfrac{1}{20}$ (10 numbers added), which equals $10\left(\dfrac{1}{20}\right) = \dfrac{1}{2}$, and GREATER than $\dfrac{1}{30} + \dfrac{1}{30} + \dfrac{1}{30} + \ldots + \dfrac{1}{30}$

(10 numbers added), which equals $10\left(\dfrac{1}{30}\right) = \dfrac{1}{3}$.

Therefore, the value of $\dfrac{1}{21} + \dfrac{1}{22} + \dfrac{1}{23} + \dots + \dfrac{1}{30}$

is between $\dfrac{1}{3}$ and $\dfrac{1}{2}$.

The correct answer is A.

PS08729

145. For every even positive integer m, $f(m)$ represents the product of all even integers from 2 to m, inclusive. For example, $f(12) = 2 \times 4 \times 6 \times 8 \times 10 \times 12$. What is the greatest prime factor of $f(24)$?

(A)   23
(B)   19
(C)   17
(D)   13
(E)   11

Arithmetic Properties of numbers

Rewriting $f(24) = 2 \times 4 \times 6 \times 8 \times 10 \times 12 \times 14 \times \dots$ $\times 20 \times 22 \times 24$ as $2 \times 4 \times 2(3) \times 8 \times 2(5) \times 12$ $\times 2(7) \times \dots \times 20 \times 2(11) \times 24$ shows that all of the prime numbers from 2 through 11 are factors of $f(24)$. The next prime number is 13, but 13 is not a factor of $f(24)$ because none of the even integers from 2 through 24 has 13 as a factor. Therefore, the largest prime factor of $f(24)$ is 11.

The correct answer is E.

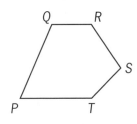

Note: Not drawn to scale.

PS08572

146. In pentagon $PQRST$, $PQ = 3$, $QR = 2$, $RS = 4$, and $ST = 5$. Which of the lengths 5, 10, and 15 could be the value of PT?

(A)   5 only
(B)   15 only
(C)   5 and 10 only
(D)   10 and 15 only
(E)   5, 10, and 15

Geometry Polygons; Triangles

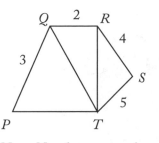

Note: Not drawn to scale.

In the figure above, diagonals $\overline{TQ}$ and $\overline{TR}$ have been drawn in to show $\triangle TRS$ and $\triangle TRQ$. Because the length of any side of a triangle must be less than the sum of the lengths of the other two sides, $RT < 5 + 4 = 9$ in $\triangle TRS$, and $QT < RT + 2$ in $\triangle TRQ$. Since $RT < 9$, then $RT + 2 < 9 + 2 = 11$, which then implies $QT < 11$. Now, $PT < QT + 3$ in $\triangle TQP$, and since $QT < 11$, $QT + 3 < 11 + 3 = 14$. It follows that $PT < 14$. Therefore, 15 cannot be the length of $\overline{PT}$ since $15 \not< 14$.

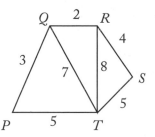

Note: Not drawn to scale.

To show that 5 can be the length of $\overline{PT}$, consider the figure above. For $\triangle TQP$, the length of any side is less than the sum of the lengths of the other two sides as shown below.

$$QT = 7 < 8 = 5 + 3 = PT + PQ$$
$$PQ = 3 < 12 = 5 + 7 = PT + TQ$$
$$PT = 5 < 10 = 3 + 7 = PQ + TQ$$

For $\triangle RQT$, the length of any side is less than the sum of the lengths of the other two sides as shown below.

$$RT = 8 < 9 = 7 + 2 = QT + QR$$
$$RQ = 2 < 15 = 7 + 8 = QT + RT$$
$$QT = 7 < 10 = 2 + 8 = QR + RT$$

For $\triangle RST$, the length of any side is less than the sum of the lengths of the other two sides as shown below.

$$RS = 4 < 13 = 8 + 5 = TR + TS$$
$$RT = 8 < 9 = 5 + 4 = ST + SR$$
$$ST = 5 < 12 = 8 + 4 = TR + RS$$

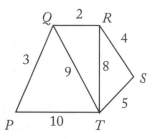

Note: Not drawn to scale.

To show that 10 can be the length of $\overline{PT}$, consider the figure above. For $\triangle TQP$, the length of any side is less than the sum of the lengths of the other two sides as shown below.

$$QT = 9 < 13 = 10 + 3 = PT + PQ$$
$$PQ = 3 < 19 = 10 + 9 = PT + TQ$$
$$PT = 10 < 12 = 3 + 9 = PQ + TQ$$

For $\triangle RQT$, the length of any side is less than the sum of the lengths of the other two sides as shown below.

$$RT = 8 < 11 = 9 + 2 = QT + QR$$
$$RQ = 2 < 17 = 9 + 8 = QT + RT$$
$$QT = 9 < 10 = 2 + 8 = QT + RT$$

For $\triangle RST$, the length of any side is less than the sum of the lengths of the other two sides as shown below.

$$RS = 4 < 13 = 8 + 5 = TR + TS$$
$$RT = 8 < 9 = 5 + 4 = ST + SR$$
$$ST = 5 < 12 = 8 + 4 = TR + RS$$

Therefore, 5 and 10 can be the length of $\overline{PT}$, and 15 cannot be the length of $\overline{PT}$.

The correct answer is C.

$$3, k, 2, 8, m, 3$$

PS07771

147. The arithmetic mean of the list of numbers above is 4. If k and m are integers and $k \neq m$ what is the median of the list?

(A)   2

(B)   2.5

(C)   3

(D)   3.5

(E)   4

Arithmetic Statistics

Since the arithmetic mean $= \dfrac{\text{sum of values}}{\text{number of values}}$, then $\dfrac{3 + k + 2 + 8 + m + 3}{6} = 4$, and so $\dfrac{16 + k + m}{6} = 4$, $16 + k + m = 24$, $k + m = 8$. Since $k \neq m$, then either $k < 4$ and $m > 4$ or $k > 4$ and $m < 4$. Because k and m are integers, either $k \leq 3$ and $m \geq 5$ or $k \geq 5$ and $m \leq 3$.

Case (i):   If $k \leq 2$, then $m \geq 6$ and the six integers in ascending order are $k, 2, 3, 3, m, 8$ or $k, 2, 3, 3, 8, m$. The two middle integers are both 3 so the median is $\dfrac{3 + 3}{2} = 3$.

Case (ii):   If $k = 3$, then $m = 5$ and the six integers in ascending order are $2, k, 3, 3, m, 8$. The two middle integers are both 3 so the median is $\dfrac{3 + 3}{2} = 3$.

Case (iii):   If $k = 5$, then $m = 3$ and the six integers in ascending order are $2, m, 3, 3, k, 8$. The two middle integers are both 3 so the median is $\dfrac{3 + 3}{2} = 3$.

Case (iv):   If $k \geq 6$, then $m \leq 2$ and the six integers in ascending order are $m, 2, 3, 3, k, 8$ or $m, 2, 3, 3, 8, k$. The two middle integers are both 3 so the median is $\dfrac{3 + 3}{2} = 3$.

The correct answer is C.

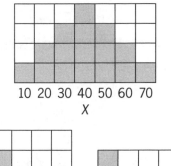

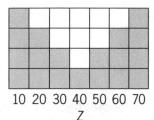

PS04987

148. If the variables *X*, *Y*, and *Z* take on only the values 10, 20, 30, 40, 50, 60, or 70 with frequencies indicated by the shaded regions above, for which of the frequency distributions is the mean equal to the median?

   (A)   *X* only

   (B)   *Y* only

   (C)   *Z* only

   (D)   *X* and *Y*

   (E)   *X* and *Z*

Arithmetic Statistics

The frequency distributions for both X and Z are symmetric about 40, and thus both X and Z have mean = median = 40. Therefore, any answer choice that does not include both X and Z can be eliminated. This leaves only answer choice E.

The correct answer is E.

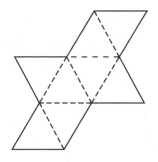

PS15538

149. When the figure above is cut along the solid lines, folded along the dashed lines, and taped along the solid lines, the result is a model of a geometric solid. This geometric solid consists of 2 pyramids, each with a square base that they share. What is the sum of the number of edges and the number of faces of this geometric solid?

   (A)   10

   (B)   18

   (C)   20

   (D)   24

   (E)   25

Geometry Solids

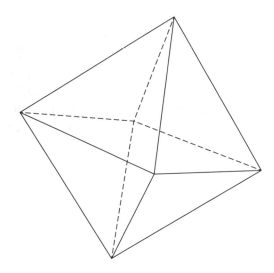

A geometric solid consisting of 2 pyramids, each with a square base that they share, is shown in the figure above. From the figure it can be seen that the solid has 12 edges and 8 faces. Therefore, the sum of the number of edges and the number of faces of the solid is $12 + 8 = 20$.

Alternatively, the solid has $7 + 5 = 12$ edges because each edge in the solid is generated from either a dashed segment (there are 7 dashed segments) or from a pair of solid segments taped together (there are $\frac{10}{2} = 5$ such pairs of solid segments), and the solid has 8 faces because there are 8 small triangles in the given figure. Therefore, the sum of the number of edges and the number of faces of the solid is $12 + 8 = 20$.

The correct answer is C.

$$2x + y = 12$$
$$|y| \le 12$$

PS03356

150. For how many ordered pairs (x,y) that are solutions of the system above are x and y both integers?

(A) 7
(B) 10
(C) 12
(D) 13
(E) 14

Algebra Absolute value

From $|y| \le 12$, if y must be an integer, then y must be in the set
$S = \{\pm 12, \pm 11, \pm 10, \ldots, \pm 3, \pm 2, \pm 1, 0\}$.

Since $2x + y = 12$, then $x = \frac{12 - y}{2}$. If x must be an integer, then $12 - y$ must be divisible by 2; that is, $12 - y$ must be even. Since 12 is even, $12 - y$ is even if and only if y is even. This eliminates all odd integers from S, leaving only the even integers $\pm 12, \pm 10, \pm 8, \pm 6, \pm 4, \pm 2,$ and 0. Thus, there are 13 possible integer y-values, each with a corresponding integer x-value and, therefore, there are 13 ordered pairs (x,y), where x and y are both integers, that solve the system.

The correct answer is D.

PS08859

151. The points R, T, and U lie on a circle that has radius 4. If the length of arc RTU is $\frac{4\pi}{3}$ what is the length of line segment RU ?

(A) $\frac{4}{3}$

(B) $\frac{8}{3}$

(C) 3

(D) 4

(E) 6

Geometry Circles; Triangles; Circumference

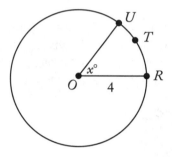

In the figure above, O is the center of the circle that contains R, T, and U and x is the degree measure of $\angle ROU$. Since the circumference of the circle is $2\pi(4) = 8\pi$ and there are 360° in the circle, the ratio of the length of arc RTU to the circumference of the circle is the same as the ratio of x to 360. Therefore, $\frac{\frac{4\pi}{3}}{8\pi} = \frac{x}{360}$. Then $x = \frac{\frac{4\pi}{3}(360)}{8\pi} = \frac{480\pi}{8\pi} = 60$. This means that $\triangle ROU$ is an isosceles triangle with side lengths $OR = OU = 4$ and vertex angle measuring 60°. The base angles of $\triangle ROU$ must have equal measures and the sum of their measures must be $180° - 60° = 120°$. Therefore, each base angle measures 60°, $\triangle ROU$ is equilateral, and $RU = 4$.

The correct answer is D.

152. A certain university will select 1 of 7 candidates eligible to fill a position in the mathematics department and 2 of 10 candidates eligible to fill 2 identical positions in the computer science department. If none of the candidates is eligible for a position in both departments, how many different sets of 3 candidates are there to fill the 3 positions?

   (A)   42
   (B)   70
   (C)   140
   (D)   165
   (E)   315

Arithmetic Elementary combinatorics

To fill the position in the math department, 1 candidate will be selected from a group of 7 eligible candidates, and so there are 7 sets of 1 candidate each to fill the position in the math department. To fill the positions in the computer science department, any one of the 10 eligible candidates can be chosen for the first position and any of the remaining 9 eligible candidates can be chosen for the second position, making a total of $10 \times 9 = 90$ sets of 2 candidates to fill the computer science positions. But, this number includes the set in which Candidate A was chosen to fill the first position and Candidate B was chosen to fill the second position as well as the set in which Candidate B was chosen for the first position and Candidate A was chosen for the second position. These sets are not different essentially since the positions are identical and in both sets Candidates A and B are chosen to fill the 2 positions. Therefore, there are $\frac{90}{2} = 45$ sets of 2 candidates to fill the computer science positions. Then, using the multiplication principle, there are $7 \times 45 = 315$ different sets of 3 candidates to fill the 3 positions.

The correct answer is E.

153. A survey of employers found that during 1993 employment costs rose 3.5 percent, where employment costs consist of salary costs and fringe-benefit costs. If salary costs rose 3 percent and fringe-benefit costs rose 5.5 percent during 1993, then fringe-benefit costs represented what percent of employment costs at the beginning of 1993 ?

   (A)   16.5%
   (B)   20%
   (C)   35%
   (D)   55%
   (E)   65%

Algebra; Arithmetic First-degree equations; Percents

Let E represent employment costs, S represent salary costs, and F represent fringe-benefit costs. Then $E = S + F$. An increase of 3 percent in salary costs and a 5.5 percent increase in fringe-benefit costs resulted in a 3.5 percent increase in employment costs. Therefore $1.03S + 1.055F = 1.035E$. But, $E = S + F$, so $1.03S + 1.055F = 1.035(S + F) = 1.035S + 1.035F$.

Combining like terms gives $(1.055 - 1.035)F = (1.035 - 1.03)S$ or $0.02F = 0.005S$. Then, $S = \frac{0.02}{0.005}F = 4F$. Thus, since $E = S + F$, it follows that $E = 4F + F = 5F$. Then, F as a percent of E is $\frac{F}{E} = \frac{F}{5F} = \frac{1}{5} = 20\%$.

The correct answer is B.

154. The subsets of the set $\{w, x, y\}$ are $\{w\}$, $\{x\}$, $\{y\}$, $\{w, x\}$, $\{w, y\}$, $\{x, y\}$, $\{w, x, y\}$, and $\{\ \}$ (the empty subset). How many subsets of the set $\{w, x, y, z\}$ contain w ?

   (A)   Four
   (B)   Five
   (C)   Seven
   (D)   Eight
   (E)   Sixteen

Arithmetic Sets

As shown in the table, the subsets of $\{w, x, y, z\}$ can be organized into two columns, those subsets of $\{w, x, y, z\}$ that do not contain w (left column) and the corresponding subsets of $\{w, x, y, z\}$ that contain w (right column), and each of these collections has the same number of sets. Therefore, there are 8 subsets of $\{w, x, y, z\}$ that contain w.

subsets not containing w	subsets containing w
{ }	$\{w\}$
$\{x\}$	$\{w, x\}$
$\{y\}$	$\{w, y\}$
$\{z\}$	$\{w, z\}$
$\{x, y\}$	$\{w, x, y\}$
$\{x, z\}$	$\{w, x, z\}$
$\{y, z\}$	$\{w, y, z\}$
$\{x, y, z\}$	$\{w, x, y, z\}$

The correct answer is D.

PS10309
155. There are 5 cars to be displayed in 5 parking spaces, with all the cars facing the same direction. Of the 5 cars, 3 are red, 1 is blue, and 1 is yellow. If the cars are identical except for color, how many different display arrangements of the 5 cars are possible?

(A)   20
(B)   25
(C)   40
(D)   60
(E)   125

Arithmetic Elementary combinatorics

There are 5 parking spaces from which 3 must be chosen to display the 3 identical red cars.

Thus, there are $\binom{5}{3} = \dfrac{5!}{3!2!} = 10$ different arrangements of the 3 identical red cars in the parking spaces. There are 2 spaces remaining for displaying the single blue car and 1 space left for displaying the single yellow car. Therefore, there are $(10)(2)(1) = 20$ arrangements possible for displaying the 5 cars in the 5 parking spaces.

The correct answer is A.

PS17461
156. The number $\sqrt{63 - 36\sqrt{3}}$ can be expressed as $x + y\sqrt{3}$ for some integers x and y. What is the value of xy?

(A)   −18
(B)   −6
(C)   6
(D)   18
(E)   27

Algebra Operations on radical expressions

Squaring both sides of $\sqrt{63 - 36\sqrt{3}} = x + y\sqrt{3}$ gives $63 - 36\sqrt{3} = x^2 + 2xy\sqrt{3} + 3y^2 = (x^2 + 3y^2) + (2xy)\sqrt{3}$, which implies that $-36 = 2xy$, or $xy = -18$. Indeed, if $-36 \neq 2xy$, or equivalently, if $36 + 2xy \neq 0$, then we could write $\sqrt{3}$ as a quotient of the two integers $63 - x^2 - 3y^2$ and $36 + 2xy$, which is not possible because $\sqrt{3}$ is an irrational number. To be more explicit, $63 - 36\sqrt{3} = x^2 + 2xy\sqrt{3} + 3y^2$ implies $63 - x^2 - 3y^2 = (36 + 2xy)\sqrt{3}$, and if $36 + 2xy \neq 0$, then we could divide both sides of the equation $63 - x^2 - 3y^2 = (36 + 2xy)\sqrt{3}$ by $36 + 2xy$ to get $\dfrac{63 - x^2 - 3y^2}{36 + 2xy} = \sqrt{3}$.

The correct answer is A.

PS01334
157. There are 10 books on a shelf, of which 4 are paperbacks and 6 are hardbacks. How many possible selections of 5 books from the shelf contain at least one paperback and at least one hardback?

(A)   75
(B)   120
(C)   210
(D)   246
(E)   252

Arithmetic Elementary combinatorics

The number of selections of 5 books containing at least one paperback and at least one hardback is equal to $T - N$, where T is the total number of selections of 5 books and N is the number of selections that do not contain both a paperback and a hardback. The value of T is

$$\binom{10}{5} = \frac{10!}{5!(10 - 5)!} = \frac{(6)(7)(8)(9)(10)}{(1)(2)(3)(4)(5)}$$

$$= (7)(2)(9)(2) = 252.$$

To find the value of N, first note that no selection of 5 books can contain all paperbacks, since there are only 4 paperback books. Thus, the value of N is equal to the number of selections of 5 books that contain all hardbacks, which is equal to 6 since there are 6 ways that a single hardback can be left out when choosing the 5 hardback books. It follows that the number of selections of 5 books containing at least one paperback and at least one hardback is $T - N = 252 - 6 = 246$.

The correct answer is D.

PS03774

158. If x is to be chosen at random from the set $\{1, 2, 3, 4\}$ and y is to be chosen at random from the set $\{5, 6, 7\}$, what is the probability that xy will be even?

(A) $\dfrac{1}{6}$

(B) $\dfrac{1}{3}$

(C) $\dfrac{1}{2}$

(D) $\dfrac{2}{3}$

(E) $\dfrac{5}{6}$

Arithmetic; Algebra Probability; Concepts of sets

By the principle of multiplication, since there are 4 elements in the first set and 3 elements in the second set, there are $(4)(3) = 12$ possible products of xy, where x is chosen from the first set and y is chosen from the second set. These products will be even EXCEPT when both x and y are odd. Since there are 2 odd numbers in the first set and 2 odd numbers in the second set, there are $(2)(2) = 4$ products of x and y that are odd. This means that the remaining $12 - 4 = 8$ products are even.

Thus, the probability that xy is even is $\dfrac{8}{12} = \dfrac{2}{3}$.

The correct answer is D.

PS04254

159. The function f is defined for each positive three-digit integer n by $f(n) = 2^x\, 3^y\, 5^z$, where x, y, and z are the hundreds, tens, and units digits of n, respectively. If m and v are three-digit positive integers such that $f(m) = 9f(v)$, then $m - v =$

(A) 8

(B) 9

(C) 18

(D) 20

(E) 80

Algebra Place value

Let the hundreds, tens, and units digits of m be A, B, and C, respectively; and let the hundreds, tens, and units digits of v be a, b, and c, respectively. From $f(m) = 9f(v)$ it follows that $2^A 3^B 5^C = 9(2^a 3^b 5^c) = 3^2(2^a 3^b 5^c) = 2^a 3^{b+2} 5^c$. Therefore, $A = a$, $B = b + 2$, and $C = c$. Now calculate $m - v$.

$m - v =$	$(100A + 10B + C)$ $- (100a + 10b + c)$	place value property
$=$	$(100a + 10(b + 2) + c)$ $- (100a + 10b + c)$	obtained above
$=$	$10(b + 2) - 10b$	combine like terms
$=$	$10b + 20 - 10b$	distributive property
$=$	20	combine like terms

The correct answer is D.

PS06312

160. If $10^{50} - 74$ is written as an integer in base 10 notation, what is the sum of the digits in that integer?

(A) 424

(B) 433

(C) 440

(D) 449

(E) 467

Arithmetic Properties of numbers

$10^2 - 74$	=	$100 - 74$	=	26
$10^3 - 74$	=	$1,000 - 74$	=	926
$10^4 - 74$	=	$10,000 - 74$	=	9,926
$10^5 - 74$	=	$100,000 - 74$	=	99,926
$10^6 - 74$	=	$1,000,000 - 74$	=	999,926

From the table above it is clear that $10^{50} - 74$ in base 10 notation will be 48 digits of 9 followed by the digits 2 and 6. Therefore, the sum of the digits of $10^{50} - 74$ is equal to $48(9) + 2 + 6 = 440$.

The correct answer is C.

PS09056

161. A certain company that sells only cars and trucks reported that revenues from car sales in 1997 were down 11 percent from 1996 and revenues from truck sales in 1997 were up 7 percent from 1996. If total revenues from car sales and truck sales in 1997 were up 1 percent from 1996, what is the ratio of revenue from car sales in 1996 to revenue from truck sales in 1996 ?

(A) 1:2

(B) 4:5

(C) 1:1

(D) 3:2

(E) 5:3

Algebra; Arithmetic First-degree equations; Percents

Let C_{96} and C_{97} represent revenues from car sales in 1996 and 1997, respectively, and let T_{96} and T_{97} represent revenues from truck sales in 1996 and 1997, respectively. A decrease of 11 percent in revenue from car sales from 1996 to 1997 can be represented as $(1 - 0.11)C_{96} = C_{97}$, and a 7 percent increase in revenue from truck sales from 1996 to 1997 can be represented as $(1 + 0.07)T_{96} = T_{97}$. An overall increase of 1 percent in revenue from car and truck sales from 1996 to 1997 can be represented as $C_{97} + T_{97} = (1 + 0.01)(C_{96} + T_{96})$. Then, by substitution of expressions for C_{97} and T_{97} that were derived above, $(1 - 0.11)C_{96} + (1 + 0.07)T_{96} = (1 + 0.01)(C_{96} + T_{96})$ and so $0.89C_{96} + 1.07T_{96} = 1.01(C_{96} + T_{96})$ or $0.89C_{96} + 1.07T_{96} = 1.01C_{96} + 1.01T_{96}$. Then, combining like terms gives $(1.07 - 1.01)T_{96} = (1.01 - 0.89)C_{96}$ or

$0.06T_{96} = 0.12C_{96}$. Thus $\dfrac{C_{96}}{T_{96}} = \dfrac{0.06}{0.12} = \dfrac{1}{2}$. The ratio of revenue from car sales in 1996 to revenue from truck sales in 1996 is 1:2.

The correct answer is A.

PS14267

162. Becky rented a power tool from a rental shop. The rent for the tool was $12 for the first hour and $3 for each additional hour. If Becky paid a total of $27, excluding sales tax, to rent the tool, for how many hours did she rent it?

(A) 5

(B) 6

(C) 9

(D) 10

(E) 12

Arithmetic Applied problems

Becky paid a total of $27 to rent the power tool. She paid $12 to rent the tool for the first hour and $27 − $12 = $15 to rent the tool for the additional hours at the rate of $3 per additional hour. It follows that she rented the tool for $\dfrac{15}{3} = 5$ additional hours and a total of $1 + 5 = 6$ hours.

The correct answer is B.

PS06959

163. If $4 < \dfrac{7 - x}{3}$, which of the following must be true?

I. $5 < x$

II. $|x + 3| > 2$

III. $-(x + 5)$ is positive.

(A) II only

(B) III only

(C) I and II only

(D) II and III only

(E) I, II, and III

Algebra Inequalities

Given that $4 < \dfrac{7-x}{3}$, it follows that $12 < 7 - x$. Then, $5 < -x$ or, equivalently, $x < -5$.

I.   If $4 < \dfrac{7-x}{3}$, then $x < -5$. If $5 < x$ were true then, by combining $5 < x$ and $x < -5$, it would follow that $5 < -5$, which cannot be true. Therefore, it is not the case that, if $4 < \dfrac{7-x}{3}$, then Statement I must be true. In fact, Statement I is never true.

II. If $4 < \dfrac{7-x}{3}$, then $x < -5$, and it follows that $x + 3 < -2$. Since $-2 < 0$, then $x + 3 < 0$ and $|x+3| = -(x+3)$. If $x + 3 < -2$, then $-(x+3) > 2$ and by substitution, $|x+3| > 2$. Therefore, Statement II must be true for every value of x such that $x < -5$. Therefore, Statement II must be true if $4 < \dfrac{7-x}{3}$.

III. If $4 < \dfrac{7-x}{3}$, then $x < -5$ and $x + 5 < 0$. But if $x + 5 < 0$, then it follows that $-(x+5) > 0$ and so $-(x+5)$ is positive. Therefore Statement III must be true if $4 < \dfrac{7-x}{3}$.

The correct answer is D.

PS08654

164. A certain right triangle has sides of length x, y, and z, where x < y < z. If the area of this triangular region is 1, which of the following indicates all of the possible values of y ?

(A) $y > \sqrt{2}$

(B) $\dfrac{\sqrt{3}}{2} < y < \sqrt{2}$

(C) $\dfrac{\sqrt{2}}{3} < y < \dfrac{\sqrt{3}}{2}$

(D) $\dfrac{\sqrt{3}}{4} < y < \dfrac{\sqrt{2}}{3}$

(E) $y < \dfrac{\sqrt{3}}{4}$

Geometry; Algebra Triangles; Area; Inequalities

Since x, y, and z are the side lengths of a right triangle and $x < y < z$, it follows that x and y are the lengths of the legs of the triangle and so the area of the triangle is $\dfrac{1}{2}xy$. But, it is given that the area is 1 and so $\dfrac{1}{2}xy = 1$. Then, $xy = 2$ and $y = \dfrac{2}{x}$. Under the assumption that x, y, and z are all positive since they are the side lengths of a triangle, $x < y$ implies $\dfrac{1}{x} > \dfrac{1}{y}$ and then $\dfrac{2}{x} > \dfrac{2}{y}$. But, $y = \dfrac{2}{x}$, so by substitution, $y > \dfrac{2}{y}$, which implies that $y^2 > 2$ since y is positive. Thus, $y > \sqrt{2}$.

Alternatively, if $x < \sqrt{2}$ and $y < \sqrt{2}$ then $xy < 2$. If $x > \sqrt{2}$ and $y > \sqrt{2}$, then $xy > 2$. But, $xy = 2$ so one of x or y must be less than $\sqrt{2}$ and the other must be greater than $\sqrt{2}$. Since $x < y$, it follows that $x < \sqrt{2} < y$ and $y > \sqrt{2}$.

The correct answer is A.

PS14397

165. On a certain day, a bakery produced a batch of rolls at a total production cost of $300. On that day, $\dfrac{4}{5}$ of the rolls in the batch were sold, each at a price that was 50 percent greater than the average (arithmetic mean) production cost per roll. The remaining rolls in the batch were sold the next day, each at a price that was 20 percent less than the price of the day before. What was the bakery's profit on this batch of rolls?

(A) $150

(B) $144

(C) $132

(D) $108

(E) $90

Arithmetic Applied problems

Let n be the number of rolls in the batch and p be the average production price, in dollars, per roll. Then the total cost of the batch is $np = 300$ dollars, and the total revenue from selling the rolls in the batch is $\left(\frac{4}{5}n\right)(1.5p) + \left(\frac{1}{5}n\right)(0.8)(1.5p) =$

$\left(\frac{4}{5}n\right)\left(\frac{3}{2}p\right) + \left(\frac{1}{5}n\right)\left(\frac{4}{5}\right)\left(\frac{3}{2}p\right) = \left(\frac{6}{5} + \frac{6}{25}\right)np$

$= \left(\frac{36}{25}\right)np$. Therefore, the profit from selling the

rolls in the batch is $\left(\frac{36}{25}\right)np - np = \left(\frac{11}{25}\right)np =$

$\left(\frac{11}{25}\right)(300)$ dollars = 132 dollars.

The correct answer is C.

PS05972

166. A set of numbers has the property that for any number t in the set, $t + 2$ is in the set. If -1 is in the set, which of the following must also be in the set?

    I. -3

    II.   1

    III.   5

(A)   I only

(B)   II only

(C)   I and II only

(D)   II and III only

(E)   I, II, and III

Arithmetic Properties of numbers

It is given that -1 is in the set and, if t is in the set, then $t + 2$ is in the set.

    I. Since $\{-1, 1, 3, 5, 7, 9, 11, \ldots\}$ contains -1 and satisfies the property that if t is in the set, then $t + 2$ is in the set, it is not true that -3 must be in the set.

    II. Since -1 is in the set, $-1 + 2 = 1$ is in the set. Therefore, it must be true that 1 is in the set.

    III. Since -1 is in the set, $-1 + 2 = 1$ is in the set. Since 1 is in the set, $1 + 2 = 3$ is in the set. Since 3 is in the set, $3 + 2 = 5$ is in the set. Therefore, it must be true that 5 is in the set.

The correct answer is D.

PS04780

167. A couple decides to have 4 children. If they succeed in having 4 children and each child is equally likely to be a boy or a girl, what is the probability that they will have exactly 2 girls and 2 boys?

(A) $\dfrac{3}{8}$

(B) $\dfrac{1}{4}$

(C) $\dfrac{3}{16}$

(D) $\dfrac{1}{8}$

(E) $\dfrac{1}{16}$

Arithmetic Probability

Representing the birth order of the 4 children as a sequence of 4 letters, each of which is B for boy and G for girl, there are 2 possibilities (B or G) for the first letter, 2 for the second letter, 2 for the third letter, and 2 for the fourth letter, making a total of $2^4 = 16$ sequences. The table below categorizes some of these 16 sequences.

# of boys	# of girls	Sequences	# of sequences
0	4	GGGG	1
1	3	BGGG, GBGG, GGBG, GGGB	4
3	1	GBBB, BGBB, BBGB, BBBG	4
4	0	BBBB	1

The table accounts for $1 + 4 + 4 + 1 = 10$ sequences. The other 6 sequences will have 2Bs and 2Gs. Therefore the probability that the couple will have exactly 2 boys and 2 girls is $\frac{6}{16} = \frac{3}{8}$.

For the mathematically inclined, if it is assumed that a couple has a fixed number of children, that the probability of having a girl each time is p, and that the sex of each child is independent of the sex of the other children, then the number of girls, x, born to a couple with n children is a random variable having the binomial probability distribution. The probability of having exactly x girls born to a couple with n children is given by the formula $\binom{n}{x} p^x (1-p)^{n-x}$. For the problem at hand, it is given that each child is equally likely to be a boy or a girl, and so $p = \dfrac{1}{2}$. Thus, the probability of having exactly 2 girls born to a couple with 4 children is

$$\binom{4}{2}\left(\frac{1}{2}\right)^2\left(\frac{1}{2}\right)^2 = \frac{4!}{2!2!}\left(\frac{1}{2}\right)^2\left(\frac{1}{2}\right)^2 =$$

$$(6)\left(\frac{1}{4}\right)\left(\frac{1}{4}\right) = \frac{6}{16} = \frac{3}{8}.$$

The correct answer is A.

PS01564

168. The closing price of Stock X changed on each trading day last month. The percent change in the closing price of Stock X from the first trading day last month to each of the other trading days last month was less than 50 percent. If the closing price on the second trading day last month was $10.00, which of the following CANNOT be the closing price on the last trading day last month?

(A) $3.00
(B) $9.00
(C) $19.00
(D) $24.00
(E) $29.00

Arithmetic Applied problems; Percents

Let P be the first-day closing price, in dollars, of the stock. It is given that the second-day closing price was $(1 + n\%)P = 10$, so $P = \dfrac{10}{1 + n\%}$, for some value of n such that $-50 < n < 50$. Therefore, P is between $\dfrac{10}{1 + 0.50} \approx 6.67$ and $\dfrac{10}{1 - 0.50} = 20$. Hence, if Q is the closing price, in dollars, of the stock on the last day, then Q is between $(0.50)(6.67) \approx 3.34$ (50% decrease from the lowest possible first-day closing price) and $(1.50)(20) = 30$ (50% increase from the greatest possible first-day closing price). The only answer choice that gives a number of dollars not between 3.34 and 30 is the first answer choice.

The correct answer is A.

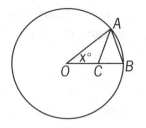

PS02389

169. In the figure above, point O is the center of the circle and $OC = AC = AB$. What is the value of x ?

(A)   40
(B)   36
(C)   34
(D)   32
(E)   30

Geometry Angles

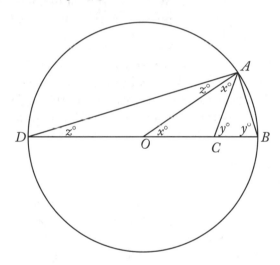

Consider the figure above, where $\overline{DB}$ is a diameter of the circle with center O and $\overline{AD}$ is a chord. Since $OC = AC$, $\triangle OCA$ is isosceles and so the base angles, $\angle AOC$ and $\angle OAC$, have the same degree measure. The measure of $\angle AOC$ is given as $x°$, so the measure of $\angle OAC$ is $x°$. Since $AC = AB$, $\triangle CAB$ is isosceles and so the base angles, $\angle ACB$ and $\angle ABC$, have the same degree measure. The measure of each is marked as $y°$. Likewise, since $\overline{OD}$ and $\overline{OA}$ are radii of the circle, $OD = OA$, and $\triangle DOA$ is isosceles with base angles, $\angle ADO$ and $\angle DAO$, each measuring $z°$. Each of the following statements is true:

(i) The measure of $\angle CAB$ is $180 - 2y$ since the sum of the measures of the angles of $\triangle CAB$ is 180.

(ii) $\angle DAB$ is a right angle (because $\overline{DB}$ is a diameter of the circle) and so $z + x + (180 - 2y) = 90$, or, equivalently, $2y - x - z = 90$.

(iii) $z + 90 + y = 180$ since the sum of the measures of the angles of right triangle $\triangle DAB$ is 180, or, equivalently, $z = 90 - y$.

(iv) $x = 2z$ because the measure of exterior angle $\angle AOC$ to $\triangle AOD$ is the sum of the measures of the two opposite interior angles, $\angle ODA$ and $\angle OAD$.

(v) $y = 2x$ because the measure of exterior angle $\angle ACB$ to $\triangle OCA$ is the sum of the measures of the two opposite interior angles, $\angle COA$ and $\angle CAO$.

Multiplying the final equation in (iii) by 2 gives $2z = 180 - 2y$. But, $x = 2z$ in (iv), so $x = 180 - 2y$. Finally, the sum of the measures of the angles of $\triangle CAB$ is 180 and so $y + y + x = 180$. Then from (v), $2x + 2x + x = 180$, $5x = 180$, and $x = 36$.

The correct answer is B.

PS16967

170. An airline passenger is planning a trip that involves three connecting flights that leave from Airports A, B, and C, respectively. The first flight leaves Airport A every hour, beginning at 8:00 a.m., and arrives at Airport B $2\frac{1}{2}$ hours later. The second flight leaves Airport B every 20 minutes, beginning at 8:00 a.m., and arrives at Airport C $1\frac{1}{6}$ hours later. The third flight leaves Airport C every hour, beginning at 8:45 a.m. What is the <u>least</u> total amount of time the passenger must spend between flights if all flights keep to their schedules?

(A) 25 min
(B) 1 hr 5 min
(C) 1 hr 15 min
(D) 2 hr 20 min
(E) 3 hr 40 min

Arithmetic Operations on rational numbers

Since the flight schedules at each of Airports A, B, and C are the same hour after hour, assume that the passenger leaves Airport A at 8:00 and arrives at Airport B at 10:30. Since flights from Airport B leave at 20-minute intervals beginning on the hour, the passenger must wait 10 minutes at Airport B for the flight that leaves at 10:40 and arrives at Airport C $1\frac{1}{6}$ hours or 1 hour 10 minutes later. Thus, the passenger arrives at Airport C at 11:50. Having arrived too late for the 11:45 flight from Airport C, the passenger must wait 55 minutes for the 12:45 flight. Thus, the least total amount of time the passenger must spend waiting between flights is $10 + 55 = 65$ minutes, or 1 hour 5 minutes.

The correct answer is B.

PS07426

171. If n is a positive integer and n^2 is divisible by 72, then the largest positive integer that must divide n is

(A) 6
(B) 12
(C) 24
(D) 36
(E) 48

Arithmetic Properties of numbers

Since n^2 is divisible by 72, $n^2 = 72k$ for some positive integer k. Since $n^2 = 72k$, then $72k$ must be a perfect square. Since $72k = (2^3)(3^2)k$, then $k = 2m^2$ for some positive integer m in order for $72k$ to be a perfect square. Then, $n^2 = 72k = (2^3)(3^2)(2m^2) = (2^4)(3^2)m^2 = [(2^2)(3)(m)]^2$, and $n = (2^2)(3)(m)$. The positive integers that MUST divide n are 1, 2, 3, 4, 6, and 12. Therefore, the largest positive integer that must divide n is 12.

The correct answer is B.

PS16977
172. A certain grocery purchased x pounds of produce for p dollars per pound. If y pounds of the produce had to be discarded due to spoilage and the grocery sold the rest for s dollars per pound, which of the following represents the gross profit on the sale of the produce?

(A) $(x - y)s - xp$

(B) $(x - y)p - ys$

(C) $(s - p)y - xp$

(D) $xp - ys$

(E) $(x - y)(s - p)$

Algebra Simplifying algebraic expressions; Applied problems

Since the grocery bought x pounds of produce for p dollars per pound, the total cost of the produce was xp dollars. Since y pounds of the produce was discarded, the grocery sold $x - y$ pounds of produce at the price of s dollars per pound, yielding a total revenue of $(x - y)s$ dollars. Then, the grocery's gross profit on the sale of the produce is its total revenue minus its total cost or $(x - y)s - xp$ dollars.

The correct answer is A.

PS16990
173. If x, y, and z are positive integers such that x is a factor of y, and x is a multiple of z, which of the following is NOT necessarily an integer?

(A) $\dfrac{x + z}{z}$

(B) $\dfrac{y + z}{x}$

(C) $\dfrac{x + y}{z}$

(D) $\dfrac{xy}{z}$

(E) $\dfrac{yz}{x}$

Arithmetic Properties of numbers

Since the positive integer x is a factor of y, then $y = kx$ for some positive integer k. Since x is a multiple of the positive integer z, then $x = mz$ for some positive integer m.

Substitute these expressions for x and/or y into each answer choice to find the one expression that is NOT necessarily an integer.

A $\dfrac{x + z}{z} = \dfrac{mz + z}{z} = \dfrac{(m + 1)z}{z} = m + 1$, which MUST be an integer

B $\dfrac{y + z}{x} = \dfrac{y}{x} + \dfrac{z}{x} = \dfrac{kx}{x} + \dfrac{z}{mz} = k + \dfrac{1}{m}$, which NEED NOT be an integer

Because only one of the five expressions need not be an integer, the expressions given in C, D, and E need not be tested. However, for completeness,

C $\dfrac{x + y}{z} = \dfrac{mz + kx}{z} = \dfrac{mz + k(mz)}{z} = \dfrac{mz(1 + k)}{z}$
$= m(1 + k)$, which MUST be an integer

D $\dfrac{xy}{z} = \dfrac{(mz)y}{z} = my$, which MUST be an integer

E $\dfrac{yz}{x} = \dfrac{(kx)(z)}{x} = kz$, which MUST be an integer

The correct answer is B.

PS08416
174. Running at their respective constant rates, Machine X takes 2 days longer to produce w widgets than Machine Y. At these rates, if the two machines together produce $\dfrac{5}{4}w$ widgets in 3 days, how many days would it take Machine X alone to produce $2w$ widgets?

(A) 4

(B) 6

(C) 8

(D) 10

(E) 12

Algebra Applied problems

If x, where $x > 2$, represents the number of days Machine X takes to produce w widgets, then Machine Y takes $x - 2$ days to produce w widgets. It follows that Machines X and Y can produce $\dfrac{w}{x}$ and $\dfrac{w}{x-2}$ widgets, respectively, in 1 day and together they can produce $\dfrac{w}{x} + \dfrac{w}{x-2}$ widgets in 1 day. Since it is given that, together, they can produce $\dfrac{5}{4}w$ widgets in 3 days, it follows that, together, they can produce $\dfrac{1}{3}\left(\dfrac{5}{4}w\right) = \dfrac{5}{12}w$ widgets in 1 day. Thus,

$$\frac{w}{x} + \frac{w}{x-2} = \frac{5}{12}w$$

$$\left(\frac{1}{x} + \frac{1}{x-2}\right)w = \frac{5}{12}w$$

$$\left(\frac{1}{x} + \frac{1}{x-2}\right) = \frac{5}{12}$$

$$12x(x-2)\left(\frac{1}{x} + \frac{1}{x-2}\right) = 12x(x-2)\left(\frac{5}{12}\right)$$

$$12[(x-2)+x] = 5x(x-2)$$

$$12(2x-2) = 5x(x-2)$$

$$24x - 24 = 5x^2 - 10x$$

$$0 = 5x^2 - 34x + 24$$

$$0 = (5x-4)(x-6)$$

$$x = \frac{4}{5} \text{ or } 6$$

Therefore, since $x > 2$, it follows that $x = 6$. Machine X takes 6 days to produce w widgets and $2(6) = 12$ days to produce $2w$ widgets.

The correct answer is E.

PS07117
175. A square wooden plaque has a square brass inlay in the center, leaving a wooden strip of uniform width around the brass square. If the ratio of the brass area to the wooden area is 25 to 39, which of the following could be the width, in inches, of the wooden strip?

  I.   1

  II.   3

  III.   4

  (A)   I only
  (B)   II only
  (C)   I and II only
  (D)   I and III only
  (E)   I, II, and III

Geometry Area

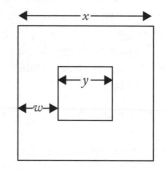

Note: Not drawn to scale.

Let x represent the side length of the entire plaque, let y represent the side length of the brass inlay, and w represent the uniform width of the wooden strip around the brass inlay, as shown in the figure above. Since the ratio of the area of the brass inlay to the area of the wooden strip is 25 to 39, the ratio of the area of the brass inlay to the area of the entire plaque is $\dfrac{y^2}{x^2} = \dfrac{25}{25+39} = \dfrac{25}{64}$.

Then, $\dfrac{y}{x} = \sqrt{\dfrac{25}{64}} = \dfrac{5}{8}$ and $y = \dfrac{5}{8}x$. Also, $x = y + 2w$ and $w = \dfrac{x-y}{2}$. Substituting $\dfrac{5}{8}x$ for y into this expression for w gives $w = \dfrac{x - \dfrac{5}{8}x}{2} = \dfrac{\dfrac{3}{8}x}{2} = \dfrac{3}{16}x$. Thus,

I. If the plaque were $\dfrac{16}{3}$ inches on a side, then the width of the wooden strip would be 1 inch, and so 1 inch is a possible width for the wooden strip.

II. If the plaque were 16 inches on a side, then the width of the wooden strip would be 3 inches, and so 3 inches is a possible width for the wooden strip.

III. If the plaque were $\dfrac{64}{3}$ inches on a side, then the width of the wooden strip would be 4 inches, and so 4 inches is a possible width for the wooden strip.

The correct answer is E.

PS16963

176. $\dfrac{2\frac{3}{5} - 1\frac{2}{3}}{\frac{2}{3} - \frac{3}{5}} =$

(A) 16

(B) 14

(C) 3

(D) 1

(E) −1

Arithmetic Operations on rational numbers

Work the problem:

$$\dfrac{2\frac{3}{5} - 1\frac{2}{3}}{\frac{2}{3} - \frac{3}{5}} =$$

$$\dfrac{\frac{13}{5} - \frac{5}{3}}{\frac{2}{3} - \frac{3}{5}} = \dfrac{\frac{39 - 25}{15}}{\frac{10 - 9}{15}} = \dfrac{\frac{14}{15}}{\frac{1}{15}} = \dfrac{14}{15} \times \dfrac{15}{1} = 14$$

The correct answer is B.

5.0 Data Sufficiency

5.0 Data Sufficiency

Data sufficiency questions appear in the Quantitative section of the GMAT® exam. Multiple-choice data sufficiency questions are intermingled with problem solving questions throughout the section. You will have 62 minutes to complete the Quantitative section of the GMAT exam, or about 2 minutes to answer each question. These questions require knowledge of the following topics:

- Arithmetic
- Elementary algebra
- Commonly known concepts of geometry

Data sufficiency questions are designed to measure your ability to analyze a quantitative problem, recognize which given information is relevant, and determine at what point there is sufficient information to solve a problem. In these questions, you are to classify each problem according to the five fixed answer choices, rather than find a solution to the problem.

Each data sufficiency question consists of a question, often accompanied by some initial information, and two statements, labeled (1) and (2), which contain additional information. You must decide whether the information in each statement is sufficient to answer the question or—if neither statement provides enough information—whether the information in the two statements together is sufficient. It is also possible that the statements, in combination do not give enough information to answer the question.

Begin by reading the initial information and the question carefully. Next, consider the first statement. Does the information provided by the first statement enable you to answer the question? Go on to the second statement. Try to ignore the information given in the first statement when you consider whether the second statement provides information that, by itself, allows you to answer the question. Now you should be able to say, for each statement, whether it is sufficient to determine the answer.

Next, consider the two statements in tandem. Do they, together, enable you to answer the question?

Look again at your answer choices. Select the one that most accurately reflects whether the statements provide the information required to answer the question.

5.1 Test-Taking Strategies

1. **Do not waste valuable time solving a problem.**

   You only need to determine whether sufficient information is given to solve it.

2. **Consider each statement separately.**

   First, decide whether each statement alone gives sufficient information to solve the problem. Be sure to disregard the information given in statement (1) when you evaluate the information given in statement (2). If either, or both, of the statements give(s) sufficient information to solve the problem, select the answer corresponding to the description of which statement(s) give(s) sufficient information to solve the problem.

3. **Judge the statements in tandem if neither statement is sufficient by itself.**

   It is possible that the two statements together do not provide sufficient information. Once you decide, select the answer corresponding to the description of whether the statements together give sufficient information to solve the problem.

4. **Answer the question asked.**

   For example, if the question asks, "What is the value of y ?" for an answer statement to be sufficient, you must be able to find one and only one value for y. Being able to determine minimum or maximum values for an answer (e.g., $y = x + 2$) is not sufficient, because such answers constitute a range of values rather than the specific value of y.

5. **Be very careful not to make unwarranted assumptions based on the images represented.**

   Figures are not necessarily drawn to scale; they are generalized figures showing little more than intersecting line segments and the relationships of points, angles, and regions. For example, if a figure described as a rectangle looks like a square, do not conclude that it is actually a square just by looking at the figure.

If statement 1 is sufficient, then the answer must be **A or D.**

If statement 2 is not sufficient, then the answer must be **A.**

If statement 2 is sufficient, then the answer must be **D.**

If statement 1 is not sufficient, then the answer must be **B, C, or E.**

If statement 2 is sufficient, then the answer must be **B.**

If statement 2 is not sufficient, then the answer must be **C or E.**

If both statements together are sufficient, then the answer must be **C.**

If both statements together are still not sufficient, then the answer must be **E.**

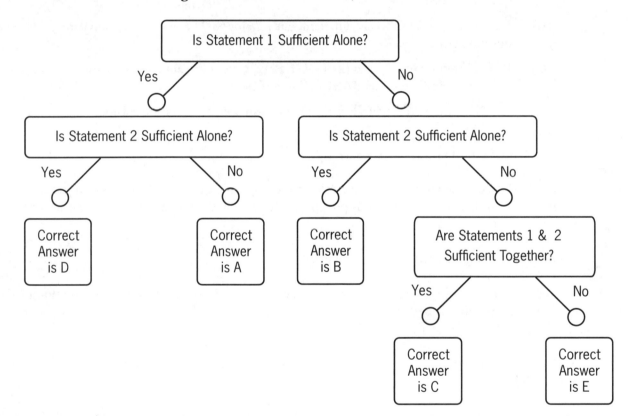

5.2 The Directions

These directions are similar to those you will see for data sufficiency questions when you take the GMAT exam. If you read the directions carefully and understand them clearly before going to sit for the test, you will not need to spend much time reviewing them when you take the GMAT exam.

Each data sufficiency problem consists of a question and two statements, labeled (1) and (2), that give data. You have to decide whether the data given in the statements are *sufficient* for answering the question. Using the data given in the statements *plus* your knowledge of mathematics and everyday facts (such as the number of days in July or the meaning of *counterclockwise*), you must indicate whether the data given in the statements are sufficient for answering the questions and then indicate one of the following answer choices:

(A)   Statement (1) ALONE is sufficient, but statement (2) alone is not sufficient to answer the question asked;

(B)   Statement (2) ALONE is sufficient, but statement (1) alone is not sufficient to answer the question asked;

(C)   BOTH statements (1) and (2) TOGETHER are sufficient to answer the question asked, but NEITHER statement ALONE is sufficient;

(D)   EACH statement ALONE is sufficient to answer the question asked;

(E)   Statements (1) and (2) TOGETHER are NOT sufficient to answer the question asked, and additional data are needed.

NOTE: In data sufficiency problems that ask for the value of a quantity, the data given in the statements are sufficient only when it is possible to determine exactly one numerical value for the quantity.

Numbers: All numbers used are real numbers.

Figures: A figure accompanying a data sufficiency problem will conform to the information given in the question but will not necessarily conform to the additional information given in statements (1) and (2).

Lines shown as straight can be assumed to be straight and lines that appear jagged can also be assumed to be straight.

You may assume that the positions of points, angles, regions, and so forth exist in the order shown and that angle measures are greater than zero degrees.

All figures lie in a plane unless otherwise indicated.

5.3 Sample Questions

Each <u>data sufficiency</u> problem consists of a question and two statements, labeled (1) and (2), which contain certain data. Using these data and your knowledge of mathematics and everyday facts (such as the number of days in July or the meaning of the word *counterclockwise*), decide whether the data given are sufficient for answering the question and then indicate one of the following answer choices:

A   Statement (1) ALONE is sufficient, but statement (2) alone is not sufficient.
B   Statement (2) ALONE is sufficient, but statement (1) alone is not sufficient.
C   BOTH statements TOGETHER are sufficient, but NEITHER statement ALONE is sufficient.
D   EACH statement ALONE is sufficient.
E   Statements (1) and (2) TOGETHER are not sufficient.

<u>Note:</u> In data sufficiency problems that ask for the value of a quantity, the data given in the statements are sufficient only when it is possible to determine exactly one numerical value for the quantity.

<u>Example:</u>

In $\triangle PQR$, what is the value of x ?

(1) $PQ = PR$

(2) $y = 40$

Explanation: According to statement (1) $PQ = PR$; therefore, $\triangle PQR$ is isosceles and $y = z$. Since $x + y + z = 180$, it follows that $x + 2y = 180$. Since statement (1) does not give a value for y, you cannot answer the question using statement (1) alone. According to statement (2), $y = 40$; therefore, $x + z = 140$. Since statement (2) does not give a value for z, you cannot answer the question using statement (2) alone. Using both statements together, since $x + 2y = 180$ and the value of y is given, you can find the value of x. Therefore, BOTH statements (1) and (2) TOGETHER are sufficient to answer the questions, but NEITHER statement ALONE is sufficient.

<u>Numbers:</u> All numbers used are real numbers.

<u>Figures:</u>
- Figures conform to the information given in the question, but will not necessarily conform to the additional information given in statements (1) and (2).
- Lines shown as straight are straight, and lines that appear jagged are also straight.
- The positions of points, angles, regions, etc., exist in the order shown, and angle measures are greater than zero.
- All figures lie in a plane unless otherwise indicated.

*DS05149
177. Does $2x + 8 = 12$?

    (1) $2x + 10 = 14$

    (2) $3x + 8 = 14$

DS01503
178. If M is a set of consecutive even integers, is 0 in set M ?

    (1)   –6 is in set M.

    (2)   –2 is in set M.

DS15510
179. Rita's monthly salary is $\frac{2}{3}$ Juanita's monthly salary. What is their combined monthly salary?

    (1)   Rita's monthly salary is $4,000.

    (2)   Either Rita's monthly salary or Juanita's monthly salary is $6,000.

DS13384
180. What is the value of the integer x ?

    (1) x rounded to the nearest hundred is 7,200.

    (2)   The hundreds digit of x is 2.

DS04644
181. Is $2x > 2y$?

    (1) $x > y$

    (2) $3x > 3y$

DS04636
182. If p and q are positive, is $\frac{p}{q}$ less than 1 ?

    (1) p is less than 4.

    (2) q is less than 4.

DS02779
183. In each quarter of 1998, Company M earned more money than in the previous quarter. What was the range of Company M's quarterly earnings in 1998?

    (1)   In the 2nd and 3rd quarters of 1998, Company M earned $4.0 million and $4.6 million, respectively.

    (2)   In the 1st and 4th quarters of 1998, Company M earned $3.8 million and $4.9 million, respectively.

DS04510
184. In a certain factory, hours worked by each employee in excess of 40 hours per week are overtime hours and are paid for at $1\frac{1}{2}$ times the employee's regular hourly pay rate. If an employee worked a total of 42 hours last week, how much was the employee's gross pay for the hours worked last week?

    (1)   The employee's gross pay for overtime hours worked last week was $30.

    (2)   The employee's gross pay for all hours worked last week was $30 more than for the previous week.

DS01104
185. Is the integer p even?

    (1)   The integer $p^2 + 1$ is odd.

    (2)   The integer $p + 2$ is even.

DS05172
186. If $x > 0$, what is the value of x^5 ?

    (1) $\sqrt{x} = 32$

    (2) $x^2 = 2^{20}$

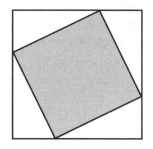

DS17640
187. In the quilting pattern shown above, a small square has its vertices on the sides of a larger square. What is the side length, in centimeters, of the larger square?

    (1)   The side length of the smaller square is 10 cm.

    (2)   Each vertex of the small square cuts 1 side of the larger square into 2 segments with lengths in the ratio of 1:2.

DS02589
188. Did Insurance Company K have more than $300 million in total net profits last year?

    (1)   Last year Company K paid out $0.95 in claims for every dollar of premiums collected.

    (2)   Last year Company K earned a total of $150 million in profits from the investment of accumulated surplus premiums from previous years.

*These numbers correlate with the online test bank question number. See the GMAT Quantitative Review Online Index in the back of this book.

157

DS15349
189. How many hours would it take Pump A and Pump B working together, each at its own constant rate, to empty a tank that was initially full?

    (1) Working alone at its constant rate, Pump A would empty the full tank in 4 hours 20 minutes.

    (2) Working alone, Pump B would empty the full tank at its constant rate of 72 liters per minute.

DS04573
190. What is the value of the integer N?

    (1) $101 < N < 103$

    (2) $202 < 2N < 206$

DS12033
191. Is zw positive?

    (1) $z + w^3 = 20$

    (2) z is positive.

DS03006
192. On the scale drawing of a certain house plan, if 1 centimeter represents x meters, what is the value of x?

    (1) A rectangular room that has a floor area of 12 square meters is represented by a region of area 48 square centimeters.

    (2) The 15-meter length of the house is represented by a segment 30 centimeters long.

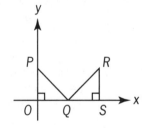

DS03939
193. In the rectangular coordinate system above, if $\triangle OPQ$ and $\triangle QRS$ have equal area, what are the coordinates of point R?

    (1) The coordinates of point P are $(0,12)$.

    (2) $OP = OQ$ and $QS = RS$.

DS07258
194. In a school that had a total of 600 students enrolled in the junior and senior classes, the students contributed to a certain fund. If all of the juniors but only half of the seniors contributed, was the total amount contributed more than $740?

    (1) Each junior contributed $1 and each senior who contributed gave $3.

    (2) There were more juniors than seniors enrolled in the school.

DS06650
195. How much did credit-card fraud cost United States banks in year X to the nearest $10 million?

    (1) In year X, counterfeit cards and telephone and mail-order fraud accounted for 39 percent of the total amount that card fraud cost the banks.

    (2) In year X, stolen cards accounted for $158.4 million, or 16 percent, of the total amount that credit-card fraud cost the banks.

DS17319
196. Is the positive integer n odd?

    (1) $n^2 + (n + 1)^2 + (n + 2)^2$ is even.

    (2) $n^2 - (n + 1)^2 - (n + 2)^2$ is even.

DS01130
197. In the xy-plane, circle C has center $(1,0)$ and radius 2. If line k is parallel to the y-axis, is line k tangent to circle C?

    (1) Line k passes through the point $(-1,0)$.

    (2) Line k passes through the point $(-1,-1)$.

DS14170
198. Company X's profits this year increased by 25% over last year's profits. Was the dollar amount of Company X's profits this year greater than the dollar amount of Company Y's?

    (1) Last year, the ratio of Company Y's profits to Company X's profits was 5:2.

    (2) Company Y experienced a 40% drop in profits from last year to this year.

DS09385
199. For all x, the expression x^* is defined to be $ax + a$, where a is a constant. What is the value of 2^*?

    (1) $3^* = 2$

    (2) $5^* = 3$

DS09260
200. Is $k + m < 0$?

    (1) $k < 0$

    (2) $km > 0$

DS08352
201. The symbol Δ represents which one of the following operations: addition, subtraction, or multiplication?

    (1) $a \Delta (b \Delta c) \neq a \Delta (c \Delta b)$ for some numbers a, b, and c.

    (2) $a \Delta (b \Delta c) \neq (a \Delta b) \Delta c$ for some numbers a, b, and c.

DS05989

202. What is the value of $2^x + 2^{-x}$?

    (1) $x > 0$
    (2) $4^x + 4^{-x} = 23$

DS13457

203. What is the ratio of c to d ?

    (1)   The ratio of $3c$ to $3d$ is 3 to 4.
    (2)   The ratio of $c + 3$ to $d + 3$ is 4 to 5.

DS15099

204. A candle company determines that, for a certain specialty candle, the supply function is $p = m_1 x + b_1$ and the demand function is $p = m_2 x + b_2$, where p is the price of each candle, x is the number of candles supplied or demanded, and m_1, m_2, b_1, and b_2 are constants. At what value of x do the graphs of the supply function and demand function intersect?

    (1) $m_1 = -m_2 = 0.005$
    (2) $b_2 - b_1 = 6$

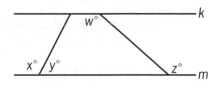

DS12862

205. In the figure shown, lines k and m are parallel to each other. Is $x = z$?

    (1) $x = w$
    (2) $y = 180 - w$

DS13097

206. If k and ℓ are lines in the xy-plane, is the slope of k less than the slope of ℓ ?

    (1)   The x-intercept of line k is positive, and the x-intercept of line ℓ is negative.
    (2)   Lines k and ℓ intersect on the positive y-axis.

DS09642

207. When the wind speed is 9 miles per hour, the wind-chill factor w is given by

$$w = -17.366 + 1.19t,$$

where t is the temperature in degrees Fahrenheit. If at noon yesterday the wind speed was 9 miles per hour, was the wind-chill factor greater than 0 ?

    (1)   The temperature at noon yesterday was greater than 10 degrees Fahrenheit.
    (2)   The temperature at noon yesterday was less than 20 degrees Fahrenheit.

DS08852

208. What is the volume of the cube above?

    (1)   The surface area of the cube is 600 square inches.
    (2)   The length of diagonal AB is $10\sqrt{3}$ inches.

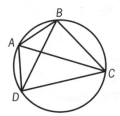

DS03989

209. In the figure shown, quadrilateral $ABCD$ is inscribed in a circle of radius 5. What is the perimeter of quadrilateral $ABCD$?

    (1)   The length of AB is 6 and the length of CD is 8.
    (2) AC is a diameter of the circle.

DS05766

210. How many members of a certain legislature voted against the measure to raise their salaries?

    (1) $\frac{1}{4}$ of the members of the legislature did not vote on the measure.
    (2)   If 5 additional members of the legislature had voted against the measure, then the fraction of members of the legislature voting against the measure would have been $\frac{1}{3}$.

DS05986

211. If $y \neq 0$, is $|x| = 1$?

    (1) $x = \dfrac{y}{|y|}$
    (2) $|x| = -x$

DS08306

212. If x is a positive integer, what is the value of x ?

    (1) $x^2 = \sqrt{x}$
    (2) $\dfrac{n}{x} = n$ and $n \neq 0$.

DS07568

213. Is the median of the five numbers a, b, c, d, and e equal to d ?

    (1) $a < c < e$
    (2) $b < d < c$

159

DS10383

214. During a certain bicycle ride, was Sherry's average speed faster than 24 kilometers per hour? (1 kilometer = 1,000 meters)

    (1)   Sherry's average speed during the bicycle ride was faster than 7 meters per second.

    (2)   Sherry's average speed during the bicycle ride was slower than 8 meters per second.

DS13907

215. Working together, Rafael and Salvador can tabulate a certain set of data in 2 hours. In how many hours can Rafael tabulate the data working alone?

    (1)   Working alone, Rafael can tabulate the data in 3 hours less time than Salvador, working alone, can tabulate the data.

    (2)   Working alone, Rafael can tabulate the data in $\frac{1}{2}$ the time that Salvador, working alone, can tabulate the data.

DS04039

216. If x and y are integers, what is the value of x?

    (1) $xy = 1$

    (2) $x \neq -1$

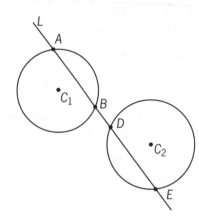

Note: Figure not drawn to scale.

DS18386

217. The figure above shows Line L, Circle 1 with center at C_1, and Circle 2 with center at C_2. Line L intersects Circle 1 at points A and B, Line L intersects Circle 2 at points D and E, and points C_1 and C_2 are equidistant from line L. Is the area of $\triangle ABC_1$ less than the area of $\triangle DEC_2$?

    (1)   The radius of Circle 1 is less than the radius of Circle 2.

    (2)   The length of chord $\overline{AB}$ is less than the length of chord $\overline{DE}$.

DS15938

218. Yesterday between 9:00 a.m. and 6:00 p.m. at Airport X, all flights to Atlanta departed at equally spaced times and all flights to New York City departed at equally spaced times. A flight to Atlanta and a flight to New York City both departed from Airport X at 1:00 p.m. yesterday. Between 1:00 p.m. and 3:00 p.m. yesterday, did another pair of flights to these 2 cities depart from Airport X at the same time?

    (1)   Yesterday at Airport X, a flight to Atlanta and a flight to New York City both departed at 10:00 a.m.

    (2)   Yesterday at Airport X, flights to New York City departed every 15 minutes between 9:00 a.m. and 6:00 p.m.

DS07206

219. Of the total number of copies of Magazine X sold last week, 40 percent were sold at full price. What was the total number of copies of the magazine sold last week?

    (1)   Last week, full price for a copy of Magazine X was $1.50 and the total revenue from full-price sales was $112,500.

    (2)   The total number of copies of Magazine X sold last week at full price was 75,000.

DS11614

220. If p, s, and t are positive, is $|ps - pt| > p(s - t)$?

    (1) $p < s$

    (2) $s < t$

DS04468

221. Is $x > y$?

    (1) $x + y > x - y$

    (2) $3x > 2y$

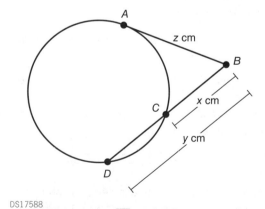

DS17588

222. In the figure above, $\overline{AB}$, which has length z cm, is tangent to the circle at point A, and $\overline{BD}$, which has length y cm, intersects the circle at point C. If $BC = x$ cm and $z = \sqrt{xy}$, what is the value of x?

    (1) $CD = x$ cm

    (2) $z = 5\sqrt{2}$

DS15863
223. Is the integer n a prime number?

    (1) $24 \le n \le 28$

    (2) n is not divisible by 2 or 3.

DS03615
224. What is the average (arithmetic mean) annual salary of the 6 employees of a toy company?

    (1)   If the 6 annual salaries were ordered from least to greatest, each annual salary would be $6,300 greater than the preceding annual salary.

    (2)   The range of the 6 annual salaries is $31,500.

DS17503
225. In a certain order, the pretax price of each regular pencil was $0.03, the pretax price of each deluxe pencil was $0.05, and there were 50% more deluxe pencils than regular pencils. All taxes on the order are a fixed percent of the pretax prices. The sum of the total pretax price of the order and the tax on the order was $44.10. What was the amount, in dollars, of the tax on the order?

    (1)   The tax on the order was 5% of the total pretax price of the order.

    (2)   The order contained exactly 400 regular pencils.

DS06785
226. If m is an integer greater than 1, is m an even integer?

    (1)   32 is a factor of m.

    (2) m is a factor of 32.

DS05657
227. If the set S consists of five consecutive positive integers, what is the sum of these five integers?

    (1)   The integer 11 is in S, but 10 is not in S.

    (2)   The sum of the even integers in S is 26.

DS17543
228. If $x > 0$, what is the value of x?

    (1) $x^3 - x = 0$

    (2) $\sqrt[3]{x} - x = 0$

DS08307
229. A total of 20 amounts are entered on a spreadsheet that has 5 rows and 4 columns; each of the 20 positions in the spreadsheet contains one amount. The average (arithmetic mean) of the amounts in row i is R_i ($1 \le i \le 5$). The average of the amounts in column j is C_j ($1 \le j \le 4$). What is the average of all 20 amounts on the spreadsheet?

    (1) $R_1 + R_2 + R_3 + R_4 + R_5 = 550$

    (2) $C_1 + C_2 + C_3 + C_4 = 440$

DS13132
230. Was the range of the amounts of money that Company Y budgeted for its projects last year equal to the range of the amounts of money that it budgeted for its projects this year?

    (1)   Both last year and this year, Company Y budgeted money for 12 projects and the least amount of money that it budgeted for a project was $400.

    (2)   Both last year and this year, the average (arithmetic mean) amount of money that Company Y budgeted per project was $2,000.

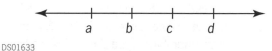

DS01633
231. If a, b, c, and d are numbers on the number line shown and if the tick marks are equally spaced, what is the value of $a + c$?

    (1) $a + b = -8$

    (2) $a + d = 0$

DS06067
232. Is $xm < ym$?

    (1) $x > y$

    (2) $m < 0$

DS02899
233. If $y = x^2 - 6x + 9$, what is the value of x?

    (1) $y = 0$

    (2) $x + y = 3$

DS06810
234. What is the probability that Lee will make exactly 5 errors on a certain typing test?

    (1)   The probability that Lee will make 5 or more errors on the test is 0.27.

    (2)   The probability that Lee will make 5 or fewer errors on the test is 0.85.

DS19208
235. If p is a positive integer, is $2^p + 1$ a prime number?

    (1) p is a prime number.

    (2) p is an even number.

DS02741
236. In the xy-plane, point (r,s) lies on a circle with center at the origin. What is the value of $r^2 + s^2$?

    (1)   The circle has radius 2.

    (2)   The point $\left(\sqrt{2}, -\sqrt{2}\right)$ lies on the circle.

DS06368

237. If r, s, and t are nonzero integers, is $r^5 s^3 t^4$ negative?

    (1) rt is negative.

    (2) s is negative.

DS13706

238. Each Type A machine fills 400 cans per minute, each Type B machine fills 600 cans per minute, and each Type C machine installs 2,400 lids per minute. A lid is installed on each can that is filled and on no can that is not filled. For a particular minute, what is the total number of machines working?

    (1)   A total of 4,800 cans are filled that minute.

    (2)   For that minute, there are 2 Type B machines working for every Type C machine working.

DS08660

239. If a and b are constants, what is the value of a ?

    (1) $a < b$

    (2) $(t - a)(t - b) = t^2 + t - 12$, for all values of t.

DS04474

240. If x is a positive integer, is $\sqrt{x}$ an integer?

    (1) $\sqrt{4x}$ is an integer.

    (2) $\sqrt{3x}$ is not an integer.

DS16456

241. If p, q, x, y, and z are different positive integers, which of the five integers is the median?

    (1) $p + x < q$

    (2) $y < z$

DS16277

242. If $w + z = 28$, what is the value of wz ?

    (1) w and z are positive integers.

    (2) w and z are consecutive odd integers.

DS02474

243. If $abc \neq 0$, is $\dfrac{\frac{a}{b}}{c} = \dfrac{a}{\frac{b}{c}}$?

    (1) $a = 1$

    (2) $c = 1$

DS14471

244. The arithmetic mean of a collection of 5 positive integers, not necessarily distinct, is 9. One additional positive integer is included in the collection and the arithmetic mean of the 6 integers is computed. Is the arithmetic mean of the 6 integers at least 10 ?

    (1)   The additional integer is at least 14.

    (2)   The additional integer is a multiple of 5.

DS11003

245. A certain list consists of 400 different numbers. Is the average (arithmetic mean) of the numbers in the list greater than the median of the numbers in the list?

    (1)   Of the numbers in the list, 280 are less than the average.

    (2)   Of the numbers in the list, 30 percent are greater than or equal to the average.

DS03678

246. In a two-month survey of shoppers, each shopper bought one of two brands of detergent, X or Y, in the first month and again bought one of these brands in the second month. In the survey, 90 percent of the shoppers who bought Brand X in the first month bought Brand X again in the second month, while 60 percent of the shoppers who bought Brand Y in the first month bought Brand Y again in the second month. What percent of the shoppers bought Brand Y in the second month?

    (1)   In the first month, 50 percent of the shoppers bought Brand X.

    (2)   The total number of shoppers surveyed was 5,000.

DS15902

247. If m and n are positive integers, is $m + n$ divisible by 4 ?

    (1) m and n are each divisible by 2.

    (2)   Neither m nor n is divisible by 4.

DS02940

248. What is the area of rectangular region R ?

    (1)   Each diagonal of R has length 5.

    (2)   The perimeter of R is 14.

DS17137

249. How many integers n are there such that $r < n < s$?

    (1) $s - r = 5$

    (2) r and s are not integers.

DS17147

250. If the total price of n equally priced shares of a certain stock was $12,000, what was the price per share of the stock?

    (1)   If the price per share of the stock had been $1 more, the total price of the n shares would have been $300 more.

    (2)   If the price per share of the stock had been $2 less, the total price of the n shares would have been 5 percent less.

DS02865
251. If n is positive, is $\sqrt{n} > 100$?

    (1) $\sqrt{n-1} > 99$

    (2) $\sqrt{n+1} > 101$

DS17150
252. Is $xy > 5$?

    (1) $1 \le x \le 3$ and $2 \le y \le 4$.

    (2) $x + y = 5$

DS17151
253. In Year X, 8.7 percent of the men in the labor force were unemployed in June compared with 8.4 percent in May. If the number of men in the labor force was the same for both months, how many men were unemployed in June of that year?

    (1)   In May of Year X, the number of unemployed men in the labor force was 3.36 million.

    (2)   In Year X, 120,000 more men in the labor force were unemployed in June than in May.

DS17112
254. If $x \ne 0$, what is the value of $\left(\dfrac{x^p}{x^q}\right)^4$?

    (1) $p = q$

    (2) $x = 3$

DS17153
255. On Monday morning a certain machine ran continuously at a uniform rate to fill a production order. At what time did it completely fill the order that morning?

    (1)   The machine began filling the order at 9:30 a.m.

    (2)   The machine had filled $\dfrac{1}{2}$ of the order by 10:30 a.m. and $\dfrac{5}{6}$ of the order by 11:10 a.m.

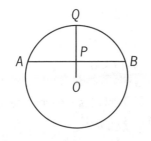

DS17107
256. What is the radius of the circle above with center O ?

    (1)   The ratio of OP to PQ is 1 to 2.

    (2) P is the midpoint of chord AB.

DS15618
257. If a and b are positive integers, what is the value of the product ab ?

    (1)   The least common multiple of a and b is 48.

    (2)   The greatest common factor of a and b is 4.

DS17095
258. What is the number of 360-degree rotations that a bicycle wheel made while rolling 100 meters in a straight line without slipping?

    (1)   The diameter of the bicycle wheel, including the tire, was 0.5 meter.

    (2)   The wheel made twenty 360-degree rotations per minute.

DS17168
259. In the equation $x^2 + bx + 12 = 0$, x is a variable and b is a constant. What is the value of b ?

    (1) $x - 3$ is a factor of $x^2 + bx + 12$.

    (2)   4 is a root of the equation $x^2 + bx + 12 = 0$.

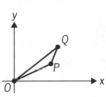

DS07715
260. In the figure above, line segment OP has slope $\dfrac{1}{2}$ and line segment PQ has slope 2. What is the slope of line segment OQ ?

    (1)   Line segment OP has length $2\sqrt{5}$.

    (2)   The coordinates of point Q are (5,4).

DS17164
261. In $\triangle XYZ$, what is the length of YZ ?

    (1)   The length of XY is 3.

    (2)   The length of XZ is 5.

DS07217
262. If the average (arithmetic mean) of n consecutive odd integers is 10, what is the least of the integers?

    (1)   The range of the n integers is 14.

    (2)   The greatest of the n integers is 17.

DS16044
263. If x, y, and z are positive numbers, is $x > y > z$?

    (1) $xz > yz$

    (2) $yx > yz$

DS06644
264. *K* is a set of numbers such that

(i) if *x* is in *K*, then −*x* is in *K*, and

(ii) if each of *x* and *y* is in *K*, then *xy* is in *K*.

Is 12 in *K*?

(1) 2 is in *K*.

(2) 3 is in *K*.

DS05637
265. If $x^2 + y^2 = 29$, what is the value of $(x − y)^2$?

(1) $xy = 10$

(2) $x = 5$

DS16470
266. After winning 50 percent of the first 20 games it played, Team A won all of the remaining games it played. What was the total number of games that Team A won?

(1) Team A played 25 games altogether.

(2) Team A won 60 percent of all the games it played.

DS17181
267. Is *x* between 0 and 1?

(1) x^2 is less than *x*.

(2) x^3 is positive.

DS04083
268. If *m* and *n* are nonzero integers, is m^n an integer?

(1) n^m is positive.

(2) n^m is an integer.

DS16034
269. What is the value of *xy*?

(1) $x + y = 10$

(2) $x − y = 6$

DS13189
270. If *n* is the least of three different integers greater than 1, what is the value of *n*?

(1) The product of the three integers is 90.

(2) One of the integers is twice one of the other two integers.

DS16461
271. Is x^2 greater than *x*?

(1) x^2 is greater than 1.

(2) *x* is greater than −1.

DS03503
272. Michael arranged all his books in a bookcase with 10 books on each shelf and no books left over. After Michael acquired 10 additional books, he arranged all his books in a new bookcase with 12 books on each shelf and no books left over. How many books did Michael have before he acquired the 10 additional books?

(1) Before Michael acquired the 10 additional books, he had fewer than 96 books.

(2) Before Michael acquired the 10 additional books, he had more than 24 books.

DS16469
273. If $xy > 0$, does $(x − 1)(y − 1) = 1$?

(1) $x + y = xy$

(2) $x = y$

DS06842
274. Last year in a group of 30 businesses, 21 reported a net profit and 15 had investments in foreign markets. How many of the businesses did not report a net profit nor invest in foreign markets last year?

(1) Last year 12 of the 30 businesses reported a net profit and had investments in foreign markets.

(2) Last year 24 of the 30 businesses reported a net profit or invested in foreign markets, or both.

DS17110
275. Is the perimeter of square *S* greater than the perimeter of equilateral triangle *T*?

(1) The ratio of the length of a side of *S* to the length of a side of *T* is 4:5.

(2) The sum of the lengths of a side of *S* and a side of *T* is 18.

DS17136
276. If $x + y + z > 0$, is $z > 1$?

(1) $z > x + y + 1$

(2) $x + y + 1 < 0$

DS07832
277. For all *z*, $\lceil z \rceil$ denotes the least integer greater than or equal to *z*. Is $\lceil x \rceil = 0$?

(1) $−1 < x < −0.1$

(2) $\lceil x + 0.5 \rceil = 1$

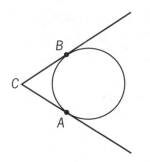

DS16464

278. The circular base of an above-ground swimming pool lies in a level yard and just touches two straight sides of a fence at points A and B, as shown in the figure above. Point C is on the ground where the two sides of the fence meet. How far from the center of the pool's base is point A ?

    (1)   The base has area 250 square feet.

    (2)   The center of the base is 20 feet from point C.

DS16050

279. If $xy = -6$, what is the value of $xy(x + y)$?

    (1) $x - y = 5$

    (2) $xy^2 = 18$

DS05519

280. $[y]$ denotes the greatest integer less than or equal to y. Is $d < 1$?

    (1) $d = y - [y]$

    (2) $[d] = 0$

DS14052

281. If N is a positive odd integer, is N prime?

    (1) $N = 2^k + 1$ for some positive integer k.

    (2) $N + 2$ and $N + 4$ are both prime.

DS01140

282. If m is a positive integer, then m^3 has how many digits?

    (1) m has 3 digits.

    (2) m^2 has 5 digits.

DS03308

283. What is the value of $x^2 - y^2$?

    (1) $(x - y)^2 = 9$

    (2) $x + y = 6$

DS01267

284. For each landscaping job that takes more than 4 hours, a certain contractor charges a total of r dollars for the first 4 hours plus $0.2r$ dollars for each additional hour or fraction of an hour, where $r > 100$. Did a particular landscaping job take more than 10 hours?

    (1)   The contractor charged a total of \$288 for the job.

    (2)   The contractor charged a total of $2.4r$ dollars for the job.

DS17600

285. If $x^2 = 2^x$, what is the value of x ?

    (1) $2x = \left(\dfrac{x}{2}\right)^3$

    (2) $x = 2^{x-2}$

DS01169

286. The sequence s_1, s_2, s_3, ..., s_n, ... is such that $s_n = \dfrac{1}{n} - \dfrac{1}{n+1}$ for all integers $n \geq 1$. If k is a positive integer, is the sum of the first k terms of the sequence greater than $\dfrac{9}{10}$?

    (1) $k > 10$

    (2) $k < 19$

DS05518

287. In the sequence S of numbers, each term after the first two terms is the sum of the two immediately preceding terms. What is the 5th term of S ?

    (1)   The 6th term of S minus the 4th term equals 5.

    (2)   The 6th term of S plus the 7th term equals 21.

DS01121

288. If 75 percent of the guests at a certain banquet ordered dessert, what percent of the guests ordered coffee?

    (1)   60 percent of the guests who ordered dessert also ordered coffee.

    (2)   90 percent of the guests who ordered coffee also ordered dessert.

DS05302

289. A tank containing water started to leak. Did the tank contain more than 30 gallons of water when it started to leak? (Note: 1 gallon = 128 ounces)

    (1)   The water leaked from the tank at a constant rate of 6.4 ounces per minute.

    (2)   The tank became empty less than 12 hours after it started to leak.

DS12752

290. In the *xy*-plane, lines *k* and *ℓ* intersect at the point (1,1). Is the *y*-intercept of *k* greater than the *y*-intercept of *ℓ* ?

(1) The slope of *k* is less than the slope of *ℓ*.

(2) The slope of *ℓ* is positive.

DS14588

291. A triangle has side lengths of *a*, *b*, and *c* centimeters. Does each angle in the triangle measure less than 90 degrees?

(1) The 3 semicircles whose diameters are the sides of the triangle have areas that are equal to 3 cm², 4 cm², and 6 cm², respectively.

(2) $c < a + b < c + 2$

DS00890

292. Each of the 45 books on a shelf is written either in English or in Spanish, and each of the books is either a hardcover book or a paperback. If a book is to be selected at random from the books on the shelf, is the probability less than $\frac{1}{2}$ that the book selected will be a paperback written in Spanish?

(1) Of the books on the shelf, 30 are paperbacks.

(2) Of the books on the shelf, 15 are written in Spanish.

DS06683

293. A small school has three foreign language classes, one in French, one in Spanish, and one in German. How many of the 34 students enrolled in the Spanish class are also enrolled in the French class?

(1) There are 27 students enrolled in the French class, and 49 students enrolled in either the French class, the Spanish class, or both of these classes.

(2) One-half of the students enrolled in the Spanish class are enrolled in more than one foreign language class.

DS04910

294. If *S* is a set of four numbers *w*, *x*, *y*, and *z*, is the range of the numbers in *S* greater than 2 ?

(1) $w - z > 2$

(2) *z* is the least number in *S*.

DS12187

295. Last year $\frac{3}{5}$ of the members of a certain club were males. This year the members of the club include all the members from last year plus some new members. Is the fraction of the members of the club who are males greater this year than last year?

(1) More than half of the new members are male.

(2) The number of members of the club this year is $\frac{6}{5}$ the number of members last year.

DS13640

296. If *a*, *b*, and *c* are consecutive integers and $0 < a < b < c$, is the product *abc* a multiple of 8 ?

(1) The product *ac* is even.

(2) The product *bc* is a multiple of 4.

DS13837

297. *M* and *N* are integers such that $6 < M < N$. What is the value of *N* ?

(1) The greatest common divisor of *M* and *N* is 6.

(2) The least common multiple of *M* and *N* is 36.

DS07575

298. Stations X and Y are connected by two separate, straight, parallel rail lines that are 250 miles long. Train P and train Q simultaneously left Station X and Station Y, respectively, and each train traveled to the other's point of departure. The two trains passed each other after traveling for 2 hours. When the two trains passed, which train was nearer to its destination?

(1) At the time when the two trains passed, train P had averaged a speed of 70 miles per hour.

(2) Train Q averaged a speed of 55 miles per hour for the entire trip.

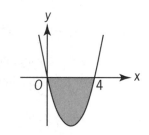

DS01613

299. In the *xy*-plane shown, the shaded region consists of all points that lie above the graph of $y = x^2 - 4x$ and below the *x*-axis. Does the point (*a*,*b*) (not shown) lie in the shaded region if $b < 0$?

(1) $0 < a < 4$

(2) $a^2 - 4a < b$

DS01685

300. If *a* and *b* are positive integers, is $\sqrt[3]{ab}$ an integer?

(1) $\sqrt{a}$ is an integer.

(2) $b = \sqrt{a}$

5.4 Answer Key

177.	D	208.	D	239.	C	270.	C
178.	E	209.	C	240.	A	271.	A
179.	A	210.	E	241.	E	272.	A
180.	E	211.	A	242.	B	273.	A
181.	D	212.	D	243.	B	274.	D
182.	E	213.	E	244.	C	275.	A
183.	B	214.	A	245.	D	276.	B
184.	A	215.	D	246.	A	277.	A
185.	D	216.	C	247.	C	278.	A
186.	D	217.	D	248.	C	279.	B
187.	C	218.	E	249.	C	280.	D
188.	E	219.	D	250.	D	281.	E
189.	E	220.	B	251.	B	282.	E
190.	D	221.	E	252.	E	283.	E
191.	E	222.	C	253.	D	284.	B
192.	D	223.	A	254.	A	285.	D
193.	C	224.	E	255.	B	286.	A
194.	E	225.	D	256.	E	287.	A
195.	B	226.	D	257.	C	288.	C
196.	D	227.	D	258.	A	289.	E
197.	D	228.	D	259.	D	290.	A
198.	C	229.	D	260.	B	291.	A
199.	D	230.	E	261.	E	292.	B
200.	C	231.	C	262.	D	293.	A
201.	D	232.	C	263.	E	294.	A
202.	B	233.	A	264.	C	295.	E
203.	A	234.	C	265.	A	296.	A
204.	C	235.	C	266.	D	297.	C
205.	D	236.	D	267.	A	298.	A
206.	C	237.	E	268.	E	299.	B
207.	E	238.	C	269.	C	300.	B

5.5 Answer Explanations

The following discussion of data sufficiency is intended to familiarize you with the most efficient and effective approaches to the kinds of problems common to data sufficiency. The particular questions in this chapter are generally representative of the kinds of data sufficiency questions you will encounter on the GMAT. Remember that it is the problem solving strategy that is important, not the specific details of a particular question.

*DS05149

177. Does $2x + 8 = 12$?

   (1) $2x + 10 = 14$

   (2) $3x + 8 = 14$

Algebra First-degree equations

We need to determine, for each of statements 1 and 2, whether the statement is sufficient for determining whether $2x + 8 = 12$. Solving for x, we see that the equation $2x + 8 = 12$ is equivalent to $2x = 12 - 8 = 4$ and is thus equivalent to $x = 2$. We thus need to find whether the statements are sufficient for determining whether $x = 2$.

   (1)   Given that $2x + 10 = 14$, it follows that $2x = 14 - 10 = 4$, and that $x = 2$; SUFFICIENT.

   (2)   Similarly, given that $3x + 8 = 14$, it follows that $3x = 14 - 8 = 6$, and that $x = 2$; SUFFICIENT.

Alternatively, for both statements 1 and 2, it is only necessary to determine that it is possible to solve each of 1 and 2 to produce a unique value for x. Care must be taken with such an approach (there are cases such as, for example, $3y = 5 + 3y$, that cannot be solved for a unique value of the variable). However, the approach can save time.

The correct answer is D;

each statement alone is sufficient.

DS01503

178. If M is a set of consecutive even integers, is 0 in set M ?

   (1)   –6 is in set M.

   (2)   –2 is in set M.

Arithmetic Series and sequences

For a set M of consecutive even integers, can we determine whether M contains the number 0 ?

   (1)   Given that –6 is in the set M, M could be a set of strictly negative integers or a set that contains both negative integers and zero (and perhaps positive integers). For example, it could be the set {–8, –6, –4} or the set {–8, –6, –4, –2, 0, 2}; NOT sufficient.

   (2)   Similarly, given that –2 is in M, M could be a set of strictly negative integers or a set that contains both negative integers and zero (and perhaps positive integers). For example, it could be the set {–4, –2} or the set {–8, –6, –4, –2, 0, 2}; NOT sufficient.

Furthermore we can see that statements 1 and 2 together are not sufficient. For example, {–8, –6, –4, –2, 0, 2} contains –6, –2, and 0, while {–8, –6, –4, –2} contains –6 and –2 but not 0.

The correct answer is E;

both statements together are not sufficient.

DS15510

179. Rita's monthly salary is $\frac{2}{3}$ Juanita's monthly salary. What is their combined monthly salary?

   (1)   Rita's monthly salary is $4,000.

   (2)   Either Rita's monthly salary or Juanita's monthly salary is $6,000.

Arithmetic Applied problems

Let R and J be Rita's and Juanita's monthly salaries, respectively, in dollars. It is given that $R = \frac{2}{3}J$. Determine the value of their combined salary, which can be expressed as $R + J = \frac{2}{3}J + J = \frac{5}{3}J$.

---

*These numbers correlate with the online test bank question number. See the GMAT Quantitative Review Online Index in the back of this book.

168

(1) Given that $R = 4,000$, it follows that $4,000 = \frac{2}{3} J$, or $J = \frac{3}{2}(4,000) = 6,000$. Therefore, $\frac{5}{3}J = \frac{5}{3}(6,000) = 10,000$; SUFFICIENT.

(2) Given that $R = 6,000$ or $J = 6,000$, then $J = \frac{3}{2}(6,000) = 9,000$ or $J = 6,000$. Thus, $\frac{5}{3}J = \frac{5}{3}(9,000) = 15,000$ or $\frac{5}{3}J = \frac{5}{3}(6,000) = 10,000$, and so it is not possible to determine the value of $\frac{5}{3}J$; NOT sufficient.

The correct answer is A;
statement 1 alone is sufficient.

DS13384
180. What is the value of the integer x?

(1) x rounded to the nearest hundred is 7,200.
(2) The hundreds digit of x is 2.

Arithmetic Rounding

(1) Given that x rounded to the nearest hundred is 7,200, the value of x cannot be determined. For example, x could be 7,200 or x could be 7,201; NOT sufficient.

(2) Given that the hundreds digit of x is 2, the value of x cannot be determined. For example, x could be 7,200 or x could be 7,201; NOT sufficient.

Taking (1) and (2) together is of no more help than either (1) or (2) taken separately because the same examples were used in both (1) and (2).

The correct answer is E;
both statements together are still not sufficient.

DS04644
181. Is $2x > 2y$?

(1) $x > y$
(2) $3x > 3y$

Algebra Inequalities

(1) It is given that $x > y$. Thus, multiplying both sides by the positive number 2, it follows that $2x > 2y$; SUFFICIENT.

(2) It is given that $3x > 3y$. Thus, multiplying both sides by the positive number $\frac{2}{3}$, it follows that $2x > 2y$; SUFFICIENT.

The correct answer is D;
each statement alone is sufficient.

DS04636
182. If p and q are positive, is $\frac{p}{q}$ less than 1?

(1) p is less than 4.
(2) q is less than 4.

Arithmetic Properties of numbers

(1) Given that p is less than 4, then it is not possible to determine whether $\frac{p}{q}$ is less than 1. For example, if $p = 1$ and $q = 2$, then $\frac{p}{q} = \frac{1}{2}$ and $\frac{1}{2}$ is less than 1. However, if $p = 2$ and $q = 1$, then $\frac{p}{q} = 2$ and 2 is not less than 1; NOT sufficient.

(2) Given that q is less than 4, then it is not possible to determine whether $\frac{p}{q}$ is less than 1. For example, if $p = 1$ and $q = 2$, then $\frac{p}{q} = \frac{1}{2}$ and $\frac{1}{2}$ is less than 1. However, if $p = 2$ and $q = 1$, then $\frac{p}{q} = 2$ and 2 is not less than 1; NOT sufficient.

Taking (1) and (2) together is of no more help than either (1) or (2) taken separately because the same examples were used in both (1) and (2).

The correct answer is E;
both statements together are still not sufficient.

DS02779
183. In each quarter of 1998, Company M earned more money than in the previous quarter. What was the range of Company M's quarterly earnings in 1998?

(1) In the 2nd and 3rd quarters of 1998, Company M earned $4.0 million and $4.6 million, respectively.

(2) In the 1st and 4th quarters of 1998, Company M earned $3.8 million and $4.9 million, respectively.

Arithmetic Statistics

We know that for each of the quarters in 1998, Company M earned more money than in the previous quarter. Is it possible to determine the range of the company's quarterly earnings in 1998?

(1) Although we are told the value of the earnings for the 2nd and 3rd quarters, Company M's 4th quarter earnings could, consistent with statement 1, be any amount that is greater than the 3rd quarter earnings. Likewise, the company's 1st quarter earnings could be any positive amount that is less than the company's 2nd quarter earnings. The difference between these two values would be the range, and we see that it cannot be determined; NOT sufficient.

(2) We are given the earnings for the 1st and 4th quarters, and we already know that, from quarter to quarter, the earnings in 1998 have always increased. We can thus infer that Company M's earnings for the 2nd and 3rd quarters are less than the 4th quarter earnings but greater than the 1st quarter earnings. The difference between the greatest quarterly earnings and the least quarter earnings for 1998 is thus the difference between the 4th quarter earnings and the 1st quarter earnings—the values $4.9 million and $3.8 million, respectively, that we have been given; SUFFICIENT.

The correct answer is B;
statement 2 alone is sufficient.

DS04510

184. In a certain factory, hours worked by each employee in excess of 40 hours per week are overtime hours and are paid for at $1\frac{1}{2}$ times the employee's regular hourly pay rate. If an employee worked a total of 42 hours last week, how much was the employee's gross pay for the hours worked last week?

(1) The employee's gross pay for overtime hours worked last week was $30.

(2) The employee's gross pay for all hours worked last week was $30 more than for the previous week.

Arithmetic Applied problems

If an employee's regular hourly rate was $R and the employee worked 42 hours last week, then the employee's gross pay for hours worked last week was $40R + 2(1.5R)$. Determine the value of $40R + 2(1.5R) = 43R$, or equivalently, the value of R.

(1) Given that the employee's gross pay for overtime hours worked last week was $30, it follows that $2(1.5R) = 30$ and $R = 10$; SUFFICIENT.

(2) Given that the employee's gross pay for all hours worked last week was $30 more than for the previous week, the value of R cannot be determined because nothing specific is known about the value of the employee's pay for all hours worked the previous week; NOT sufficient.

The correct answer is A;
statement (1) alone is sufficient.

DS01104

185. Is the integer p even?

(1) The integer $p^2 + 1$ is odd.

(2) The integer $p + 2$ is even.

Arithmetic Properties of integers

(1) For any odd number m, $m - 1$ must be even. Therefore, given that $p^2 + 1$ is odd, p^2 must be even. Now, if in this case p were odd, p would not be divisible by 2 and so would not have 2 as one of its prime factors. p^2 would also not have 2 as one of its prime factors, and so, if p were odd, p^2 would be odd. Therefore, given that $p^2 + 1$ is odd (and p^2 is even), p must not be odd. That is, p must be even; SUFFICIENT.

(2) Given that $p + 2$ is even, it follows that $p + 2$ is divisible by 2. That is, $p + 2 = 2k$, where k is an integer. Thus, $p = 2k - 2 = 2(k - 1)$, where $k - 1$ is an integer. The integer p is thus divisible by 2 and is therefore even; SUFFICIENT.

The correct answer is D;
each statement alone is sufficient.

DS05172
186. If $x > 0$, what is the value of x^5 ?

(1) $\sqrt{x} = 32$

(2) $x^2 = 2^{20}$

Algebra Exponents

(1) Given that $\sqrt{x} = 32$, it follows that $x = 32^2$ and $x^5 = (32^2)^5$; SUFFICIENT.

(2) Given that $x^2 = 2^{20}$, since x is positive, it follows that $x = \sqrt{2^{20}} = 2^{10}$ and $x^5 = (2^{10})^5$; SUFFICIENT.

The correct answer is D; each statement alone is sufficient.

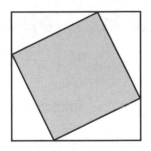

DS17640
187. In the quilting pattern shown above, a small square has its vertices on the sides of a larger square. What is the side length, in centimeters, of the larger square?

(1) The side length of the smaller square is 10 cm.

(2) Each vertex of the small square cuts 1 side of the larger square into 2 segments with lengths in the ratio of 1:2.

Geometry Triangles; Pythagorean theorem

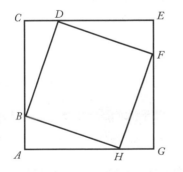

Determine the side length of the larger square or, in the figure above, determine $AG = AH + HG$. Note that $\triangle BAH$, $\triangle DCB$, $\triangle FED$, and $\triangle HGF$ are the same size and shape and that $AB = CD = EF = GH$ and $BC = DE = FG = HA$.

(1) This indicates that $HF = 10$, but it is possible that $HG = 6$ and $GF = 8$ $\left(\sqrt{6^2 + 8^2} = 10\right)$, from which it follows that the side length of the larger square is $6 + 8 = 14$, and it is possible that $HG = 1$ and $GF = \sqrt{99}$ $\left(\sqrt{1^2 + \left(\sqrt{99}\right)^2} = 10\right)$, from which it follows that the side length of the larger square is $1 + \sqrt{99}$; NOT sufficient.

(2) This indicates that if $HG = x$, then $AH = 2x$. If $x = 2$, then the side length of the larger square is $2 + 2(2) = 6$, but if $x = 5$, then the side length of the larger square is $5 + 2(5) = 15$; NOT sufficient.

Taking (1) and (2) together, $10 = \sqrt{x^2 + (2x)^2}$, which can be solved for x. Then taking 3 times the value of x gives the side length of the larger square.

The correct answer is C; both statements together are sufficient.

DS02589
188. Did Insurance Company K have more than $300 million in total net profits last year?

(1) Last year Company K paid out $0.95 in claims for every dollar of premiums collected.

(2) Last year Company K earned a total of $150 million in profits from the investment of accumulated surplus premiums from previous years.

Arithmetic Applied problems

Letting R and E, respectively, represent the company's total revenue and total expenses last year, determine if $R - E > \$300$ million.

(1) This indicates that, for $\$x$ in premiums collected, the company paid $\$0.95x$ in claims, but gives no information about other sources of revenue or other types of expenses; NOT sufficient.

(2) This indicates that the company's profits from the investment of accumulated surplus premiums was $150 million last year, but gives no information about other sources of revenue or other types of expenses; NOT sufficient.

Taking (1) and (2) together gives information on profit resulting from collecting premiums and paying claims as well as profit resulting from investments from accumulated surplus premiums, but gives no indication whether there were other sources of revenue or other types of expenses.

**The correct answer is E;
both statements together are still not sufficient.**

DS15349

189. How many hours would it take Pump A and Pump B working together, each at its own constant rate, to empty a tank that was initially full?

(1) Working alone at its constant rate, Pump A would empty the full tank in 4 hours 20 minutes.

(2) Working alone, Pump B would empty the full tank at its constant rate of 72 liters per minute.

Arithmetic Applied problems

Determine how long it would take Pumps A and B working together, each at its own constant rate, to empty a full tank.

(1) This indicates how long it would take Pump A to empty the tank, but gives no information about Pump B's constant rate; NOT sufficient.

(2) This indicates the rate at which Pump B can empty the tank, but without information about the capacity of the tank or Pump A's rate, it is not possible to determine how long both pumps working together would take to empty the tank; NOT sufficient.

Taking (1) and (2) together gives the amount of time it would take Pump A to empty the tank and the rate at which Pump B can empty the tank, but without knowing the capacity of the tank, it is not possible to determine how long the pumps working together would take to empty the tank.

**The correct answer is E;
both statements together are still not sufficient.**

DS04573

190. What is the value of the integer N?

(1) $101 < N < 103$

(2) $202 < 2N < 206$

Arithmetic Inequalities

(1) Given that N is an integer and $101 < N < 103$, it follows that $N = 102$; SUFFICIENT.

(2) Given that N is an integer and $202 < 2N < 206$, it follows that $101 < N < 103$ and $N = 102$; SUFFICIENT.

**The correct answer is D;
each statement alone is sufficient.**

DS12033

191. Is zw positive?

(1) $z + w^3 = 20$

(2) z is positive.

Arithmetic Properties of numbers

(1) Given that $z + w^3 = 20$, if $z = 1$ and $w = \sqrt[3]{19}$ then $z + w^3 = 20$ and zw is positive. However, if $z = 20$ and $w = 0$, then $z + w^3 = 20$ and zw is not positive; NOT sufficient.

(2) Given that z is positive, if $z = 1$ and $w = \sqrt[3]{19}$, then zw is positive. However, if $z = 20$ and $w = 0$, then zw is not positive; NOT sufficient.

Taking (1) and (2) together is of no more help than either (1) or (2) taken separately because the same examples were used in both (1) and (2).

**The correct answer is E;
both statements together are still not sufficient.**

DS03006

192. On the scale drawing of a certain house plan, if 1 centimeter represents x meters, what is the value of x?

(1) A rectangular room that has a floor area of 12 square meters is represented by a region of area 48 square centimeters.

(2) The 15-meter length of the house is represented by a segment 30 centimeters long.

Arithmetic Ratio and proportion

It is given that on the scale drawing, 1 centimeter represents x meters. Determine the value of x. Note that 1 cm² represents x^2 m².

(1) This indicates that an area of 12 m² is represented by an area of 48 cm². Then,

dividing both 12 and 48 by 48, it follows

that an area of $\frac{12}{48} = \frac{1}{4}$ m² is represented

by an area of $\frac{48}{48} = 1$ cm² and so $x^2 = \frac{1}{4}$ or

$x = \frac{1}{2}$; SUFFICIENT.

(2) This indicates that a length of 15 m is represented by a length of 30 cm. Then, dividing both 15 and 30 by 30, it follows

that a length of $\frac{15}{30} = \frac{1}{2}$ m is represented

by a length of $\frac{30}{30} = 1$ cm and so $x = \frac{1}{2}$;
SUFFICIENT.

**The correct answer is D;
each statement alone is sufficient.**

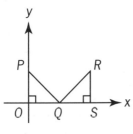

DS03939

193. In the rectangular coordinate system above, if ΔOPQ and ΔQRS have equal area, what are the coordinates of point R ?

(1) The coordinates of point P are (0,12).

(2) OP = OQ and QS = RS.

Geometry Coordinate geometry; Triangles

Since the area of ΔOPQ is equal to the area of

ΔQRS, it follows that $\frac{1}{2}$ (OQ)(OP) =
$\frac{1}{2}$(QS)(SR), or (OQ)(OP) = (QS)(SR). Also, if
both OS and SR are known, then the coordinates of point R will be known.

(1) Given that the y-coordinate of P is 12, it is not possible to determine the coordinates of point R. For example, if OQ = QS = SR = 12, then the equation (OQ)(OP) = (QS)(SR) becomes (12)(12) = (12)(12), which is true, and the x-coordinate of R is OQ + QS = 24 and the y-coordinate of R is SR = 12. However, if

OQ = 12, QS = 24, and SR = 6, then the equation (OQ)(OP) = (QS)(SR) becomes (12)(12) = (24)(6), which is true, and the x-coordinate of R is OQ + QS = 36 and the y-coordinate of R is SR = 6; NOT sufficient.

(2) Given that OP = OQ and QS = RS, it is not possible to determine the coordinates of point R, since everything given would still be true if all the lengths were doubled, but doing this would change the coordinates of point R; NOT sufficient.

Taking (1) and (2) together, it follows that OP = OQ = 12. Therefore, (OQ)(OP) = (QS)(SR) becomes (12)(12) = (QS)(SR), or 144 = (QS)(SR). Using QS = RS in the last equation gives 144 = (QS)², or 12 = QS. Thus, OQ = QS = SR = 12 and point R has coordinates (24,12).

**The correct answer is C;
both statements together are sufficient.**

DS07258

194. In a school that had a total of 600 students enrolled in the junior and senior classes, the students contributed to a certain fund. If all of the juniors but only half of the seniors contributed, was the total amount contributed more than $740 ?

(1) Each junior contributed $1 and each senior who contributed gave $3.

(2) There were more juniors than seniors enrolled in the school.

Arithmetic Applied problems

The task in this question is to determine whether the respective statements are sufficient for answering the question of whether the total amount contributed was more than $740. In making this determination, it is important to remember that we are to use only the information that has been given. For example, it may seem plausible to assume that the number of seniors at the school is roughly equal to the number of juniors. However, because no such information has been provided, we cannot assume that this assumption holds. With this in mind, consider statements 1 and 2.

(1) If it were the case that half of the 600 students were seniors, then, given that half of the 300 seniors would have contributed

$3, there would have been $150 \times \$3 = \$450$ in contributions from the seniors and $300 \times \$1 = \$300$ in contributions from the juniors, for a total of $750—more than the figure of $740 with which the question is concerned. However, as noted, we cannot make such an assumption. To test the conditions that we have actually been given, we can consider extreme cases, which are often relatively simple. For example, given the information provided, it is possible that only two of the students are seniors and the other 598 students are juniors. If this were the case, then the contributions from the juniors would be $598 ($1 per student) and the contributions from the seniors would be $3 ($3 for the one senior who contributes, given that only half of the 2 seniors contribute). The total contributions would then be $598 + \$3 = \$601$; NOT sufficient.

(2) Merely with this statement—and not statement 1—we have no information as to how much the students contributed. We therefore cannot determine the total amount contributed; NOT sufficient.

We still need to consider whether statements 1 and 2 are sufficient *together* for determining whether a minimum of $740 has been contributed. However, note that the reasoning in connection with statement 1 applies here as well. We considered there the possibility that the 600 students included only two seniors, with the other 598 students being juniors. Because this scenario also satisfies statement 2, we see that statements 1 and 2 taken together are not sufficient.

The correct answer is E;

both statements together are still not sufficient.

DS06650

195. How much did credit-card fraud cost United States banks in year X to the nearest $10 million?

(1) In year X, counterfeit cards and telephone and mail-order fraud accounted for 39 percent of the total amount that card fraud cost the banks.

(2) In year X, stolen cards accounted for $158.4 million, or 16 percent, of the total amount that credit-card fraud cost the banks.

Arithmetic Percents

(1) It is given that certain parts of the total fraud cost have a total that is 39% of the total fraud cost, but since no actual dollar amounts are specified, it is not possible to estimate the total fraud cost to the nearest $10 million; NOT sufficient.

(2) Given that $158.4 million represents 16% of the total fraud cost, it follows that the total fraud cost equals $158.4 million divided by 0.16; SUFFICIENT.

The correct answer is B;

statement 2 alone is sufficient.

DS17319

196. Is the positive integer n odd?

(1) $n^2 + (n + 1)^2 + (n + 2)^2$ is even.

(2) $n^2 - (n + 1)^2 - (n + 2)^2$ is even.

Arithmetic Properties of numbers

The positive integer n is either odd or even. Determine if it is odd.

(1) This indicates that the sum of the squares of three consecutive integers, n^2, $(n + 1)^2$, and $(n + 2)^2$, is even. If n is even, then $n + 1$ is odd and $n + 2$ is even. It follows that n^2 is even, $(n + 1)^2$ is odd, and $(n + 2)^2$ is even and, therefore, that $n^2 + (n + 1)^2 + (n + 2)^2$ is odd. But, this contradicts the given information, and so, n must be odd; SUFFICIENT.

(2) This indicates that $n^2 - (n + 1)^2 - (n + 2)^2$ is even. Adding the even number represented by $2(n + 1)^2 + 2(n + 2)^2$ to the even number represented by $n^2 - (n + 1)^2 - (n + 2)^2$ gives the even number represented by $n^2 + (n + 1)^2 + (n + 2)^2$. This is Statement (1); SUFFICIENT.

The correct answer is D;

each statement alone is sufficient.

DS01130

197. In the xy-plane, circle C has center (1,0) and radius 2. If line k is parallel to the y-axis, is line k tangent to circle C ?

(1) Line k passes through the point (–1,0).

(2) Line k passes through the point (–1,–1).

Geometry Coordinate geometry

Can we determine whether line k, which is parallel to the y-axis, is tangent to the circle C?

(1) Given that line k passes through the point $(-1,0)$, we can represent the scenario in the following diagram, which is not drawn to scale.

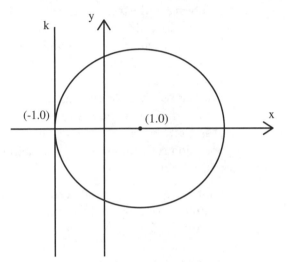

The points $(1,0)$ and $(-1,0)$ are two units apart on the x axis. We therefore know that circle C, with center $(1,0)$ and radius 2, passes through the point $(-1,0)$ and that, given that k passes through the point $(-1,0)$, the circle intersects line k at this point. Furthermore, the radial line from the center $(1,0)$ of the circle to point $(-1,0)$ on the circle rests on the x-axis and is therefore perpendicular to the y-axis. Line k, being parallel to the y-axis, must also be perpendicular to this radial line. Therefore, because line k both intersects the circle at a point at which a radial line intersects the circle and is perpendicular to this radial line, we see that that line k must be tangent to circle C; SUFFICIENT.

(2) The sufficiency of statement 2 follows from the sufficiency of statement 1. For, if k is perpendicular to the y-axis and passes through point $(-1,-1)$, then k must also pass through point $(-1,0)$; k is simply the line $x = -1$. The reasoning for statement 1 now applies; SUFFICIENT.

The correct answer is D;

Each statement alone is sufficient.

DS14170

198. Company X's profits this year increased by 25% over last year's profits. Was the dollar amount of Company X's profits this year greater than the dollar amount of Company Y's?

(1) Last year, the ratio of Company Y's profits to Company X's profits was 5:2.

(2) Company Y experienced a 40% drop in profits from last year to this year.

Algebra Applied problems

Let P_X and P'_X, respectively, be the profits of Company X last year and this year, and let P_Y and P'_Y, respectively, be the profits of Company Y last year and this year. Then $P'_X = 1.25 P_X$. Is $P'_X > P'_Y$?

(1) Given that $\frac{P_Y}{P_X} = \frac{5}{2}$, it is not possible to determine whether $P'_X > P'_Y$ because nothing is known about the value of P'_Y other than P'_Y is positive; NOT sufficient.

(2) Given that $P'_Y = 0.6 P_Y$, it is not possible to determine whether $P'_X > P'_Y$ because nothing is known that relates the profits of Company X for either year to the profits of Company Y for either year; NOT sufficient.

Taking (1) and (2) together, it is given that $P'_X = 1.25 P_X$ and from (1) it follows that $\frac{P_Y}{P_X} = \frac{5}{2}$, or $P_X = \frac{2}{5} P_Y$, and thus $P'_X = (1.25)\left(\frac{2}{5} P_Y\right)$. From (2) it follows that $P'_Y = 0.6 P_Y$, or $P_Y = \frac{1}{0.6} P'_Y$, and thus $P'_X = (1.25)\left(\frac{2}{5}\right)\left(\frac{1}{0.6} P'_Y\right)$. Since the last equation expresses P'_X as a specific number times P'_Y, it follows that it can be determined whether or not $P'_X > P'_Y$. Note that

$$(1.25)\left(\frac{2}{5}\right)\left(\frac{1}{0.6}\right) = \left(\frac{5}{4}\right)\left(\frac{2}{5}\right)\left(\frac{5}{3}\right) = \frac{5}{6},$$ and so the answer to the question "Is $P'_X > P'_Y$" is no.

The correct answer is C;

both statements together are sufficient.

199. For all x, the expression x* is defined to be ax + a, where a is a constant. What is the value of 2* ?

    (1) $3^* = 2$

    (2) $5^* = 3$

Algebra Linear equations

Determine the value of $2^* = (a)(2) + a = 3a$, or equivalently, determine the value of a.

    (1)   Given that $3^* = 2$, it follows that $(a)(3) + a = 2$, or $4a = 2$, or $a = \dfrac{1}{2}$; SUFFICIENT.

    (2)   Given that $5^* = 3$, it follows that $(a)(5) + a = 3$, or $6a = 3$, or $a = \dfrac{1}{2}$; SUFFICIENT.

The correct answer is D;
each statement alone is sufficient.

200. Is $k + m < 0$?

    (1) $k < 0$

    (2) $km > 0$

Arithmetic Properties of numbers

    (1)   Given that k is negative, it is not possible to determine whether $k + m$ is negative. For example, if $k = -2$ and $m = 1$, then $k + m$ is negative. However, if $k = -2$ and $m = 3$, then $k + m$ is not negative; NOT sufficient.

    (2)   Given that km is positive, it is not possible to determine whether $k + m$ is negative. For example, if $k = -2$ and $m = -1$, then km is positive and $k + m$ is negative. However, if $k = 2$ and $m = 1$, then km is positive and $k + m$ is not negative; NOT sufficient.

Taking (1) and (2) together, k is negative and km is positive, it follows that m is negative. Therefore, both k and m are negative, and hence $k + m$ is negative.

The correct answer is C;
both statements together are sufficient.

201. The symbol Δ represents which one of the following operations: addition, subtraction, or multiplication?

    (1) $a \Delta (b \Delta c) \neq a \Delta (c \Delta b)$ for some numbers a, b, and c.

    (2) $a \Delta (b \Delta c) \neq (a \Delta b) \Delta c$ for some numbers a, b, and c.

Arithmetic Arithmetic operations

Can we determine which of the operations—addition, subtraction, or multiplication—is the operation Δ?

    (1)   Given the condition that Δ has the property that, for some numbers a, b, and c, $a \Delta (b \Delta c) \neq a \Delta (c \Delta b)$, we can infer that, for some numbers b and c, $b \Delta c \neq c \Delta b$. Both addition and multiplication have the commutative property, whereby, for any numbers x and y, $x + y = y + x$ and $x \times y = y \times x$. For example, $7 + 2 = 9 = 2 + 7$, and $7 \times 2 = 14 = 2 \times 7$. We thus see that, for *all* numbers x, y, and z, both of the statements $x + (y + z) = x + (z + y)$ and $x \times (y \times z) = x \times (z \times y)$ are true. The operation Δ therefore cannot be addition or multiplication.

        Subtraction, on the other hand, lacks the commutative property; for example, $7 - 2 = 5$ and $2 - 7 = -5$. The operation Δ could therefore be subtraction. Subtraction is therefore the one operation among addition, subtraction, and multiplication that satisfies statement 1; SUFFICIENT.

    (2)   The reasoning in this case is similar to the reasoning for statement 1, but concerning the associative property rather than the commutative property. Both addition and multiplication have this property. For any numbers x, y, and z, the statements $x + (y + z) = (x + y) + z$ and $x \times (y \times z) = (x \times y) \times z$ are always true. For example, in the case of multiplication, $2 \times (3 \times 5) = 2 \times 15 = 30 = 6 \times 5 = (2 \times 3) \times 5$. However, in contrast to addition and multiplication, the operation of subtraction does not have the associative property. For example, for the numbers 2, 3, and 5, $2 - (3 - 5) = 2 - (-2) = 4$, whereas $(2 - 3) - 4 = -1 - 4 = -5$. Subtraction is therefore the one operation among addition, subtraction, and multiplication that satisfies statement 2; SUFFICIENT.

The correct answer is D;
each statement alone is sufficient.

DS05989

202. What is the value of $2^x + 2^{-x}$?

    (1) $x > 0$

    (2) $4^x + 4^{-x} = 23$

Algebra Equations

Can we determine the value of $2^x + 2^{-x}$?

    (1)   The condition $x > 0$ by itself is not sufficient for determining the value of $2^x + 2^{-x}$. For example, if $x = 1$, then $2^x + 2^{-x} = 2^1 + 2^{-1} = 2\frac{1}{2}$. And if $x = 2$, then $2^x + 2^{-x} = 2^2 + 2^{-2} = 4\frac{1}{4}$; NOT sufficient.

    (2)   Given $4^x + 4^{-x} = 23$, it may be tempting to reason that this is an equation with only one unknown, and that it is therefore possible to determine the value of x and then the value of $2^x + 2^{-x}$. However, this reasoning can often produce erroneous results. For example the equation $(y - 1)(y - 3) = 0$ has only one unknown but is consistent with two values for y (1 and 3). To be sure that the statement $4^x + 4^{-x} = 23$ is sufficient for determining the value of $2^x + 2^{-x}$, consider first the square of $2^x + 2^{-x}$.

$$(2^x + 2^{-x})^2 = (2^x)^2 + (2^{-x})^2 + 2(2^x)(2^{-x})$$

$$= 2^{2x} + 2^{-2x} + 2(2^{x-x})$$

$$= (2^2)^x + (2^{-2})^x + 2$$

$$= 4^x + 4^{-x} + 2.$$

So $4^x + 4^{-x} = (2^x + 2^{-x})^2 - 2$. The condition that $4^x + 4^{-x} = 23$ thus becomes

$(2^x + 2^{-x})^2 - 2 = 23$, or $(2^x + 2^{-x})^2 = 25$. And because we know that $2^x + 2^{-x} > 0$ (because both $2^x > 0$ and $2^{-x} > 0$), we see that statement 1 implies $(2^x + 2^{-x}) = \sqrt{25} = 5$; SUFFICIENT.

The correct answer is B;
statement 2 alone is sufficient.

DS13457

203. What is the ratio of c to d ?

    (1)   The ratio of $3c$ to $3d$ is 3 to 4.

    (2)   The ratio of $c + 3$ to $d + 3$ is 4 to 5.

Arithmetic Ratio and proportion

Determine the value of $\frac{c}{d}$.

    (1)   Given that $\frac{3c}{3d} = \frac{3}{4}$, it follows that $\frac{3c}{3d} = \frac{c}{d} = \frac{3}{4}$; SUFFICIENT.

    (2)   Given that $\frac{c+3}{d+3} = \frac{4}{5}$, then it is not possible to determine the value of $\frac{c}{d}$. For example, if $c = 1$ and $d = 2$, then $\frac{c+3}{d+3} = \frac{4}{5}$ and $\frac{c}{d} = \frac{1}{2}$. However, if $c = 5$ and $d = 7$, then $\frac{c+3}{d+3} = \frac{8}{10} = \frac{4}{5}$ and $\frac{c}{d} = \frac{5}{7}$; NOT sufficient.

The correct answer is A;
statement (1) alone is sufficient.

DS15099

204. A candle company determines that, for a certain specialty candle, the supply function is $p = m_1 x + b_1$ and the demand function is $p = m_2 x + b_2$, where p is the price of each candle, x is the number of candles supplied or demanded, and m_1, m_2, b_1, and b_2 are constants. At what value of x do the graphs of the supply function and demand function intersect?

    (1) $m_1 = -m_2 = 0.005$

    (2) $b_2 - b_1 = 6$

Algebra First-degree equations

The graphs will intersect at the value of x such that $m_1 x + b_1 = m_2 x + b_2$ or $(m_1 - m_2)x = b_2 - b_1$.

    (1)   This indicates that $m_1 = -m_2 = 0.005$. It follows that $m_1 - m_2 = 0.01$, and so $0.01x = b_2 - b_1$ or $x = 100(b_2 - b_1)$, which can vary as the values of b_2 and b_1 vary; NOT sufficient.

    (2)   This indicates that $b_2 - b_1 = 6$. It follows that $(m_1 - m_2)x = 6$. This implies that $m_1 \neq m_2$, and so $x = \dfrac{b_2 - b_1}{m_1 - m_2} = \dfrac{6}{m_1 - m_2}$, which can vary as the values of m_1 and m_2 vary; NOT sufficient.

Taking (1) and (2) together, $m_1 - m_2 = 0.01$ and $b_2 - b_1 = 6$ and so the value of x is $\dfrac{6}{0.01} = 600$.

The correct answer is C;
both statements together are sufficient.

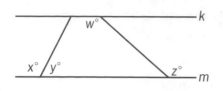

DS12862

205. In the figure shown, lines k and m are parallel to each other. Is $x = z$?

(1) $x = w$
(2) $y = 180 - w$

Geometry Angles

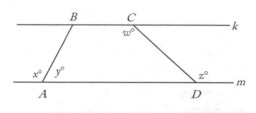

Since lines k and m are parallel, it follows from properties of parallel lines that in the diagram above x is the degree measure of $\angle ABC$ in quadrilateral $ABCD$. Therefore, because $y = 180 - x$, the four interior angles of quadrilateral $ABCD$ have degree measures $(180 - x)$, x, w, and $(180 - z)$.

(1)   Given that $x = w$, then because the sum of the degree measures of the angles of the quadrilateral $ABCD$ is 360, it follows that $(180 - x) + x + x + (180 - z) = 360$, or $x - z = 0$, or $x = z$; SUFFICIENT.

(2)   Given that $y = 180 - w$, then because $y = 180 - x$, it follows that $180 - w = 180 - x$, or $x = w$. However, it is shown in (1) that $x = w$ is sufficient; SUFFICIENT.

**The correct answer is D;
each statement alone is sufficient.**

DS13097

206. If k and ℓ are lines in the xy-plane, is the slope of k less than the slope of ℓ ?

(1)   The x-intercept of line k is positive, and the x-intercept of line ℓ is negative.
(2)   Lines k and ℓ intersect on the positive y-axis.

Geometry Simple coordinate geometry

Can we determine, for lines k and l in the xy plane, whether the slope of k is less than the slope of l ?

(1)   Given that the x-intercept of k is positive and the x-intercept of line l is negative, we cannot determine whether the slope of k is less than the slope of l. For example, in the case of line k, we have only been told where (within a certain range) line k intersects another line (the x-axis). Although a line with only a single x-intercept would not be horizontal, the line k could have any non-horizontal slope. Likewise in the case of line l. For example, the slope of k could be positive and the slope of l negative, or vice versa; NOT sufficient.

(2)   Given that k and l intersect on the positive y-axis, we cannot determine whether the slope of k is less than the slope of l. The point here is the same as the point with statement 1. With statement 2, we have only been given, for each of lines k and l, a condition on where the two lines intersect. And, given only that a line passes through a particular point (and regardless of whether another line happens to pass through this point), the line could have any slope. For example, again, the slope of k could be positive and the slope of l negative, or vice versa; NOT sufficient.

Considering statements 1 and 2 together, we have, for each of lines k and l, a condition on two of the points that the line passes through. As illustrated in the diagram, the two conditions together are sufficient for determining the relationship in question.

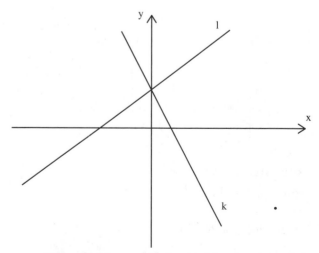

Because k intersects the positive y-axis and the positive x-axis, its slope must be downward (negative). And because l intersects the negative x-axis and the positive y-axis, its slope must be upward (positive). The slope of *k* is therefore less than the slope of *l*.

The correct answer is C;
both statements together are sufficient.

DS09642

207. When the wind speed is 9 miles per hour, the wind-chill factor *w* is given by

$$w = -17.366 + 1.19t,$$

where *t* is the temperature in degrees Fahrenheit. If at noon yesterday the wind speed was 9 miles per hour, was the wind-chill factor greater than 0 ?

(1) The temperature at noon yesterday was greater than 10 degrees Fahrenheit.

(2) The temperature at noon yesterday was less than 20 degrees Fahrenheit.

Algebra Applied problems

Determine whether $-17.366 + 1.19t$ is greater than 0.

(1) Given that $t > 10$, it follows that $-17.366 + 1.19t > -17.366 + 1.19(10)$, or $-17.366 + 1.19t > -5.466$. However, it is not possible to determine whether $-17.366 + 1.19t$ is greater than 0. For example, if $t = 19$, then $-17.366 + 1.19t = 5.244$ is greater than 0. However, if $t = 11$, then $-17.366 + 1.19t = -4.276$, which is not greater than 0; NOT sufficient.

(2) Given that $t < 20$, the same examples used in (1) show that it is not possible to determine whether $-17.366 + 1.19t$ is greater than 0; NOT sufficient.

Taking (1) and (2) together is of no more help than either (1) or (2) taken separately because the same examples were used in both (1) and (2).

The correct answer is E;
both statements together are still not sufficient.

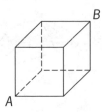

DS08852

208. What is the volume of the cube above?

(1) The surface area of the cube is 600 square inches.

(2) The length of diagonal *AB* is $10\sqrt{3}$ inches.

Geometry Volume

This problem can be solved by determining the side length, *s*, of the cube.

(1) This indicates that $6s^2 = 600$, from which it follows that $s^2 = 100$ and $s = 10$; SUFFICIENT.

(2) To determine diagonal *AB*, first determine diagonal *AN* by applying the Pythagorean theorem to $\triangle AMN$: $AN = \sqrt{s^2 + s^2} = \sqrt{2s^2}$. Now determine *AB* by applying the Pythagorean theorem to $\triangle ANB$: $AB = \sqrt{(AN)^2 + (NB)^2} = \sqrt{2s^2 + s^2} = \sqrt{3s^2} = s\sqrt{3}$. It is given that $AB = 10\sqrt{3}$, and so $s = 10$; SUFFICIENT.

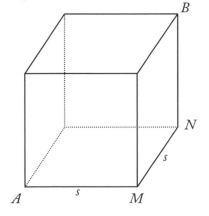

The correct answer is D;
each statement alone is sufficient.

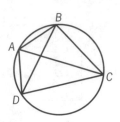

DS03989

209. In the figure shown, quadrilateral *ABCD* is inscribed in a circle of radius 5. What is the perimeter of quadrilateral *ABCD* ?

(1) The length of *AB* is 6 and the length of *CD* is 8.

(2) *AC* is a diameter of the circle.

Geometry Quadrilaterals; Perimeter; Pythagorean theorem

Determine the perimeter of quadrilateral *ABCD*, which is given by $AB + BC + CD + DA$.

(1) This indicates that $AB = 6$ and $CD = 8$, but gives no information about *BC* or *DA*.

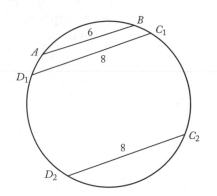

For example, the perimeter of ABC_1D_1 is clearly different than the perimeter of ABC_2D_2 and $\overline{CD}$ could be positioned where $\overline{C_1D_1}$ is on the diagram or it could be positioned where $\overline{C_2D_2}$ is on the diagram; NOT sufficient.

(2) This indicates that $AC = 2(5) = 10$ since *AC* is a diameter of the circle and the radius of the circle is 5. It also indicates that $\angle ABC$ and $\angle ADC$ are right angles since each is inscribed in a semicircle. However, there is no information about *AB*, *BC*, *CD*, or *DA*. For example, if $AB = CD = 6$, then $BC = DA = \sqrt{10^2 - 6^2} = \sqrt{64} = 8$ and the perimeter of *ABCD* is $2(6 + 8) = 28$. However, if $AB = DA = 2$, then $BC = CD = \sqrt{10^2 - 2^2} = \sqrt{96}$ and the perimeter of $ABCD = 2(2 + \sqrt{96})$; NOT sufficient.

Taking (1) and (2) together, $\triangle ABC$ is a right triangle with $AC = 10$ and $AB = 6$. It follows from the Pythagorean theorem that $BC = \sqrt{10^2 - 6^2} = \sqrt{64} = 8$. Likewise, $\triangle ADC$ is a right triangle with $AC = 10$ and $CD = 8$. It follows from the Pythagorean theorem that $DA = \sqrt{10^2 - 8^2} = \sqrt{36} = 6$. Thus, the perimeter of quadrilateral *ABCD* can be determined.

The correct answer is C; both statements together are sufficient.

DS05766

210. How many members of a certain legislature voted against the measure to raise their salaries?

(1) $\frac{1}{4}$ of the members of the legislature did not vote on the measure.

(2) If 5 additional members of the legislature had voted against the measure, then the fraction of members of the legislature voting against the measure would have been $\frac{1}{3}$.

Arithmetic Ratio and proportion

The task in this question is to determine whether, on the basis of statements 1 and 2, it is possible to calculate the number of members of the legislature who voted against a certain measure.

(1) This statement, that $\frac{1}{4}$ of the members of the legislature did not vote on the measure, is compatible with any number of members of the legislature voting against the measure. After all, any number among the $\frac{3}{4}$ of the remaining members could have voted against the measure. Furthermore, based on statement 1, we do not know the number of members of the legislature (although we do know, based on this statement, that the number of members of the legislature is divisible by 4); NOT sufficient.

(2) This statement describes a scenario, of 5 additional members of the legislature voting against the measure, and stipulates that $\frac{1}{3}$ of the members of the legislature would have voted against the measure in the scenario. Given this condition, we know that the number of members of the legislature was divisible by 3, and that the

legislature had at least 15 members (to allow for the "5 additional members of the legislature" that could have voted against the measure, for a total of $\frac{1}{3}$ of the members voting against it). However, beyond this we know essentially nothing from statement 2. In particular, depending on the number of members of the legislature (which we have not been given), any number of members could have voted against the measure. For example, exactly one member could have voted against the measure, in which case the legislature would have had $(1 + 5) \times 3 = 18$ members. Exactly two members could have voted against the measure, in which case the legislature would have had $(2 + 5) \times 3 = 21$ members, and so on for 3 members voting against, 4 members voting against, etc.; NOT sufficient.

Considering the statements 1 and 2 together, the reasoning is similar to the reasoning for statement 2, but with the further condition that the total number of members of the legislature is divisible by 12 (so as to allow that both exactly $\frac{1}{4}$ of the members did not vote on the measure while exactly $\frac{1}{3}$ could have voted against the measure). For example, it could have been the case that the legislature had 24 members. In this case, $\frac{1}{3}$ of the members would have been 8 members, and, consistent with statements 1 and 2, 3 of the members (8 – 5) could have voted against the measure. Or the legislature could have had 36 members, in which case, consistent with statements 1 and 2, $\frac{1}{3}(36) - 5 = 12 - 5 = 7$ members could have voted against the measure.

The correct answer is E;

both statements together are still not sufficient.

DS05986

211. If $y \neq 0$, is $|x| = 1$?

(1) $x = \dfrac{y}{|y|}$

(2) $|x| = -x$

Algebra Absolute value

Can we determine whether $|x| = 1$?

(1) Given that $x = \dfrac{y}{|y|}$, we consider two cases: $y > 0$ and $y < 0$. If $y > 0$, then $|y| = y$ and $\dfrac{y}{|y|} = \dfrac{y}{y} = 1$. So if $y > 0$, then $x = 1$ and, of course, $|x| = 1$. If $y < 0$, then $|y| = (-1)\,y$ and $x = \dfrac{y}{|y|} = \dfrac{y}{(-1)\,y} = (-1)\dfrac{y}{y} = (-1)(1) = -1$. So $|x| = 1$. If $y < 0$, then $|x| = 1$. In both of the two cases, $|x| = 1$; SUFFICIENT.

(2) Given that $|x| = -x$, all we know is that x is not positive. For example, both –4 and –5 satisfy this condition on x: $|-4| = 4 = -(-4)$ and $|-5| = 5 = -(-5)$; NOT sufficient.

The correct answer is A;

statement 1 alone is sufficient.

DS08306

212. If x is a positive integer, what is the value of x ?

(1) $x^2 = \sqrt{x}$

(2) $\dfrac{n}{x} = n$ and $n \neq 0$.

Algebra Operations with radicals

(1) It is given that x is a positive integer. Then,

$$
\begin{array}{ll}
x^2 = \sqrt{x} & \text{given} \\
x^4 = x & \text{square both sides} \\
x^4 - x = 0 & \text{subtract } x \text{ from both sides} \\
x(x - 1)(x^2 + x + 1) = 0 & \text{factor left side}
\end{array}
$$

Thus, the positive integer value of x being sought will be a solution of this equation. One solution of this equation is $x = 0$, which is not a positive integer. Another solution is $x = 1$, which is a positive integer. Also, $x^2 + x + 1$ is a positive integer for all positive integer values of x, and so $x^2 + x + 1 = 0$ has no positive integer solutions. Thus, the only possible positive integer value of x is 1; SUFFICIENT.

(2) It is given that $n \neq 0$. Then,

$$
\begin{array}{ll}
\dfrac{n}{x} = n & \text{given} \\
n = nx & \text{multiply both sides by } x \\
1 = x & \text{divide both sides by } n, \text{ where } n \neq 0
\end{array}
$$

Thus, $x = 1$; SUFFICIENT.

The correct answer is D;
each statement alone is sufficient.

DS07568

213. Is the median of the five numbers *a*, *b*, *c*, *d*, and *e* equal to *d*?

   (1) $a < c < e$

   (2) $b < d < c$

Arithmetic Statistics

Determine if the median of the five numbers, *a*, *b*, *c*, *d*, and *e*, is equal to *d*.

   (1)   This indicates that $a < c < e$, but does not indicate a relationship of *b* and *d* with *a*, *c*, and *e*. For example, if $a = 5$, $b = 1$, $c = 10$, $d = 7$, and $e = 15$, then $a < c < e$, and *d* is the median. However, if $a = 5$, $b = 1$, $c = 10$, $d = 2$, and $e = 15$, then $a < c < e$, and *a*, not *d*, is the median; NOT sufficient.

   (2)   This indicates that $b < d < c$, but does not indicate a relationship of *a* and *e* with *b*, *d*, and *c*. For example, if $a = 5$, $b = 1$, $c = 10$, $d = 7$, and $e = 15$, then $b < d < c$, and *d* is the median. However, if $a = 5$, $b = 1$, $c = 10$, $d = 2$, and $e = 15$, then $b < d < c$, and *a*, not *d*, is the median; NOT sufficient.

Taking (1) and (2) together is of no more help than either (1) or (2) taken separately since the same examples used to show that (1) is not sufficient also show that (2) is not sufficient.

The correct answer is E;
both statements together are still not sufficient.

DS10383

214. During a certain bicycle ride, was Sherry's average speed faster than 24 kilometers per hour? (1 kilometer = 1,000 meters)

   (1)   Sherry's average speed during the bicycle ride was faster than 7 meters per second.

   (2)   Sherry's average speed during the bicycle ride was slower than 8 meters per second.

Arithmetic Applied problems

This problem can be solved by converting 24 kilometers per hour into meters per second. First, 24 kilometers is equivalent to 24,000 meters and 1 hour is equivalent to 3,600 seconds. Then, traveling 24 kilometers in 1 hour is equivalent to traveling 24,000 meters in 3,600 seconds, or $\dfrac{24,000}{3,600} = 6\dfrac{2}{3}$ meters per second.

   (1)   This indicates that Sherry's average speed was faster than 7 meters per second, which is faster than $6\dfrac{2}{3}$ meters per second and, therefore, faster than 24 kilometers per hour; SUFFICIENT.

   (2)   This indicates that Sherry's average speed was slower than 8 meters per second. Her average speed could have been 7 meters per second (since $7 < 8$), in which case her average speed was faster than $6\dfrac{2}{3}$ meters per second and, therefore, faster than 24 kilometers per hour. Or her average speed could have been 5 meters per second (since $5 < 8$), in which case her average speed was not faster than $6\dfrac{2}{3}$ meters per second and, therefore, not faster than 24 kilometers per hour; NOT sufficient.

The correct answer is A;
statement 1 alone is sufficient.

DS13907

215. Working together, Rafael and Salvador can tabulate a certain set of data in 2 hours. In how many hours can Rafael tabulate the data working alone?

   (1)   Working alone, Rafael can tabulate the data in 3 hours less time than Salvador, working alone, can tabulate the data.

   (2)   Working alone, Rafael can tabulate the data in $\dfrac{1}{2}$ the time that Salvador, working alone, can tabulate the data.

Algebra Simultaneous equations

We are given that Rafael and Salvador, working together, can tabulate the set of data in two hours. That is, if Rafael tabulates data at the rate of *R* units of data per hour and Salvador tabulates the data at the rate of *S* units per hour, then, if the set of data is made up of *D* units, then $2R + 2S = D$. Can we determine how much time, in hours, it takes Rafael to tabulate the data if working alone?

(1) First of all, note that the choice of units used to measure the amounts of data doesn't matter. In particular, we can define one unit of data to be D. Thus, $2R + 2S = 1$. With this in mind, consider the condition that Rafael, when working alone, can tabulate the data in 3 hours less time than Salvador can when working alone. Given that Rafael tabulates R units of data per unit time, he takes $\frac{1}{R}$ units of time to tabulate one unit of data. Similarly, Salvador takes $\frac{1}{S}$ units of time to tabulate one unit of data. This unit, as defined, is simply the entire set of data. Our given condition thus becomes $\frac{1}{R} = \frac{1}{S} - 3$, and we have the set of simultaneous equations made up of this equation and the equation $2R + 2S = 1$.

One way to determine the number of hours it would take Rafael to tabulate the data is to solve one of these equations for S and then substitute this solution into the other equation. Considering the first of these equations, we multiply both sides by RS and then manipulate the result as follows.

$$S = R - 3RS$$
$$S + 3RS = R$$
$$S(1 + 3R) = R$$
$$S = \frac{R}{1 + 3R}$$

Substituting into the equation $2R + 2S = 1$,

$$2R + \frac{2R}{1 + 3R} = 1$$

Multiplying both sides by $1 + 3R$ to eliminate the fraction,

$$2R(1 + 3R) + 2R = 1 + 3R$$
$$2R + 6R^2 = 1 + R$$
$$6R^2 + R - 1 = 0$$
$$(3R - 1)(2R + 1) = 0$$

This equation has two solutions, $-\frac{1}{2}$ and $\frac{1}{3}$. However, because the rate R cannot be negative, we find that Rafael tabulates $\frac{1}{3}$ of a unit of data every hour. Since one unit is the entire set, it takes Rafael 3 hours to tabulate the entire set; SUFFICIENT.

(2) We are given that Rafael, working alone, can tabulate the data in $\frac{1}{2}$ the amount of time it takes Salvador, working alone, to tabulate the data. As in the discussion of statement 1, we have that Rafael tabulates R units of data every hour, and takes $\frac{1}{R}$ hours to tabulate one unit of data. Similarly, it takes Salvador $\frac{1}{S}$ hours to tabulate one unit of data. One unit of data has been defined to be the size of the entire set to be tabulated, so statement 2 becomes the expression

$$\frac{1}{R} = \frac{1}{2} \times \frac{1}{S} = \frac{1}{2S}$$

We thus have $2S = R$. Substituting this value for $2S$ in the equation $2R + 2S = 1$, we have $R + 2R = 1$, and $3R = 1$. Solving for R we get $\frac{1}{3}$; SUFFICIENT.

Note that, for both statements 1 and 2, it would have been possible to stop calculating once we had determined whether it was possible to find a unique value for R. The ability to make such judgments accurately is part of what the test has been designed to measure.

The correct answer is D;

each statement alone is sufficient.

DS04039

216. If x and y are integers, what is the value of x ?

(1) $xy = 1$

(2) $x \neq -1$

Arithmetic Properties of integers

Given that x and y are integers, determine the value of x.

(1) If $x = y = -1$, then $xy = 1$, and if $x = y = 1$, then $xy = 1$; NOT sufficient.

(2) Given that $x \neq -1$, the value of x could be any other integer; NOT sufficient.

Taking (1) and (2) together, since the two possibilities for the value of x are $x = -1$ or $x = 1$ by (1), and $x \neq -1$ by (2), then $x = 1$.

The correct answer is C;
both statements together are sufficient.

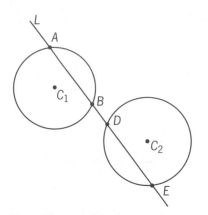

Note: Figure not drawn to scale.

DS18386

217. The figure above shows Line L, Circle 1 with center at C_1, and Circle 2 with center at C_2. Line L intersects Circle 1 at points A and B, Line L intersects Circle 2 at points D and E, and points C_1 and C_2 are equidistant from line L. Is the area of $\triangle ABC_1$ less than the area of $\triangle DEC_2$?

   (1)   The radius of Circle 1 is less than the radius of Circle 2.

   (2)   The length of chord $\overline{AB}$ is less than the length of chord $\overline{DE}$.

Geometry Triangles

We are given various elements of information that apply regardless of whether we assume that statements 1, 2, or both are true, and asked whether it is possible, when considering one or both of these statements, to determine if the area of triangle $\triangle ABC_1$ is less than the area of $\triangle DEC_2$.

   (1)   Given the condition that the radius of Circle 1 is less than the radius of Circle 2, it may be useful to consider the following diagrams of the triangles, in which they have been rotated so as to have the sides AB and DE represented as horizontal and on the bottom. The diagrams are not drawn to scale.

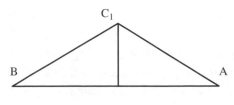

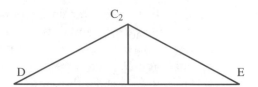

Note that the radius of the Circle 1 is equal to (the length) $C_1B (= C_1A)$ and that the radius of Circle 2 is equal to $C_2D (= C_2E)$. Furthermore, because line L is equidistant from points C_1 and C_2, we know that the respective heights of the triangles (distances from C_1 and C_2 to the respective bases BA and DE) are the same. However, because (with statement 1) the radius of Circle 1 is less than the radius of Circle 2, we know that C_1B and C_1A are less than C_2D and C_2E. Because the triangles have the same height, triangle $\triangle ABC_1$ must be less "wide" than $\triangle DEC_2$ and must thus have a lesser base (length). And because the area of a triangle is always $\frac{1}{2} \times$ base $\times$ height, we can infer that the area of $\triangle ABC_1$ is less than the area of $\triangle DEC_2$; SUFFICIENT.

   (2)   Given that AB is less than DE, we can infer that the area of $\triangle ABC_1$ is less than the area of $\triangle DEC_2$. After all, we know that the heights of the two triangles are the same (because, as discussed in connection with statement 1, line L is equidistant from C_1 and C_2). The formula for the area of a triangle, $\frac{1}{2} \times$ base $\times$ height, thus allows us to make our inference; SUFFICIENT.

The correct answer is D; each statement alone is sufficient.

DS15938

218. Yesterday between 9:00 a.m. and 6:00 p.m. at Airport X, all flights to Atlanta departed at equally spaced times and all flights to New York City departed at equally spaced times. A flight to Atlanta and a flight to New York City both departed from Airport X at 1:00 p.m. yesterday. Between 1:00 p.m. and 3:00 p.m. yesterday, did another pair of flights to these 2 cities depart from Airport X at the same time?

   (1)   Yesterday at Airport X, a flight to Atlanta and a flight to New York City both departed at 10:00 a.m.

   (2)   Yesterday at Airport X, flights to New York City departed every 15 minutes between 9:00 a.m. and 6:00 p.m.

Arithmetic Applied problems

It is useful to note that although the departures discussed all lie between 9:00 a.m. and 6:00 p.m., there is no information concerning when the first departures took place during this time other than what is necessary for the information to be consistent. For example, since departures to both Atlanta and New York City took place at 1:00 p.m., the first departure to either of these cities could not have occurred after 1:00 p.m.

(1) Given that departures to both Atlanta and New York City took place at 10:00 a.m., it is not possible to determine whether simultaneous departures to these cities occurred between 1:00 p.m. and 3:00 p.m. For example, it is possible that departures to both Atlanta and New York City took place every 15 minutes beginning at 9:15 a.m., and thus it is possible that simultaneous departures to both these cities occurred between 1:00 p.m. and 3:00 p.m. However, it is also possible that departures to Atlanta took place every 3 hours beginning at 10:00 a.m. and departures to New York City took place every 15 minutes beginning at 9:15 a.m., and thus it is possible that no simultaneous departures to these cities occurred between 1:00 p.m. and 3:00 p.m.; NOT sufficient.

(2) Given that departures to New York City took place every 15 minutes, the same examples used in (1) can be used to show that it is not possible to determine whether simultaneous departures to these cities occurred between 1:00 p.m. and 3:00 p.m.; NOT sufficient.

Taking (1) and (2) together, it is still not possible to determine whether simultaneous departures to these cities occurred between 1:00 p.m. and 3:00 p.m. because both (1) and (2) are true for the examples above.

The correct answer is E;

both statements together are still not sufficient.

DS07206
219. Of the total number of copies of Magazine X sold last week, 40 percent were sold at full price. What was the total number of copies of the magazine sold last week?

(1) Last week, full price for a copy of Magazine X was $1.50 and the total revenue from full-price sales was $112,500.

(2) The total number of copies of Magazine X sold last week at full price was 75,000.

Algebra Applied problems

For the copies of Magazine X sold last week, let n be the total number of copies sold and let $\$p$ be the full price of each copy. Then for Magazine X last week, a total of $0.4n$ copies were each sold at price $\$p$. What is the value of n?

(1) Given that $\$p = 1.50$ and $(0.4n)(\$p) = \$112,500$, it follows that $(0.4n)(1.5) = 112,500$, or $0.6n = 112,500$, or $n = \dfrac{112,500}{0.6}$; SUFFICIENT.

(2) Given that $0.4n = 75,000$, it follows that $n = \dfrac{75,000}{0.4}$; SUFFICIENT.

The correct answer is D;

each statement alone is sufficient.

DS11614
220. If p, s, and t are positive, is $|ps - pt| > p(s - t)$?

(1) $p < s$

(2) $s < t$

Algebra Absolute value

Since p is positive, it follows that $|p(s - t)| = |p||s - t| = p|s - t|$. Therefore, the task is to determine if $|s - t| > s - t$. Since $|s - t| = s - t$ if and only if $s - t \geq 0$, it follows that $|s - t| > s - t$ if and only if $s - t < 0$.

(1) This indicates that $p < s$ but does not provide information about the relationship between s and t. For example, if $p = 5$, $s = 10$, and $t = 15$, then $p < s$ and $s < t$, but if $p = 5$, $s = 10$, and $t = 3$, then $p < s$ and $s > t$; NOT sufficient.

(2) This indicates that $s < t$, or equivalently, $s - t < 0$; SUFFICIENT.

The correct answer is B;

statement 2 alone is sufficient.

221. Is $x > y$?

(1) $x + y > x - y$

(2) $3x > 2y$

Algebra Inequalities

(1) Given that $x + y > x - y$, it follows that $y > -y$, or $2y > 0$, or $y > 0$. However, nothing is known about the value of x. If $x = 2$ and $y = 1$, then $x + y > x - y$ and the answer to the question is yes. However, if $x = 1$ and $y = 1$, then $x + y > x - y$ and the answer to the question is no; NOT sufficient.

(2) Given that $3x > 2y$, then $x = 2$ and $y = 1$ is possible and the answer to the question is yes. However, if $3x > 2y$, then $x = 1$ and $y = 1$ is also possible and the answer to the question is no; NOT sufficient.

Taking (1) and (2) together is of no more help than either (1) or (2) taken separately because the same examples used to show that (1) is not sufficient also show that (2) is not sufficient.

The correct answer is E;
both statements together are still not sufficient.

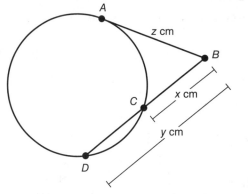

222. In the figure above, $\overline{AB}$, which has length z cm, is tangent to the circle at point A, and $\overline{BD}$, which has length y cm, intersects the circle at point C. If $BC = x$ cm and $z = \sqrt{xy}$, what is the value of x ?

(1) $CD = x$ cm

(2) $z = 5\sqrt{2}$

Geometry Circles

(1) Given that $CD = x$ cm, it is not possible to determine the value of x because all the given information continues to hold when all the parts of the figure increase in length by any given nonzero factor; NOT sufficient.

(2) Given that $z = 5\sqrt{2}$, the value of x will vary when the radius of the circle varies and $\overline{CD}$ is a diameter and thus passes through the center of the circle. To see this, let r be the radius, in centimeters, of the circle and let O be the center of the circle, as shown in the figure below. Then, because $\overline{CD}$ is a diameter, it follows that $CD = 2r$ and $y = x + CD = x + 2r$. Also, $\triangle OAB$ is a right triangle and the Pythagorean theorem gives $(OA)^2 + (AB)^2 = (OB)^2$, or $r^2 + (5\sqrt{2})^2 = (x + r)^2$, or $r^2 + 50 = x^2 + 2xr + r^2$, or $x(x + 2r) = 50$, which implies that $xy = z^2$ and $z = \sqrt{xy}$, since $y = x + 2r$ and $z = 5\sqrt{2}$. Therefore, if $z = 5\sqrt{2}$ and $\overline{CD}$ is a diameter, then $z = \sqrt{xy}$ holds, and the value of x can vary.

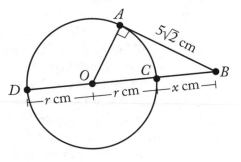

This can be seen by considering the equation $x(x + 2r) = 50$, or $x = \dfrac{50}{x + 2r}$. If the value of r changes slightly to a new value R, then the value of x must also change. Otherwise, there would be two different numbers, namely $\dfrac{50}{x + 2r}$ and $\dfrac{50}{x + 2R}$, equal to each other, which is a contradiction; NOT sufficient.

Taking (1) and (2) together, $y = x + CD = x + x = 2x$ and $z = 5\sqrt{2}$, so $z = \sqrt{xy}$ becomes $5\sqrt{2} = \sqrt{x(2x)}$, or $(5\sqrt{2})^2 = (\sqrt{x(2x)})^2$, or $50 = x(2x)$, or $x^2 = 25$, or $x = 5$.

The correct answer is C;
both statements together are sufficient.

223. Is the integer *n* a prime number?

    (1) $24 \leq n \leq 28$
    (2) *n* is not divisible by 2 or 3.

Arithmetic Properties of numbers

Determine if the integer *n* is a prime number.

(1) This indicates that *n* is between 24 and 28, inclusive. It follows that the value of *n* can be 24, 25, 26, 27, or 28. Each of these is NOT a prime number. Thus, it can be determined that *n* is NOT a prime number; SUFFICIENT.

(2) This indicates that *n* is not divisible by 2 or 3. If *n* = 7, then *n* is not divisible by 2 or 3 and is a prime number. However, if *n* = 25, then *n* is not divisible by 2 or 3 and is a not prime number since 25 has a factor, namely 5, other than 1 and itself; NOT sufficient.

The correct answer is A; statement 1 alone is sufficient.

224. What is the average (arithmetic mean) annual salary of the 6 employees of a toy company?

    (1) If the 6 annual salaries were ordered from least to greatest, each annual salary would be $6,300 greater than the preceding annual salary.
    (2) The range of the 6 annual salaries is $31,500.

Arithmetic Statistics

Can we determine the arithmetic mean of the annual salaries of the 6 employees?

(1) Given only that the 6 annual salaries can be put into a sequence from least to greatest, with a difference of $6,300 between adjacent members of the sequence, we can infer certain things about the mean of the salaries. For example, because none of the salaries would be negative, we know from statement 1 that the mean of the salaries is greater than or equal to

$$\frac{0 + \$6,300 + \$12,600 + \$18,900 + \$25,200 + \$31,500}{6}.$$

(It is not necessary to perform this calculation.) However, depending on what the least of the salaries is—that is, the value at which the sequence of salaries begins—

the average of the salaries could, consistent with condition 1, take on any value greater than this quotient; NOT sufficient.

(2) Given the statement that the range of the salaries is $31,500, reasoning similar to the reasoning for statement 1 applies. A difference between least salary and greatest salary of $31,500 is consistent with any value for the least salary, so long as the greatest salary is $31,500 greater than the least salary. Furthermore, even if we knew what the least and the greatest salaries are, it would be impossible to determine the mean merely from the range; NOT sufficient.

As reflected in the numerator of the quotient in the discussion of statement 1, we can see that statement 1 implies statement 2. In the sequence of 6 salaries with a difference of $6,300 between adjacent members of the sequence, the difference between the least salary and the greatest salary is 5 × $6,300 = $31,500. Therefore, because statement 1 is insufficient for determining the mean of the salaries, the combination of statement 1 and statement 2 is also insufficient for determining the mean of the salaries.

The correct answer is E; both statements together are not sufficient.

225. In a certain order, the pretax price of each regular pencil was $0.03, the pretax price of each deluxe pencil was $0.05, and there were 50% more deluxe pencils than regular pencils. All taxes on the order are a fixed percent of the pretax prices. The sum of the total pretax price of the order and the tax on the order was $44.10. What was the amount, in dollars, of the tax on the order?

    (1) The tax on the order was 5% of the total pretax price of the order.
    (2) The order contained exactly 400 regular pencils.

Arithmetic Percents

Let *n* be the number of regular pencils in the order and let *r*% be the tax rate on the order as a percent of the pretax price. Then the order contains 1.5*n* deluxe pencils, the total pretax price of the order is ($0.03)*n* + ($0.05)(1.5*n*) = $0.105*n*, and the sum of the total pretax price of the order and the tax on the order is $\left(1+\dfrac{r}{100}\right)(\$0.105n)$. Given that

$\left(1+\dfrac{r}{100}\right)(\$0.105n) = \$44.10$, what is the value

of $\left(\dfrac{r}{100}\right)(\$0.105n)$?

(1)   Given that $r = 5$, then $\left(1+\dfrac{r}{100}\right)(\$0.105n)$

   $= \$44.10$ becomes $(1.05)(0.105n) = 44.10$,
   which is a first-degree equation that can be
   solved for n. Since the value of r is known
   and the value of n can be determined, it

   follows that the value of $\left(\dfrac{r}{100}\right)(\$0.105n)$

   can be determined; SUFFICIENT.

(2)   Given that $n = 400$, then

   $\left(1+\dfrac{r}{100}\right)(\$0.105n) = \$44.10$ becomes

   $\left(1+\dfrac{r}{100}\right)(0.105)(400) = 44.10$, which is a

   first-degree equation that can be solved
   for r. Since the value of r can be determined
   and the value of n is known, it follows

   that the value of $\left(\dfrac{r}{100}\right)(\$0.105n)$ can be

   determined; SUFFICIENT.

The correct answer is D;
each statement alone is sufficient.

DS06785

226. If m is an integer greater than 1, is m an even integer?

(1)   32 is a factor of m.

(2) m is a factor of 32.

Arithmetic Properties of numbers

(1)   Given that 32 is a factor of m, then each of
   the factors of 32, including 2, is a factor of m.
   Since 2 is a factor of m, it follows that m is
   an even integer; SUFFICIENT.

(2)   Given that m is a factor of 32 and m is
   greater than 1, it follows that $m = 2, 4, 8, 16$,
   or 32. Since each of these is an even integer,
   m must be an even integer; SUFFICIENT.

The correct answer is D;
each statement alone is sufficient.

DS05657

227. If the set S consists of five consecutive positive
integers, what is the sum of these five integers?

(1)   The integer 11 is in S, but 10 is not in S.

(2)   The sum of the even integers in S is 26.

Arithmetic Sequences

(1)   This indicates that the least integer in
   S is 11 since S consists of consecutive
   integers and 11 is in S, but 10 is not in S.
   Thus, the integers in S are 11, 12, 13, 14,
   and 15, and their sum can be determined;
   SUFFICIENT.

(2)   This indicates that the sum of the even
   integers in S is 26. In a set of 5 consecutive
   integers, either two of the integers or three of
   the integers are even. If there are three even
   integers, then the first integer in S must be

   even. Also, since $\dfrac{26}{3} = 8\dfrac{2}{3}$, the three even

   integers must be around 8. The three even
   integers could be 6, 8, and 10, but are not
   because their sum is less than 26; or they
   could be 8, 10, and 12, but are not because
   their sum is greater than 26. Therefore, S
   cannot contain three even integers and
   must contain only two even integers. Those
   integers must be 12 and 14 since $12 + 14$
   $= 26$. It follows that the integers in S are
   11, 12, 13, 14, and 15, and their sum can be
   determined; SUFFICIENT.

Alternately, if $n, n + 1, n + 2, n + 3$, and $n + 4$
represent the five consecutive integers and three
of them are even, then $n + (n + 2) + (n + 4) = 26$,

or $3n = 20$, or $n = \dfrac{20}{3}$, which is not an integer.

On the other hand, if two of the integers are
even, then $(n + 1) + (n + 3) = 26$, or $2n = 22$, or
$n = 11$. It follows that the integers are 11, 12, 13,
14, and 15, and their sum can be determined;
SUFFICIENT.

The correct answer is D;
each statement alone is sufficient.

DS17543

228. If $x > 0$, what is the value of x ?

(1) $x^3 - x = 0$

(2) $\sqrt[3]{x} - x = 0$

Algebra Factoring; Operations with radical expressions

(1) Given that $x^3 - x = 0$, factoring gives $x(x^2 - 1) = x(x - 1)(x + 1) = 0$. Hence, $x = 0$, $x = 1$, or $x = -1$. Since $x > 0$, the value of x cannot be 0 or -1, and so $x = 1$; SUFFICIENT.

(2) Given that $\sqrt[3]{x} - x = 0$, it follows that $\sqrt[3]{x} = x$, or $(\sqrt[3]{x})^3 = x^3$, or $x = x^3$. Therefore, $x^3 - x = 0$ and the discussion in (1) shows that the only positive value of x is $x = 1$; SUFFICIENT.

The correct answer is D; each statement alone is sufficient.

DS08307
229. A total of 20 amounts are entered on a spreadsheet that has 5 rows and 4 columns; each of the 20 positions in the spreadsheet contains one amount. The average (arithmetic mean) of the amounts in row i is R_i ($1 \le i \le 5$). The average of the amounts in column j is C_j ($1 \le j \le 4$). What is the average of all 20 amounts on the spreadsheet?

(1) $R_1 + R_2 + R_3 + R_4 + R_5 = 550$

(2) $C_1 + C_2 + C_3 + C_4 = 440$

Arithmetic Statistics

It is given that R_i represents the average of the amounts in row i. Since there are four amounts in each row, $4R_i$ represents the total of the amounts in row i. Likewise, it is given that C_j represents the average of the amounts in column j. Since there are five amounts in each column, $5C_j$ represents the total of the amounts in column j.

(1) It is given that $R_1 + R_2 + R_3 + R_4 + R_5 = 550$, and so $4(R_1 + R_2 + R_3 + R_4 + R_5) = 4R_1 + 4R_2 + 4R_3 + 4R_4 + 4R_5 = 4(550) = 2{,}200$. Therefore, 2,200 is the sum of all 20 amounts (4 amounts in each of 5 rows), and the average of all 20 amounts is $\frac{2{,}200}{20} = 110$; SUFFICIENT.

(2) It is given that $C_1 + C_2 + C_3 + C_4 = 440$, and so $5(C_1 + C_2 + C_3 + C_4) = 5C_1 + 5C_2 + 5C_3 + 5C_4 = 5(440) = 2{,}200$. Therefore, 2,200 is the sum of all 20 amounts (5 amounts in each of

4 columns), and the average of all 20 amounts is $\frac{2{,}200}{20} = 110$; SUFFICIENT.

The correct answer is D; each statement alone is sufficient.

DS13132
230. Was the range of the amounts of money that Company Y budgeted for its projects last year equal to the range of the amounts of money that it budgeted for its projects this year?

(1) Both last year and this year, Company Y budgeted money for 12 projects and the least amount of money that it budgeted for a project was $400.

(2) Both last year and this year, the average (arithmetic mean) amount of money that Company Y budgeted per project was $2,000.

Arithmetic Statistics

Let G_1 and L_1 represent the greatest and least amounts, respectively, of money that Company Y budgeted for its projects last year, and let G_2 and L_2 represent the greatest and least amounts, respectively, of money that Company Y budgeted for its projects this year. Determine if the range of the amounts of money Company Y budgeted for its projects last year is equal to the range of amounts budgeted for its projects this year; that is, determine if $G_1 - L_1 = G_2 - L_2$.

(1) This indicates that $L_1 = L_2 = \$400$, but does not give any information about G_1 or G_2; NOT sufficient.

(2) This indicates that the average amount Company Y budgeted for its projects both last year and this year was $2,000 per project, but does not give any information about the least and greatest amounts that it budgeted for its projects either year; NOT sufficient.

Taking (1) and (2) together, it is known that $L_1 = L_2 = \$400$ and that the average amount Company Y budgeted for its projects both last year and this year was $2,000 per project, but there is no information about G_1 or G_2. For example, if, for each year, Company Y budgeted $400 for each of 2 projects and $2,320 for each of the 10 others, then (1) and (2) are true and the range for each year was $2,320 – $400 = $1,920. However, if, last year, Company Y budgeted $400 for each of 2 projects and $2,320 for each of the 10 others, and, this year, budgeted $400 for each of 11 projects and $19,600 for 1 project, then (1) and (2) are true, but the range for last year was $1,920 and the range for this year was $19,600 – $400 = $19,200.

The correct answer is E;
both statements together are still not sufficient.

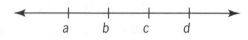

DS01633

231. If a, b, c, and d are numbers on the number line shown and if the tick marks are equally spaced, what is the value of $a + c$?

(1) $a + b = -8$

(2) $a + d = 0$

Algebra Sequences

It is given that the distance between a and b is the same as the distance between b and c, which is the same as the distance between c and d. Letting q represent this distance, then $b = a + q$, $c = a + 2q$, and $d = a + 3q$. The value of $a + c$ can be determined if the value of $a + (a + 2q) = 2a + 2q$ can be determined.

(1)   It is given that $a + b = -8$. Then, $a + (a + q) = 2a + q = -8$. From this, the value of $2a + 2q$ cannot be determined. For example, the values of a and q could be -5 and 2, respectively, or they could be -6 and 4, respectively; NOT sufficient.

(2)   It is given that $a + d = 0$. Then, $a + (a + 3q) = 2a + 3q = 0$. From this, the value of $2a + 2q$ cannot be determined. For example, the values of a and q could be -3 and 2, respectively, or they could be -6 and 4, respectively; NOT sufficient.

Taking (1) and (2) together, adding the equations, $2a + q = -8$ and $2a + 3q = 0$ gives $4a + 4q = -8$ and so $2a + 2q = \dfrac{-8}{2} = -4$.

The correct answer is C;
both statements together are sufficient.

DS06067

232. Is $xm < ym$?

(1) $x > y$

(2) $m < 0$

Algebra Inequalities

(1)   Given that $x > y$, the inequality $xm < ym$ can be true (for example, if $m = -1$, then $xm < ym$ becomes $-x < -y$, or $x > y$, which is true by assumption) and it is possible that the inequality $xm < ym$ can be false (for example, if $m = 0$, then $xm < ym$ becomes $0 < 0$, which is false); NOT sufficient.

(2)   Given that $m < 0$, the inequality $xm < ym$ can be true (for example, if $m = -1$, $x = 2$, and $y = 1$, then $xm < ym$ becomes $-2 < -1$, which is true) and it is possible that the inequality $xm < ym$ can be false (for example, if $m = -1$, $x = 1$, and $y = 2$, then $xm < ym$ becomes $-1 < -2$, which is false); NOT sufficient.

Taking (1) and (2) together, multiplying both sides of the inequality $x > y$ by m reverses the inequality sign (since $m < 0$), which gives $xm < ym$.

The correct answer is C;
both statements together are sufficient.

DS02899

233. If $y = x^2 - 6x + 9$, what is the value of x ?

(1) $y = 0$

(2) $x + y = 3$

Algebra Second-degree equations

Given that $y = x^2 - 6x + 9 = (x - 3)^2$, what is the value of x ?

(1)   Given that $y = 0$, it follows that $(x - 3)^2 = 0$, or $x = 3$; SUFFICIENT.

(2)   Given that $x + y = 3$, or $y = 3 - x$, then $x = 3$ and $y = 0$ are possible, since $y = (x - 3)^2$ becomes $0 = (3 - 3)^2$, which is true, and $y = 3 - x$ becomes $0 = 3 - 3$, which is true. However, $x = 2$ and $y = 1$ are also possible, since $y = (x - 3)^2$ becomes $1 = (2 - 3)^2$, which is true, and $y = 3 - x$ becomes $1 = 3 - 2$, which is true; NOT sufficient.

Note: The values for x and y used in (2) above can be found by solving $(x-3)^2 = 3 - x$, which can be rewritten as $x^2 - 6x + 9 = 3 - x$, or $x^2 - 5x + 6 = 0$, or $(x-3)(x-2) = 0$.

The correct answer is A;
statement 1 alone is sufficient.

DS06810

234. What is the probability that Lee will make exactly 5 errors on a certain typing test?

(1) The probability that Lee will make 5 or more errors on the test is 0.27.

(2) The probability that Lee will make 5 or fewer errors on the test is 0.85.

Arithmetic Probability

(1) Given that 0.27 is the probability that Lee will make 5 or more errors on the test, it is clearly not possible to determine the probability that Lee will make exactly 5 errors on the test; NOT sufficient.

(2) Given that 0.85 is the probability that Lee will make 5 or fewer errors on the test, it is clearly not possible to determine the probability that Lee will make exactly 5 errors on the test; NOT sufficient.

Taking (1) and (2) together, let E be the event that Lee will make 5 or more errors on the test and let F be the event that Lee will make 5 or fewer errors on the test. Then $P(E \text{ or } F) = 1$, since it will always be the case that, when taking the test, Lee will make at least 5 errors or at most 5 errors. Also, (1) and (2) can be expressed as $P(E) = 0.27$ and $P(F) = 0.85$, and the question asks for the value of $P(E \text{ and } F)$. Using the identity $P(E \text{ or } F) = P(E) + P(F) - P(E \text{ and } F)$, it follows that $1 = 0.27 + 0.85 - P(E \text{ and } F)$, or $P(E \text{ and } F) = 0.27 + 0.85 - 1 = 0.12$. Therefore, the probability that Lee will make exactly 5 errors on the test is 0.12.

The correct answer is C;
both statements together are sufficient.

DS19208

235. If p is a positive integer, is $2^p + 1$ a prime number?

(1) p is a prime number.

(2) p is an even number.

Arithmetic Properties of integers

Given that p is a positive integer, can we determine whether $2^p + 1$ is a prime number?

(1) Given that p is a prime number, we don't have enough information to determine whether $2^p + 1$ is a prime number. To see this, it best to consider some cases. If $p = 2$, then $2^p + 1 = 2^2 + 1 = 2 \times 2 + 1 = 4 + 1 = 5$, which is prime. And if $p = 3$, then $2^p + 1 = 2^3 + 1 = 2 \times 2 \times 2 + 1 = 8 + 1 = 9$, which is not prime (it is equal to 3×3); NOT sufficient.

(2) Given that p is an even number, we can again consider cases and see that it is impossible to determine whether $2^p + 1$ is a prime number. If $p = 2$ then $2^p + 1 = 2^2 + 1 = 4 + 1 = 5$, which, again, is prime. And if $p = 6$, then $2^p + 1 = 2^6 + 1 = 2 \times 2 \times 2 \times 2 \times 2 \times 2 + 1 = (2 \times 2 \times 2) \times (2 \times 2 \times 2) + 1 = 8 \times 8 + 1 = 64 + 1 = 65$, which is not prime (it is equal to 13×5); NOT sufficient.

Considering the two statements together, we have that p is both prime and even. The only even number that is not divisible by some other positive integer besides 1 is 2. That is, the only prime even integer is 2. $2^p + 1$ is therefore equal to $2^2 + 1 = 5$, which is prime.

The correct answer is C;
both statements together are sufficient.

DS02741

236. In the xy-plane, point (r,s) lies on a circle with center at the origin. What is the value of $r^2 + s^2$?

(1) The circle has radius 2.

(2) The point $\left(\sqrt{2}, -\sqrt{2}\right)$ lies on the circle.

Geometry Simple coordinate geometry

Let R be the radius of the circle. A right triangle with legs of lengths $|r|$ and $|s|$ can be formed so that the line segment with endpoints (r,s) and $(0,0)$ is the hypotenuse. Since the length of the hypotenuse is R, the Pythagorean theorem for this right triangle gives $R^2 = r^2 + s^2$. Therefore, to determine the value of $r^2 + s^2$, it is sufficient to determine the value of R.

(1) It is given that $R = 2$; SUFFICIENT.

(2) It is given that $\left(\sqrt{2}, -\sqrt{2}\right)$ lies on the circle. A right triangle with legs each of length $\sqrt{2}$ can be formed so that the line segment with endpoints $\left(\sqrt{2}, -\sqrt{2}\right)$ and $(0,0)$ is the hypotenuse. Since the length of the hypotenuse is the radius of the circle, which is R, where $R^2 = r^2 + s^2$, the Pythagorean theorem for this right triangle gives $R^2 = \left(\sqrt{2}\right)^2 + \left(\sqrt{2}\right)^2 = 2 + 2 = 4$. Therefore, $r^2 + s^2 = 4$; SUFFICIENT.

The correct answer is D; each statement alone is sufficient.

DS06368

237. If r, s, and t are nonzero integers, is $r^5 s^3 t^4$ negative?

(1) rt is negative.

(2) s is negative.

Arithmetic Properties of numbers

Since $r^5 s^3 t^4 = (rt)^4 r s^3$ and $(rt)^4$ is positive, $r^5 s^3 t^4$ will be negative if and only if $r s^3$ is negative, or if and only if r and s have opposite signs.

(1) It is given that rt is negative, but nothing can be determined about the sign of s. If the sign of s is the opposite of the sign of r, then $r^5 s^3 t^4 = (rt)^4 r s^3$ will be negative. However, if the sign of s is the same as the sign of r, then $r^5 s^3 t^4 = (rt)^4 r s^3$ will be positive; NOT sufficient.

(2) It is given that s is negative, but nothing can be determined about the sign of r. If r is positive, then $r^5 s^3 t^4 = (rt)^4 r s^3$ will be negative. However, if r is negative, then $r^5 s^3 t^4 = (rt)^4 r s^3$ will be positive; NOT sufficient.

Given (1) and (2), it is still not possible to determine whether r and s have opposite signs. For example, (1) and (2) hold if r is positive, s is negative, and t is negative, and in this case r and s have opposite signs. However, (1) and (2) hold if r is negative, s is negative, and t is positive, and in this case r and s have the same sign.

The correct answer is E; both statements together are still not sufficient.

DS13706

238. Each Type A machine fills 400 cans per minute, each Type B machine fills 600 cans per minute, and each Type C machine installs 2,400 lids per minute. A lid is installed on each can that is filled and on no can that is not filled. For a particular minute, what is the total number of machines working?

(1) A total of 4,800 cans are filled that minute.

(2) For that minute, there are 2 Type B machines working for every Type C machine working.

Algebra Simultaneous equations

(1) Given that 4,800 cans were filled that minute, it is possible that 12 Type A machines, no Type B machines, and 2 Type C machines were working, for a total of 14 machines, since $(12)(400) + (0)(600) = 4,800$ and $(2)(2,400) = 4,800$. However, it is also possible that no Type A machines, 8 Type B machines, and 2 Type C machines were working, for a total of 10 machines, since $(0)(400) + (8)(600) = 4,800$ and $(2)(2,400) = 4,800$; NOT sufficient.

(2) Given that there are 2 Type B machines working for every Type C machine working, it is possible that there are 6 machines working—3 Type A machines, 2 Type B machines, and 1 Type C machine. This gives $3(400) + 2(600) = 2,400$ cans and $1(2,400) = 2,400$ lids. It is also possible that there are 12 machines working—6 Type A machines, 4 Type B machines, and 2 Type C machines. This gives $6(400) + 4(600) = 4,800$ cans and $2(2,400) = 4,800$ lids; NOT sufficient.

Taking (1) and (2) together, since there were 4,800 cans filled that minute, there were 4,800 lids installed that minute. It follows that 2 Type C machines were working that minute, since $(2)(2,400) = 4,800$. Since there were twice this number of Type B machines working that minute, it follows that 4 Type B machines were working that minute. These 4 Type B machines filled $(4)(600) = 2,400$ cans that minute, leaving $4,800 - 2,400 = 2,400$ cans to be filled by Type A machines. Therefore, the number of Type A machines working that minute was $\dfrac{2,400}{400} = 6$, and it follows that the total number of machines working that minute was $2 + 4 + 6 = 12$.

**The correct answer is C;
both statements together are sufficient.**

DS08660

239. If a and b are constants, what is the value of a ?

(1)　$a < b$

(2)　$(t - a)(t - b) = t^2 + t - 12$, for all values of t.

Algebra Second-degree equations

(1) Given that $a < b$, it is not possible to determine the value of a. For example, $a < b$ is true when $a = 1$ and $b = 2$, and $a < b$ is true when $a = 2$ and $b = 3$; NOT sufficient.

(2) By factoring, what is given can be expressed as $(t - a)(t - b) = (t + 4)(t - 3)$, so either $a = -4$ and $b = 3$, or $a = 3$ and $b = -4$; NOT sufficient.

Taking (1) and (2) together, the relation $a < b$ is satisfied by only one of the two possibilities given in the discussion of (2) above, namely $a = -4$ and $b = 3$. Therefore, the value of a is -4.

**The correct answer is C;
both statements together are sufficient.**

DS04474

240. If x is a positive integer, is $\sqrt{x}$ an integer?

(1)　$\sqrt{4x}$ is an integer.

(2)　$\sqrt{3x}$ is not an integer.

Algebra Radicals

(1) It is given that $\sqrt{4x} = n$, or $4x = n^2$, for some positive integer n. Since $4x$ is the square of an integer, it follows that in the prime factorization of $4x$, each distinct prime factor is repeated an even number of times. Therefore, the same must be true for the prime factorization of x, since the prime factorization of x only differs from the prime factorization of $4x$ by two factors of 2, and hence by an even number of factors of 2; SUFFICIENT.

(2) Given that $\sqrt{3x}$ is not an integer, it is possible for $\sqrt{x}$ to be an integer (for example, $x = 1$) and it is possible for $\sqrt{x}$ to not be an integer (for example, $x = 2$); NOT sufficient.

**The correct answer is A;
statement 1 alone is sufficient.**

DS16456

241. If p, q, x, y, and z are different positive integers, which of the five integers is the median?

(1)　$p + x < q$

(2)　$y < z$

Arithmetic Statistics

Since there are five different integers, there are two integers greater and two integers less than the median, which is the middle number.

(1) No information is given about the order of y and z with respect to the other three numbers; NOT sufficient.

(2) This statement does not relate y and z to the other three integers; NOT sufficient.

Because (1) and (2) taken together do not relate p, x, and q to y and z, it is impossible to tell which is the median. For example, if $p = 3$, $x = 4$, $q = 8$, $y = 9$, and $z = 10$, then the median is 8, but if $p = 3$, $x = 4$, $q = 8$, $y = 1$, and $z = 2$, then the median is 3.

**The correct answer is E;
both statements together are still not sufficient.**

DS16277

242. If $w + z = 28$, what is the value of wz ?

(1)　w and z are positive integers.

(2)　w and z are consecutive odd integers.

Arithmetic Arithmetic operations

(1) The fact that w and z are both positive integers does not allow the values of w and z to be determined because, for example, if $w = 20$ and $z = 8$, then $wz = 160$, and if $w = 10$ and $z = 18$, then $wz = 180$; NOT sufficient.

(2) Since w and z are consecutive odd integers whose sum is 28, it is reasonable to consider the possibilities for the sum of consecutive odd integers: $\ldots, (-5) + (-3) = -8$, $(-3) + (-1) = -4, (-1) + 1 = 0, 1 + 3 = 4, \ldots,$ $9 + 11 = 20, 11 + 13 = 24, 13 + 15 = 28,$ $15 + 17 = 32, \ldots.$ From this list it follows that only one pair of consecutive odd integers has 28 for its sum, and hence there is exactly one possible value for wz.

This problem can also be solved algebraically by letting the consecutive odd integers w and

z be represented by $2n + 1$ and $2n + 3$, where n can be any integer. Since $28 = w + z$, it follows that

$$28 = (2n+1)+(2n+3)$$

$28 = 4n + 4$ simplify

$24 = 4n$ subtract 4 from both sides

$6 = n$ divide both sides by 4

Thus, $w = 2(6) + 1 = 13$, $z = 2(6) + 3 = 15$, and hence exactly one value can be determined for wz; SUFFICIENT.

**The correct answer is B;
statement 2 alone is sufficient.**

DS02474

243. If $abc \neq 0$, is $\dfrac{\frac{a}{b}}{c} = \dfrac{a}{\frac{b}{c}}$?

  (1) $a = 1$

  (2) $c = 1$

Algebra Fractions

Since $\dfrac{\frac{a}{b}}{c} = \dfrac{a}{b} \div c = \dfrac{a}{b} \times \dfrac{1}{c} = \dfrac{a}{bc}$ and

$\dfrac{a}{\frac{b}{c}} = a \div \dfrac{b}{c} = a \times \dfrac{c}{b} = \dfrac{ac}{b}$, it is to be

determined whether $\dfrac{a}{bc} = \dfrac{ac}{b}$.

  (1)   Given that $a = 1$, the equation to be

investigated, $\dfrac{a}{bc} = \dfrac{ac}{b}$, is $\dfrac{1}{bc} = \dfrac{c}{b}$. This equation can be true for some nonzero values of b and c (for example, $b = c = 1$) and false for other nonzero values of b and c (for example, $b = 1$ and $c = 2$); NOT sufficient.

  (2)   Given that $c = 1$, the equation to be

investigated, $\dfrac{a}{bc} = \dfrac{ac}{b}$, is $\dfrac{a}{b} = \dfrac{a}{b}$. This equation is true for all nonzero values of a and b; SUFFICIENT.

**The correct answer is B;
statement 2 alone is sufficient.**

DS14471

244. The arithmetic mean of a collection of 5 positive integers, not necessarily distinct, is 9. One additional positive integer is included in the collection and the arithmetic mean of the 6 integers is computed. Is the arithmetic mean of the 6 integers at least 10 ?

  (1)   The additional integer is at least 14.

  (2)   The additional integer is a multiple of 5.

Arithmetic Statistics

Since the arithmetic mean of the 5 integers is 9, the sum of the 5 integers divided by 5 is equal to 9, and hence the sum of the 5 integers is equal to $(5)(9) = 45$. Let x be the additional positive integer. Then the sum of the 6 integers is $45 + x$, and the arithmetic mean of the 6 integers is $\dfrac{45+x}{6}$. Determine whether $\dfrac{45+x}{6} \geq 10$, or equivalently, whether $45 + x \geq 60$, or equivalently, whether $x \geq 15$.

  (1)   Given that $x \geq 14$, then x could equal 14 and $x \geq 15$ is not true, or x could equal 15 and $x \geq 15$ is true; NOT sufficient.

  (2)   Given that x is a multiple of 5, then x could equal 10 and $x \geq 15$ is not true, or x could equal 15 and $x \geq 15$ is true; NOT sufficient.

Taking (1) and (2) together, then x is a multiple of 5 that is greater than or equal to 14, and so x could equal one of the numbers 15, 20, 25, 30, ... Each of these numbers is greater than or equal to 15.

**The correct answer is C;
both statements together are sufficient.**

DS11003

245. A certain list consists of 400 different numbers. Is the average (arithmetic mean) of the numbers in the list greater than the median of the numbers in the list?

  (1)   Of the numbers in the list, 280 are less than the average.

  (2)   Of the numbers in the list, 30 percent are greater than or equal to the average.

Arithmetic Statistics

In a list of 400 numbers, the median will be halfway between the 200th and the 201st numbers in the list when the numbers are ordered from least to greatest.

(1) This indicates that 280 of the 400 numbers in the list are less than the average of the 400 numbers. This means that both the 200th and the 201st numbers, as well as the median, are less than the average and, therefore, that the average is greater than the median; SUFFICIENT.

(2) This indicates that $(0.3)(400) = 120$ of the numbers are greater than or equal to the average. This means that the other $400 - 120 = 280$ numbers are less than the average, which is the same as the information in (1); SUFFICIENT.

The correct answer is D; each statement alone is sufficient.

DS03678

246. In a two-month survey of shoppers, each shopper bought one of two brands of detergent, X or Y, in the first month and again bought one of these brands in the second month. In the survey, 90 percent of the shoppers who bought Brand X in the first month bought Brand X again in the second month, while 60 percent of the shoppers who bought Brand Y in the first month bought Brand Y again in the second month. What percent of the shoppers bought Brand Y in the second month?

(1) In the first month, 50 percent of the shoppers bought Brand X.

(2) The total number of shoppers surveyed was 5,000.

Arithmetic Percents

This problem can be solved by using the following contingency table where A and B represent, respectively, the number of shoppers who bought Brand X and the number of shoppers who bought Brand Y in the first month; C and D represent, respectively, the number of shoppers who bought Brand X and the number of shoppers who bought Brand Y in the second month; and T represents the total number of shoppers in the survey. Also in the table, $0.9A$ represents the 90% of the shoppers who bought Brand X in the first month and also bought it in the second month, and $0.1A$ represents the $(100 - 90)\% = 10\%$ of the shoppers who bought Brand X in the first month and Brand Y in the second month. Similarly, $0.6B$ represents the 60% of the shoppers who bought Brand Y in the first month and also bought it in the second month, and $0.4B$ represents the $(100 - 60)\% = 40\%$ of the shoppers who bought Brand Y in the first month and Brand X in the second month.

		Second Month		
		X	Y	Total
First Month	X	$0.9A$	$0.1A$	A
	Y	$0.4B$	$0.6B$	B
	Total	C	D	T

Determine the value of $\dfrac{D}{T}$ as a percentage.

(1) This indicates that 50% of the shoppers bought Brand X in the first month, so $A = 0.5T$. It follows that the other 50% of the shoppers bought Brand Y in the first month, so $B = 0.5T$. Then, $D = 0.1A + 0.6B = 0.1(0.5T) + 0.6(0.5T) = 0.05T + 0.30T = 0.35T$. It follows that $\dfrac{D}{T} = \dfrac{0.35T}{T} = 0.35$, which is 35%; SUFFICIENT.

(2) This indicates that $T = 5,000$, as shown in the following table:

		Second Month		
		X	Y	Total
First Month	X	$0.9A$	$0.1A$	A
	Y	$0.4B$	$0.6B$	B
	Total	C	D	5,000

But not enough information is given to be able to determine D or D as a percentage of 5,000; NOT sufficient.

The correct answer is A; statement 1 alone is sufficient.

DS15902

247. If m and n are positive integers, is $m + n$ divisible by 4 ?

(1) m and n are each divisible by 2.

(2) Neither m nor n is divisible by 4.

Arithmetic Properties of numbers

Determine whether the sum of the positive integers m and n is divisible by 4.

(1) It is given that m is divisible by 2 and n is divisible by 2. If, for example, $m = 2$ and $n = 2$, then each of m and n is divisible by 2 and $m + n = 2 + 2 = 4$, which is divisible by 4.

However, if $m = 2$ and $n = 4$, then each of m and n is divisible by 2 and $m + n = 2 + 4 = 6$, which is not divisible by 4; NOT sufficient.

(2) It is given that neither m nor n is divisible by 4. If, for example, $m = 3$ and $n = 5$, then neither m nor n is divisible by 4 and $m + n = 3 + 5 = 8$, which is divisible by 4. On the other hand, if $m = 3$ and $n = 6$, then neither m nor n is divisible by 4 and $m + n = 3 + 6 = 9$, which is not divisible by 4; NOT sufficient.

Taking (1) and (2) together, m is not divisible by 4, so $m = 4q + r$, where q is a positive integer and $0 < r < 4$. However, m is divisible by 2, so r must be even. Since the only positive even integer less than 4 is 2, then $r = 2$ and $m = 4q + 2$. Similarly, since n is divisible by 2 but not by 4, $n = 4s + 2$. It follows that $m + n = (4q + 2) + (4s + 2) = 4q + 4s + 4 = 4(q + s + 1)$, and $m + n$ is divisible by 4.

The correct answer is C;
both statements together are sufficient.

DS02940
248. What is the area of rectangular region R?

(1) Each diagonal of R has length 5.
(2) The perimeter of R is 14.

Geometry Rectangles

Let L and W be the length and width of the rectangle, respectively. Determine the value of LW.

(1) It is given that a diagonal's length is 5. Thus, by the Pythagorean theorem, it follows that $L^2 + W^2 = 5^2 = 25$. The value of LW cannot be determined, however, because $L = \sqrt{15}$ and $W = \sqrt{10}$ satisfy $L^2 + W^2 = 25$ with $LW = \sqrt{150}$, and $L = \sqrt{5}$ and $W = \sqrt{20}$ satisfy $L^2 + W^2 = 25$ with $LW = \sqrt{100}$; NOT sufficient.

(2) It is given that $2L + 2W = 14$, or $L + W = 7$, or $L = 7 - W$. Therefore, $LW = (7 - W)W$, which can vary in value. For example, if $L = 3$ and $W = 4$, then $L + W = 7$ and $LW = 12$. However, if $L = 2$ and $W = 5$, then $L + W = 7$ and $LW = 10$; NOT sufficient.

Given (1) and (2) together, it follows from (2) that $(L + W)^2 = 7^2 = 49$, or $L^2 + W^2 + 2LW = 49$. Using (1), 25 can be substituted for $L^2 + W^2$ to obtain $25 + 2LW = 49$, or $2LW = 24$, or $LW = 12$. Alternatively, $7 - W$ can be substituted for L in

$L^2 + W^2 = 25$ to obtain the quadratic equation $(7 - W)^2 + W^2 = 25$, or $49 - 14W + W^2 + W^2 = 25$, or $2W^2 - 14W + 24 = 0$, or $W^2 - 7W + 12 = 0$. The left side of the last equation can be factored to give $(W - 4)(W - 3) = 0$. Therefore, $W = 4$, which gives $L = 7 - W = 7 - 4 = 3$ and $LW = (3)(4) = 12$, or $W = 3$, which gives $L = 7 - W = 7 - 3 = 4$ and $LW = (4)(3) = 12$. Since $LW = 12$ in either case, a unique value for LW can be determined.

The correct answer is C;
both statements together are sufficient.

DS17137
249. How many integers n are there such that $r < n < s$?

(1) $s - r = 5$
(2) r and s are not integers.

Arithmetic Properties of numbers

(1) The difference between s and r is 5. If r and s are integers (e.g., 7 and 12), the number of integers between them (i.e., n could be 8, 9, 10, or 11) is 4. If r and s are not integers (e.g., 6.5 and 11.5), then the number of integers between them (i.e., n could be 7, 8, 9, 10, or 11) is 5. No information is given that allows a determination of whether s and r are integers; NOT sufficient.

(2) No information is given about the difference between r and s. If $r = 0.4$ and $s = 0.5$, then r and s have no integers between them. However, if $r = 0.4$ and $s = 3.5$, then r and s have 3 integers between them; NOT sufficient.

Using the information from both (1) and (2), it can be determined that, because r and s are not integers, there are 5 integers between them.

The correct answer is C;
both statements together are sufficient.

DS17147
250. If the total price of n equally priced shares of a certain stock was $12,000, what was the price per share of the stock?

(1) If the price per share of the stock had been $1 more, the total price of the n shares would have been $300 more.
(2) If the price per share of the stock had been $2 less, the total price of the n shares would have been 5 percent less.

Arithmetic Arithmetic operations; Percents

Since the price per share of the stock can be expressed as $\dfrac{\$12,000}{n}$, determining the value of n is sufficient to answer this question.

(1) A per-share increase of $1 and a total increase of $300 for n shares of stock mean together that $n(\$1) = \$300$. It follows that $n = 300$; SUFFICIENT.

(2) If the price of each of the n shares had been reduced by $2, the total reduction in price would have been 5 percent less or $0.05(\$12,000)$. The equation $2n = 0.05(\$12,000)$ expresses this relationship. The value of n can be determined to be 300 from this equation; SUFFICIENT.

**The correct answer is D;
each statement alone is sufficient.**

DS02865

251. If n is positive, is $\sqrt{n} > 100$?

(1) $\sqrt{n-1} > 99$

(2) $\sqrt{n+1} > 101$

Algebra Radicals

Determine if $\sqrt{n} > 100$ or equivalently, if $n > (100)(100) = 10,000$.

(1) Given that $\sqrt{n-1} > 99$, or equivalently, $n - 1 > (99)(99)$, it follows from

$$(99)(99) = 99(100-1)$$
$$= 9,900 - 99$$
$$= 9,801$$

that $\sqrt{n-1} > 99$ is equivalent to $n - 1 > 9,801$, or $n > 9,802$. Since $n > 9,802$ allows for values of n that are greater than 10,000 and $n > 9,802$ allows for values of n that are not greater than 10,000, it cannot be determined if $n > 10,000$; NOT sufficient.

(2) Given that $\sqrt{n+1} > 101$, or equivalently, $n + 1 > (101)(101)$, it follows from

$$(101)(101) = 101(100+1)$$
$$= 10,100 + 101$$
$$= 10,201$$

that $\sqrt{n+1} > 101$ is equivalent to $n + 1 > 10,201$, or $n > 10,200$. Since $10,200 > 10,000$, it can be determined that $n > 10,000$; SUFFICIENT.

**The correct answer is B;
statement 2 alone is sufficient.**

DS17150

252. Is $xy > 5$?

(1) $1 \le x \le 3$ and $2 \le y \le 4$.

(2) $x + y = 5$

Algebra Inequalities

(1) While it is known that $1 \le x \le 3$ and $2 \le y \le 4$, xy could be $(3)(4) = 12$, which is greater than 5, or xy could be $(1)(2) = 2$, which is not greater than 5; NOT sufficient.

(2) Given that $x + y = 5$, xy could be 6 (when $x = 2$ and $y = 3$), which is greater than 5, and xy could be 4 (when $x = 1$ and $y = 4$), which is not greater than 5; NOT sufficient.

Both (1) and (2) together are not sufficient since the two examples given in (2) are consistent with both statements.

**The correct answer is E;
both statements together are still not sufficient.**

DS17151

253. In Year X, 8.7 percent of the men in the labor force were unemployed in June compared with 8.4 percent in May. If the number of men in the labor force was the same for both months, how many men were unemployed in June of that year?

(1) In May of Year X, the number of unemployed men in the labor force was 3.36 million.

(2) In Year X, 120,000 more men in the labor force were unemployed in June than in May.

Arithmetic Percents

Since 8.7 percent of the men in the labor force were unemployed in June, the number of unemployed men could be calculated if the total number of men in the labor force was known. Let t represent the total number of men in the labor force.

(1) This implies that for May $(8.4\%)t = 3,360,000$, from which the value of t can be determined; SUFFICIENT.

(2) This implies that $(8.7\% - 8.4\%)t = 120{,}000$ or $(0.3\%)t = 120{,}000$. This equation can be solved for t; SUFFICIENT.

The correct answer is D; each statement alone is sufficient.

DS17112

254. If $x \neq 0$, what is the value of $\left(\dfrac{x^p}{x^q}\right)^4$?

(1) $p = q$

(2) $x = 3$

Arithmetic; Algebra Arithmetic operations; Simplifying expressions

(1)   Since $p = q$, it follows that $\left(\dfrac{x^p}{x^q}\right)^4 = \left(\dfrac{x^p}{x^p}\right)^4 = (1)^4$; SUFFICIENT.

(2)   Since $x = 3$ (and, therefore, $x \neq 1$) and the values of p or q are unknown, the value of the expression $\left(\dfrac{x^p}{x^q}\right)^4$ cannot be determined; NOT sufficient.

The correct answer is A; statement 1 alone is sufficient.

DS17153

255. On Monday morning a certain machine ran continuously at a uniform rate to fill a production order. At what time did it completely fill the order that morning?

(1)   The machine began filling the order at 9:30 a.m.

(2)   The machine had filled $\dfrac{1}{2}$ of the order by 10:30 a.m. and $\dfrac{5}{6}$ of the order by 11:10 a.m.

Arithmetic Arithmetic operations

(1)   This merely states what time the machine began filling the order; NOT sufficient.

(2)   In the 40 minutes between 10:30 a.m. and 11:10 a.m., $\dfrac{5}{6} - \dfrac{1}{2} = \dfrac{1}{3}$ of the order was filled. Therefore, the entire order was completely filled in $3 \times 40 = 120$ minutes, or 2 hours. Since half the order took 1 hour and was filled by 10:30 a.m., the second half of the order, and thus the entire order, was filled by 11:30 a.m.; SUFFICIENT.

The correct answer is B; statement 2 alone is sufficient.

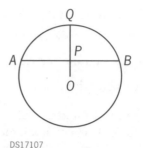

DS17107

256. What is the radius of the circle above with center O ?

(1)   The ratio of OP to PQ is 1 to 2.

(2) P is the midpoint of chord AB.

Geometry Circles

(1)   It can be concluded only that the radius is 3 times the length of OP, which is unknown; NOT sufficient.

(2)   It can be concluded only that $AP = PB$, and the chord is irrelevant to the radius; NOT sufficient.

Together, (1) and (2) do not give the length of any line segment shown in the circle. In fact, if the circle and all the line segments were uniformly expanded by a factor of, say, 5, the resulting circle and line segments would still satisfy both (1) and (2). Therefore, the radius of the circle cannot be determined from (1) and (2) together.

The correct answer is E; both statements together are still not sufficient.

DS15618

257. If a and b are positive integers, what is the value of the product ab ?

(1)   The least common multiple of a and b is 48.

(2)   The greatest common factor of a and b is 4.

Arithmetic Properties of numbers

Determine the value of the product of positive integers a and b.

(1)   This indicates that the least common multiple (lcm) of a and b is 48, which means that 48 is the least integer that is a multiple of both a and b. If $a = 24$ and $b = 16$, then the multiples of a are 24, 48, 72, ..., and the multiples of b are 16, 32, 48, 64, ... So, 48 is the lcm of 24 and 16, and $ab = (24)(16)$. However, if $a = 48$ and $b = 16$, then the multiples of a are 48, 96, ..., and the multiples of b are 16, 32, 48, 64,

. . . . So, 48 is the lcm of 48 and 16, and $ab =$ (48)(16); NOT sufficient.

(2) This indicates that 4 is the greatest common factor (gcf) of a and b, which means that 4 is the greatest integer that is a factor of both a and b. If $a = 4$ and $b = 4$, then 4 is the gcf a and b, and $ab = (4)(4)$. However, if $a = 4$ and $b = 16$, then 4 is the gcf of a and b, and $ab = (4)(16)$; NOT sufficient.

Taking (1) and (2) together, each of a and b is a multiple of 4 (which means that each of a and b is divisible by 4) and 48 is a multiple of each of a and b (which means that 48 is divisible by each of a and b). It follows that the only possible values for a and b are 4, 8, 12, 16, 24, and 48. The following table shows all possible pairs of these values and that only 4 of them ($a = 4$ and $b = 48$, $a = 12$ and $b = 16$, $a = 16$ and $b = 12$, $a = 48$ and $b = 4$), satisfy both (1) and (2).

		b					
		4	**8**	**12**	**16**	**24**	**48**
a	**4**	lcm is 4, not 48	lcm is 8, not 48	lcm is 12, not 48	lcm is 16, not 48	lcm is 24, not 48	lcm is 48, gcf is 4
	8	lcm is 8, not 48	lcm is 8, not 48	lcm is 24, not 48	gcf is 8, not 4	gcf is 8, not 4	gcf is 8, not 4
	12	lcm is 12, not 48	lcm is 24, not 48	gcf is 12, not 4	lcm is 48, gcf is 4	gcf is 12, not 4	gcf is 12, not 4
	16	lcm is 16, not 48	gcf is 8, not 4	lcm is 48, gcf is 4	gcf is 16, not 4	gcf is 8, not 4	gcf is 16, not 4
	24	lcm is 24, not 48	gcf is 8, not 4	gcf is 12, not 4	gcf is 8, not 4	gcf is 24, not 4	gcf is 24, not 4
	48	lcm is 48, gcf is 4	gcf is 8, not 4	gcf is 12, not 4	gcf is 16, not 4	gcf is 24, not 4	gcf is 48, not 4

In each case where both (1) and (2) are satisfied, $ab = 192$.

Alternatively,

(1) Using prime factorizations, since the least common multiple of a and b is 48 and

$48 = 2^4 \cdot 3^1$, it follows that $a = 2^p \cdot 3^q$, where $p \leq 4$ and $q \leq 1$, and $b = 2^r \cdot 3^s$, where $r \leq 4$ and $s \leq 1$. Since the least common multiple of two positive integers is the product of the highest power of each prime in the prime factorizations of the two integers, one of p or r must be 4 and one of q or s must be 1. If, for example, $p = 4$, $q = 1$, and $r = s = 0$, then $a = 2^4 \cdot 3^1 = 48$, $b = 2^0 \cdot 3^0 = 1$, and $ab = (48)(1) = 48$. However, if $p = 4$, $q = 1$, $r = 4$, and $s = 1$, then $a = 2^4 \cdot 3^1 = 48$, $b = 2^4 \cdot 3^1 = 48$, and $ab = (48)(48) = 2,304$; NOT sufficient.

(2) If $a = 4$ and $b = 4$, then the greatest common factor of a and b is 4 and $ab = (4)(4) = 16$. However, if $a = 4$ and $b = 12$, then the greatest common factor of a and b is 4 and $ab = (4)(12) = 48$; NOT sufficient.

Taking (1) and (2) together, by (1), $a = 2^p \cdot 3^q$, where $p \leq 4$ and $q \leq 1$, and $b = 2^r \cdot 3^s$, where $r \leq 4$ and $s \leq 1$. Since the least common multiple of two positive integers is the product of the highest power of each prime in the prime factorizations of the two integers, exactly one of p or r must be 4 and the other one must be 2. Otherwise, either the least common multiple of a and b would not be 48 or the greatest common factor would not be 4. Likewise, exactly one of q or s must be 1 and the other one must be 0. The following table gives all possible combinations of values for p, q, r, and s along with corresponding values of a, b, and ab.

p	q	r	s	$a = 2^p \cdot 3^q$	$b = 2^r \cdot 3^s$	ab
2	0	4	1	$2^2 \cdot 3^0 = 4$	$2^4 \cdot 3^1 = 48$	192
2	1	4	0	$2^2 \cdot 3^1 = 12$	$2^4 \cdot 3^0 = 16$	192
4	0	2	1	$2^4 \cdot 3^0 = 16$	$2^2 \cdot 3^1 = 12$	192
4	1	2	0	$2^4 \cdot 3^1 = 48$	$2^2 \cdot 3^0 = 4$	192

In each case, $ab = 192$.

The correct answer is C; both statements together are sufficient.

DS17095

258. What is the number of 360-degree rotations that a bicycle wheel made while rolling 100 meters in a straight line without slipping?

(1) The diameter of the bicycle wheel, including the tire, was 0.5 meter.

(2) The wheel made twenty 360-degree rotations per minute.

Geometry Circles

For each 360-degree rotation, the wheel has traveled a distance equal to its circumference. Given either the circumference of the wheel or the means to calculate its circumference, it is thus possible to determine the number of times the circumference of the wheel was laid out along the straight-line path of 100 meters.

(1) The circumference of the bicycle wheel can be determined from the given diameter using the equation $C = \pi d$, where $d =$ the diameter; SUFFICIENT.

(2) The speed of the rotations is irrelevant, and no dimensions of the wheel are given; NOT sufficient.

The correct answer is A; statement 1 alone is sufficient.

DS17168

259. In the equation $x^2 + bx + 12 = 0$, x is a variable and b is a constant. What is the value of b ?

(1) $x - 3$ is a factor of $x^2 + bx + 12$.

(2) 4 is a root of the equation $x^2 + bx + 12 = 0$.

Algebra First- and second-degree equations

(1) Method 1: If $x - 3$ is a factor, then $x^2 + bx + 12 = (x - 3)(x + c)$ for some constant c. Equating the constant terms (or substituting $x = 0$), it follows that $12 = -3c$, or $c = -4$. Therefore, the quadratic polynomial is $(x - 3)(x - 4)$, which is equal to $x^2 - 7x + 12$, and hence $b = -7$.

Method 2: If $x - 3$ is a factor of $x^2 + bx + 12$, then 3 is a root of $x^2 + bx + 12 = 0$. Therefore, $3^2 + 3b + 12 = 0$, which can be solved to get $b = -7$.

Method 3: The value of b can be found by long division:

$$x - 3 \overline{)\,x^2 + bx + 12\,} \quad x + (b + 3)$$

$$\underline{x^2 - 3x}$$
$$(b + 3)x + 12$$
$$\underline{(b + 3)x - 3b - 9}$$
$$3b + 21$$

These calculations show that the remainder is $3b + 21$. Since the remainder must be 0, it follows that $3b + 21 = 0$, or $b = -7$; SUFFICIENT.

(2) If 4 is a root of the equation, then 4 can be substituted for x in the equation $x^2 + bx + 12 = 0$, yielding $4^2 + 4b + 12 = 0$. This last equation can be solved to obtain a unique value for b; SUFFICIENT.

The correct answer is D; each statement alone is sufficient.

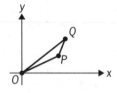

DS07715

260. In the figure above, line segment OP has slope $\frac{1}{2}$ and line segment PQ has slope 2. What is the slope of line segment OQ ?

(1) Line segment OP has length $2\sqrt{5}$.

(2) The coordinates of point Q are (5,4).

Geometry Coordinate geometry

Let P have coordinates (a,b) and Q have coordinates (x,y). Since the slope of $\overline{OP}$ is $\frac{1}{2}$, it follows that $\frac{b - 0}{a - 0} = \frac{1}{2}$, or $a = 2b$. What is the slope of $\overline{OQ}$?

(1) Given that $\overline{OP}$ has length $2\sqrt{5}$, it follows from the Pythagorean theorem that $a^2 + b^2 = \left(2\sqrt{5}\right)^2$, or $(2b)^2 + b^2 = 20$, or $5b^2 = 20$. The only positive solution of this equation is $b = 2$, and therefore $a = 2b = 4$

and the coordinates of P are $(a,b) = (4,2)$. However, nothing is known about how far Q is from P. If Q is close to P, then the slope of $\overline{OQ}$ will be close to $\frac{1}{2}$ (the slope of $\overline{OP}$), and if Q is far from P, then the slope of $\overline{OQ}$ will be close to 2 (the slope of $\overline{PQ}$). To be explicit, since the slope of $\overline{PQ}$ is 2, it follows that $\frac{y-2}{x-4} = 2$, or $y = 2x - 6$. Choosing $x = 4.1$ and $y = 2(4.1) - 6 = 2.2$ gives $(x,y) = (4.1, 2.2)$, and the slope of $\overline{OQ}$ is $\frac{2.2}{4.1}$, which is close to $\frac{1}{2}$. On the other hand, choosing $x = 100$ and $y = 2(100) - 6 = 194$ gives $(x,y) = (100,194)$, and the slope of $\overline{OQ}$ is $\frac{194}{100}$, which is close to 2; NOT sufficient.

(2) Given that the coordinates of point Q are $(5,4)$, it follows that the slope of $\overline{OQ}$ is $\frac{4-0}{5-0} = \frac{4}{5}$; SUFFICIENT.

The correct answer is B; statement 2 alone is sufficient.

DS17164

261. In $\triangle XYZ$, what is the length of YZ?

(1) The length of XY is 3.

(2) The length of XZ is 5.

Geometry Triangles

Given the length of one side of a triangle, it is known that the sum of the lengths of the other two sides is greater than that given length. The length of either of the other two sides, however, can be any positive number.

(1) Only the length of one side, XY, is given, and that is not enough to determine the length of YZ; NOT sufficient.

(2) Again, only the length of one side, XZ, is given and that is not enough to determine the length of YZ; NOT sufficient.

Even by using the triangle inequality stated above, only a range of values for YZ can be determined from (1) and (2). If the length of side YZ is represented by k, then it is known both that $3 + 5 > k$ and that $3 + k > 5$, or $k > 2$. Combining

these inequalities to determine the length of k yields only that $8 > k > 2$.

The correct answer is E; both statements together are still not sufficient.

DS07217

262. If the average (arithmetic mean) of n consecutive odd integers is 10, what is the least of the integers?

(1) The range of the n integers is 14.

(2) The greatest of the n integers is 17.

Arithmetic Statistics

Let k be the least of the n consecutive odd integers. Then the n consecutive odd integers are $k, k+2, k+4, \ldots, k+2(n-1)$, where $k+2(n-1)$ is the greatest of the n consecutive odd integers and $[k+2(n-1)] - k = 2(n-1)$ is the range of the n consecutive odd integers. Determine the value of k.

(1) Given that the range of the odd integers is 14, it follows that $2(n-1) = 14$, or $n-1 = 7$, or $n = 8$. It is also given that the average of the 8 consecutive odd integers is 10, and so, $\frac{k + (k+2) + (k+4) + \ldots + (k+14)}{8} = 10$ from which a unique value for k can be determined; SUFFICIENT.

(2) Given that the greatest of the odd integers is 17, it follows that the n consecutive odd integers can be expressed as $17, 17-2, 17-4, \ldots, 17-2(n-1)$. Since the average of the n consecutive odd integers is 10, then
$$\frac{17 + (17-2) + (17-4) + \ldots + [17-2(n-1)]}{n} = 10,$$
or
$$17 + (17-2) + (17-4) + \ldots + [17-2(n-1)] = 10n \text{ (i)}$$
The n consecutive odd integers can also be expressed as $k, k+2, k+4, \ldots, k+2(n-1)$.

Since the average of the n consecutive odd integers is 10, then
$$\frac{k + (k+2) + (k+4) + \ldots + [k+2(n-1)]}{n} = 10,$$
or
$$k + (k+2) + (k+4) + \ldots + [k+2(n-1)] = 10n \text{ (ii)}$$

Adding equations (i) and (ii) gives

$$(17 + k) + (17 + k) + (17 + k) + \ldots + (17 + k) = 20n$$

$$n(17 + k) = 20n$$

$$17 + k = 20$$

$$k = 3$$

Alternatively, because the numbers are consecutive odd integers, they form a data set that is symmetric about its average, and so the average of the numbers is the average of the least and greatest numbers. Therefore, $10 = \dfrac{k+17}{2}$, from which a unique value for k can be determined; SUFFICIENT.

The correct answer is D; each statement alone is sufficient.

DS16044

263. If x, y, and z are positive numbers, is $x > y > z$?

(1) $xz > yz$

(2) $yx > yz$

Algebra Inequalities

(1) Dividing both sides of the inequality by z yields $x > y$. However, there is no information relating z to either x or y; NOT sufficient.

(2) Dividing both sides of the inequality by y yields only that $x > z$, with no further information relating y to either x or z; NOT sufficient.

From (1) and (2) it can be determined that x is greater than both y and z. Since it still cannot be determined which of y or z is the least, the correct ordering of the three numbers also cannot be determined.

The correct answer is E; both statements together are still not sufficient.

DS06644

264. K is a set of numbers such that

(i)   if x is in K, then $-x$ is in K, and

(ii) if each of x and y is in K, then xy is in K.

Is 12 in K ?

(1) 2 is in K.

(2) 3 is in K.

Arithmetic Properties of numbers

(1) Given that 2 is in K, it follows that K could be the set of all real numbers, which contains 12. However, if K is the set $\{\ldots, -16, -8, -4, -2, 2, 4, 8, 16, \ldots\}$, then K contains 2 and K satisfies both (i) and (ii), but K does not contain 12. To see that K satisfies (ii), note that K can be written as $\{\ldots, -2^4, -2^3, -2^2, -2^1, 2^1, 2^2, 2^3, 2^4, \ldots\}$, and thus a verification of (ii) can reduce to verifying that the sum of two positive integer exponents is a positive integer exponent; NOT sufficient.

(2) Given that 3 is in K, it follows that K could be the set of all real numbers, which contains 12. However, if K is the set $\{\ldots, -81, -27, -9, -3, 3, 9, 27, 81, \ldots\}$, then K contains 3 and K satisfies both (i) and (ii), but K does not contain 12. To see that K satisfies (ii), note that K can be written as $\{\ldots, -3^4, -3^3, -3^2, -3^1, 3^1, 3^2, 3^3, 3^4, \ldots\}$, and thus a verification of (ii) can reduce to verifying that the sum of two positive integer exponents is a positive integer exponent; NOT sufficient.

Given (1) and (2), it follows that both 2 and 3 are in K. Thus, by (ii), $(2)(3) = 6$ is in K. Therefore, by (ii), $(2)(6) = 12$ is in K.

The correct answer is C; both statements together are sufficient.

DS05637

265. If $x^2 + y^2 = 29$, what is the value of $(x - y)^2$?

(1) $xy = 10$

(2) $x = 5$

Algebra Simplifying algebraic expressions

Since $(x - y)^2 = (x^2 + y^2) - 2xy$ and it is given that $x^2 + y^2 = 29$, it follows that $(x - y)^2 = 29 - 2xy$. Therefore, the value of $(x - y)^2$ can be determined if and only if the value of xy can be determined.

(1) Since the value of xy is given, the value of $(x - y)^2$ can be determined; SUFFICIENT.

(2) Given only that $x = 5$, it is not possible to determine the value of xy. Therefore, the value of $(x - y)^2$ cannot be determined; NOT sufficient.

The correct answer is A; statement 1 alone is sufficient.

DS16470

266. After winning 50 percent of the first 20 games it played, Team A won all of the remaining games it played. What was the total number of games that Team A won?

(1) Team A played 25 games altogether.

(2) Team A won 60 percent of all the games it played.

Arithmetic Percents

Let r be the number of the remaining games played, all of which the team won. Since the team won $(50\%)(20) = 10$ of the first 20 games and the r remaining games, the total number of games the team won is $10 + r$. Also, the total number of games the team played is $20 + r$. Determine the value of r.

(1) Given that the total number of games played is 25, it follows that $20 + r = 25$, or $r = 5$; SUFFICIENT.

(2) It is given that the total number of games won is $(60\%)(20 + r)$, which can be expanded as $12 + 0.6r$. Since it is also known that the number of games won is $10 + r$, it follows that $12 + 0.6r = 10 + r$. Solving this equation gives $12 - 10 = r - 0.6r$, or $2 = 0.4r$, or $r = 5$; SUFFICIENT.

**The correct answer is D;
each statement alone is sufficient.**

DS17181

267. Is x between 0 and 1 ?

(1) x^2 is less than x.

(2) x^3 is positive.

Arithmetic Arithmetic operations

(1) Since x^2 is always nonnegative, it follows that here x must also be nonnegative, that is, greater than or equal to 0. If $x = 0$ or 1, then $x^2 = x$. Furthermore, if x is greater than 1, then x^2 is greater than x. Therefore, x must be between 0 and 1; SUFFICIENT.

(2) If x^3 is positive, then x is positive, but x can be any positive number; NOT sufficient.

**The correct answer is A;
statement 1 alone is sufficient.**

DS04083

268. If m and n are nonzero integers, is m^n an integer?

(1) n^m is positive.

(2) n^m is an integer.

Arithmetic Properties of numbers

It is useful to note that if $m > 1$ and $n < 0$, then $0 < m^n < 1$, and therefore m^n will not be an integer. For example, if $m = 3$ and $n = -2$, then $m^n = 3^{-2} = \frac{1}{3^2} = \frac{1}{9}$.

(1) Although it is given that n^m is positive, m^n can be an integer or m^n can fail to be an integer. For example, if $m = 2$ and $n = 2$, then $n^m = 2^2 = 4$ is positive and $m^n = 2^2 = 4$ is an integer. However, if $m = 2$ and $n = -2$, then $n^m = (-2)^2 = 4$ is positive and $m^n = 2^{-2} = \frac{1}{2^2} = \frac{1}{4}$ is not an integer; NOT sufficient.

(2) Although it is given that n^m is an integer, m^n can be an integer or m^n can fail to be an integer. For example, if $m = 2$ and $n = 2$, then $n^m = 2^2 = 4$ is an integer and $m^n = 2^2 = 4$ is an integer. However, if $m = 2$ and $n = -2$, then $n^m = (-2)^2 = 4$ is an integer and $m^n = 2^{-2} = \frac{1}{2^2} = \frac{1}{4}$ is not an integer; NOT sufficient.

Taking (1) and (2) together, it is still not possible to determine if m^n is an integer, since the same examples are used in both (1) and (2) above.

**The correct answer is E;
both statements together are still not sufficient.**

DS16034

269. What is the value of xy ?

(1) $x + y = 10$

(2) $x - y = 6$

Algebra First- and second-degree equations; Simultaneous equations

(1) Given $x + y = 10$, or $y = 10 - x$, it follows that $xy = x(10 - x)$, which does not have a unique value. For example, if $x = 0$, then $xy = (0)(10) = 0$, but if $x = 1$, then $xy = (1)(9) = 9$; NOT sufficient.

(2) Given $x - y = 6$, or $y = x - 6$, it follows that $xy = x(x - 6)$, which does not have a unique value. For example, if $x = 0$, then $xy = (0)(-6) = 0$, but if $x = 1$, then $xy = (1)(-5) = -5$; NOT sufficient.

Using (1) and (2) together, the two equations can be solved simultaneously for x and y. One way to do this is by adding the two equations, $x + y = 10$ and $x - y = 6$, to get $2x = 16$, or $x = 8$. Then substitute into either of the equations to obtain an equation that can be solved to get $y = 2$. Thus, xy can be determined to have the value $(8)(2) = 16$. Alternatively, the two equations correspond to a pair of nonparallel lines in the (x,y) coordinate plane, which have a unique point in common.

The correct answer is C;
both statements together are sufficient.

DS13189

270. If n is the least of three different integers greater than 1, what is the value of n?

(1) The product of the three integers is 90.

(2) One of the integers is twice one of the other two integers.

Arithmetic Operations with integers

Given that n is the least of three different integers n, p, and q, where $1 < n < p < q$, determine the value of n.

(1) This indicates that the product of the three integers is 90. The integers could be 2, 5, and 9 since $(2)(5)(9) = 90$, and n would be 2. However, the integers could be 3, 5, and 6 since $(3)(5)(6) = 90$, and n would be 3; NOT sufficient.

(2) This indicates that one of the integers is twice one of the others. It could be that $p = 2n$, or $q = 2n$, or $q = 2p$. For example, if $n = 2$, $p = 4$, and $q = 5$, then $p = 2n$, and the value of n would be 2. If $n = 3$, $p = 4$, and $q = 6$, then $q = 2n$, and the value of n would be 3; NOT sufficient.

Taking (1) and (2) together, if $p = 2n$, then $npq = (n)(2n)(q) = 90$, or $n^2q = 45$. It follows that $n = 3$, $p = (2)(3) = 6$, and $q = 5$. The value of n is 3. If $q = 2n$, then $npq = (n)(p)(2n) = 90$ or $n^2p = 45$. It follows that $n = 3$, $p = 5$, and $q = (2)(3) = 6$. The value of n is 3. If $q = 2p$, then $npq = (n)(p)(2p) = 90$ or $np^2 = 45$. It follows that $n = 5$, $p = 3$, and $q = (2)(3) = 6$, and this case can be eliminated because n is not the least of the three integers. Therefore, the value of n is 3.

Alternatively, taking (1) and (2) together, the integers n, p, and q are among 2, 3, 5, 6, 9, 10, 15, 18, 30, and 45 since they are factors of 90 from (1). Because all three integers are different and $90 = (2)(3)(15) = (2)(3^2)(5)$, n, p, and q must be among the integers 2, 3, 5, 9, 10, and 15. Only two pairs of these integers satisfy (2): 3 and 6 since $6 = (2)(3)$ and 5 and 10 since $10 = (2)(5)$. However, for each possible value for n, $(n)(5)(10) > 90$. Therefore, the only pair that satisfies both (1) and (2) is 3 and 6, and the third integer is then $\dfrac{90}{(3)(6)} = 5$. Thus, the value of n is 3.

The correct answer is C;
both statements together are sufficient.

DS16461

271. Is x^2 greater than x?

(1) x^2 is greater than 1.

(2) x is greater than -1.

Arithmetic; Algebra Exponents; Inequalities

(1) Given $x^2 > 1$, it follows that either $x > 1$ or $x < -1$. If $x > 1$, then multiplying both sides of the inequality by the positive number x gives $x^2 > x$. On the other hand, if $x < -1$, then x is negative and x^2 is positive (because $x^2 > 1$), which also gives $x^2 > x$; SUFFICIENT.

(2) Given $x > -1$, x^2 can be greater than x (for example, $x = 2$) and x^2 can fail to be greater than x (for example, $x = 0$); NOT sufficient.

The correct answer is A;
statement 1 alone is sufficient.

DS03503

272. Michael arranged all his books in a bookcase with 10 books on each shelf and no books left over. After Michael acquired 10 additional books, he arranged all his books in a new bookcase with 12 books on each shelf and no books left over. How many books did Michael have before he acquired the 10 additional books?

(1) Before Michael acquired the 10 additional books, he had fewer than 96 books.

(2) Before Michael acquired the 10 additional books, he had more than 24 books.

Arithmetic Properties of numbers

If x is the number of books Michael had before he acquired the 10 additional books, then x is a multiple of 10. After Michael acquired the 10 additional books, he had $x + 10$ books and $x + 10$ is a multiple of 12.

(1) If $x < 96$, where x is a multiple of 10, then $x = 10, 20, 30, 40, 50, 60, 70, 80,$ or 90 and $x + 10 = 20, 30, 40, 50, 60, 70, 80, 90,$ or 100. Since $x + 10$ is a multiple of 12, then $x + 10 = 60$ and $x = 50$; SUFFICIENT.

(2) If $x > 24$, where x is a multiple of 10, then x must be one of the numbers $30, 40, 50, 60, 70, 80, 90, 100, 110, \ldots,$ and $x + 10$ must be one of the numbers $40, 50, 60, 70, 80, 90, 100, 110, 120, \ldots$. Since there is more than one multiple of 12 among these numbers (for example, 60 and 120), the value of $x + 10$, and therefore the value of x, cannot be determined; NOT sufficient.

The correct answer is A;
statement 1 alone is sufficient.

DS16469

273. If $xy > 0$, does $(x - 1)(y - 1) = 1$?

(1) $x + y = xy$
(2) $x = y$

Algebra First- and second-degree equations

By expanding the product $(x - 1)(y - 1)$, the question is equivalent to whether $xy - y - x + 1 = 1$, or $xy - y - x = 0$, when $xy > 0$.

(1) If $x + y = xy$, then $xy - y - x = 0$, and hence by the remarks above, $(x - 1)(y - 1) = 1$; SUFFICIENT.

(2) If $x = y$, then $(x - 1)(y - 1) = 1$ can be true $(x = y = 2)$ and $(x - 1)(y - 1) = 1$ can be false $(x = y = 1)$; NOT sufficient.

The correct answer is A;
statement 1 alone is sufficient.

DS06842

274. Last year in a group of 30 businesses, 21 reported a net profit and 15 had investments in foreign markets. How many of the businesses did not report a net profit nor invest in foreign markets last year?

(1) Last year 12 of the 30 businesses reported a net profit and had investments in foreign markets.

(2) Last year 24 of the 30 businesses reported a net profit or invested in foreign markets, or both.

Arithmetic Concepts of sets

Consider the Venn diagram below in which x represents the number of businesses that reported a net profit and had investments in foreign markets. Since 21 businesses reported a net profit, $21 - x$ businesses reported a net profit only. Since 15 businesses had investments in foreign markets, $15 - x$ businesses had investments in foreign markets only. Finally, since there is a total of 30 businesses, the number of businesses that did not report a net profit and did not invest in foreign markets is $30 - (21 - x + x + 15 - x) = x - 6$.

Determine the value of $x - 6$, or equivalently, the value of x.

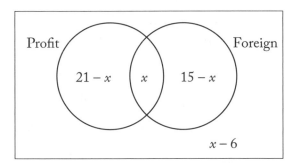

(1) It is given that $12 = x$; SUFFICIENT.

(2) It is given that $24 = (21 - x) + x + (15 - x)$. Therefore, $24 = 36 - x$, or $x = 12$.

Alternatively, the information given is exactly the number of businesses that are not among those to be counted in answering the question posed in the problem, and therefore the number of businesses that are to be counted is $30 - 24 = 6$; SUFFICIENT.

The correct answer is D;
each statement alone is sufficient.

DS17110

275. Is the perimeter of square S greater than the perimeter of equilateral triangle T?

(1) The ratio of the length of a side of S to the length of a side of T is 4:5.

(2) The sum of the lengths of a side of S and a side of T is 18.

Geometry Perimeter

Letting s and t be the side lengths of square S and triangle T, respectively, the task is to determine if $4s > 3t$, which is equivalent (divide both sides by $4t$) to determining if $\frac{s}{t} > \frac{3}{4}$.

(1) It is given that $\frac{s}{t} = \frac{4}{5}$. Since $\frac{4}{5} > \frac{3}{4}$, it follows that $\frac{s}{t} > \frac{3}{4}$; SUFFICIENT.

(2) Many possible pairs of numbers have the sum of 18. For some of these (s,t) pairs it is the case that $\frac{s}{t} > \frac{3}{4}$ (for example, $s = t = 9$), and for others of these pairs it is not the case that $\frac{s}{t} > \frac{3}{4}$ (for example, $s = 1$ and $t = 17$); NOT sufficient.

**The correct answer is A;
statement 1 alone is sufficient.**

DS17136

276. If $x + y + z > 0$, is $z > 1$?

(1) $z > x + y + 1$

(2) $x + y + 1 < 0$

Algebra Inequalities

(1) The inequality $x + y + z > 0$ gives $z > -x - y$. Adding this last inequality to the given inequality, $z > x + y + 1$, gives $2z > 1$, or $z > \frac{1}{2}$, which suggests that (1) is not sufficient. Indeed, z could be 2 ($x = y = 0$ and $z = 2$ satisfy both $x + y + z > 0$ and $z > x + y + 1$), which is greater than 1, and z could be $\frac{3}{4}$ ($x = y = -\frac{1}{4}$ and $z = \frac{3}{4}$ satisfy both $x + y + z > 0$ and $z > x + y + 1$), which is not greater than 1; NOT sufficient.

(2) It follows from the inequality $x + y + z > 0$ that $z > -(x + y)$. It is given that $x + y + 1 < 0$, or $(x + y) < -1$, or $-(x + y) > 1$. Therefore, $z > -(x + y)$ and $-(x + y) > 1$, from which it follows that $z > 1$; SUFFICIENT.

**The correct answer is B;
statement 2 alone is sufficient.**

DS07832

277. For all z, $\lceil z \rceil$ denotes the least integer greater than or equal to z. Is $\lceil x \rceil = 0$?

(1) $-1 < x < -0.1$

(2) $\lceil x + 0.5 \rceil = 1$

Algebra Operations with real numbers

Determining if $\lceil x \rceil = 0$ is equivalent to determining if $-1 < x \le 0$. This can be inferred by examining a few representative examples, such as $\lceil -1.1 \rceil = -1, \lceil -1 \rceil = -1, \lceil -0.9 \rceil = 0, \lceil -0.1 \rceil = 0$, $\lceil 0 \rceil = 0$, and $\lceil 0.1 \rceil = 1$.

(1) Given $-1 < x < -0.1$, it follows that $-1 < x \le 0$, since $-1 < x \le 0$ represents all numbers x that satisfy $-1 < x < -0.1$ along with all numbers x that satisfy $-0.1 \le x \le 0$; SUFFICIENT.

(2) Given $\lceil x + 0.5 \rceil = 1$, it follows from the same reasoning used just before (1) above that this equality is equivalent to $0 < x + 0.5 \le 1$, which in turn is equivalent to $-0.5 < x \le 0.5$. Since from among these values of x it is possible for $-1 < x \le 0$ to be true (for example, $x = -0.1$) and it is possible for $-1 < x \le 0$ to be false (for example, $x = 0.1$), it cannot be determined if $\lceil x \rceil = 0$; NOT sufficient.

**The correct answer is A;
statement 1 alone is sufficient.**

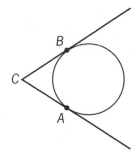

DS16464

278. The circular base of an above-ground swimming pool lies in a level yard and just touches two straight sides of a fence at points A and B, as shown in the figure above. Point C is on the ground where the two sides of the fence meet. How far from the center of the pool's base is point A ?

(1) The base has area 250 square feet.

(2) The center of the base is 20 feet from point C.

Geometry Circles

Let Q be the center of the pool's base and r be the distance from Q to A, as shown in the figure below.

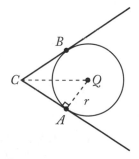

Since A is a point on the circular base, QA is a radius (r) of the base.

(1) Since the formula for the area of a circle is area = πr^2, this information can be stated as $250 = \pi r^2$ or $\sqrt{\dfrac{250}{\pi}} = r$; SUFFICIENT.

(2) Since $\overline{CA}$ is tangent to the base, $\triangle QAC$ is a right triangle. It is given that $QC = 20$, but there is not enough information to use the Pythagorean theorem to determine the length of $\overline{QA}$; NOT sufficient.

**The correct answer is A;
statement 1 alone is sufficient.**

DS16050

279. If $xy = -6$, what is the value of $xy(x + y)$?

(1) $x - y = 5$

(2) $xy^2 = 18$

Algebra First- and second-degree equations

By substituting -6 as the value of xy, the question can be simplified to "What is the value of $-6(x + y)$?"

(1) Adding y to both sides of $x - y = 5$ gives $x = y + 5$. When $y + 5$ is substituted for x in the equation $xy = -6$, the equation yields $(y + 5)y = -6$, or $y^2 + 5y + 6 = 0$. Factoring the left side of this equation gives $(y + 2)(y + 3) = 0$. Thus, y may have a value of -2 or -3. Since a unique value of y is not determined, neither the value of x nor the value of xy can be determined; NOT sufficient.

(2) Since $xy^2 = (xy)y$ and $xy^2 = 18$, it follows that $(xy)y = 18$. When -6 is substituted for xy, this equation yields $-6y = 18$, and hence $y = -3$. Since $y = -3$ and $xy = -6$, it follows that $-3x = -6$, or $x = 2$. Therefore, the value of $x + y$, and hence the value of $xy(x + y) = -6(x + y)$ can be determined; SUFFICIENT.

**The correct answer is B;
statement 2 alone is sufficient.**

DS05519

280. [y] denotes the greatest integer less than or equal to y. Is $d < 1$?

(1) $d = y - [y]$

(2) $[d] = 0$

Algebra Operations with real numbers

(1) It is given $d = y - [y]$. If y is an integer, then $y = [y]$, and thus $y - [y] = 0$, which is less than 1. If y is not an integer, then y lies between two consecutive integers, the smaller of which is equal to $[y]$. Since each of these two consecutive integers is at a distance of less than 1 from y, it follows that $[y]$ is at a distance of less than 1 from y, or $y - [y] < 1$. Thus, regardless of whether y is an integer or y is not an integer, it can be determined that $d < 1$; SUFFICIENT.

(2) It is given that $[d] = 0$, which is equivalent to $0 \le d < 1$. This can be inferred by examining a few representative examples, such as $[-0.1] = -1$, $[0] = 0$, $[0.1] = 0$, $[0.9] = 0$, and $[1.1] = 1$. From $0 \le d < 1$, it follows that $d < 1$; SUFFICIENT.

**The correct answer is D;
each statement alone is sufficient.**

DS14052

281. If N is a positive odd integer, is N prime?

(1) $N = 2^k + 1$ for some positive integer k.
(2) $N + 2$ and $N + 4$ are both prime.

Arithmetic Properties of numbers

Determine whether the positive odd integer N is prime.

(1) This indicates that $N = 2^k + 1$ for some positive integer k. If $k = 1$, then $N = 2^1 + 1 = 3$ and N is prime. However, if $k = 3$, then $N = 2^3 + 1 = 9$ and N is not prime; NOT sufficient.

(2) This indicates that both $N + 2$ and $N + 4$ are prime. If $N = 3$, then $N + 2 = 5$ and $N + 4 = 7$ are both prime and N is prime. However, if $N = 9$, then $N + 2 = 11$ and $N + 4 = 13$ are both prime and N is not prime; NOT sufficient.

Taking (1) and (2) together is of no more help than (1) and (2) taken separately since the same examples were used to show that neither (1) nor (2) is sufficient.

**The correct answer is E;
both statements together are still not sufficient.**

DS01140

282. If m is a positive integer, then m^3 has how many digits?

(1) m has 3 digits.
(2) m^2 has 5 digits.

Arithmetic Properties of numbers

(1) Given that m has 3 digits, then m could be 100 and $m^3 = 1{,}000{,}000$ would have 7 digits, or m could be 300 and $m^3 = 27{,}000{,}000$ would have 8 digits; NOT sufficient.

(2) Given that m^2 has 5 digits, then m could be 100 (because $100^2 = 10{,}000$ has 5 digits) or m could be 300 (because $300^2 = 90{,}000$ has 5 digits). In the former case, $m^3 = 1{,}000{,}000$

has 7 digits and in the latter case, $m^3 = 27{,}000{,}000$ has 8 digits; NOT sufficient.

Given (1) and (2), it is still possible for m to be 100 or for m to be 300, and thus m^3 could have 7 digits or m^3 could have 8 digits.

**The correct answer is E;
both statements together are still not sufficient.**

DS03308

283. What is the value of $x^2 - y^2$?

(1) $(x - y)^2 = 9$
(2) $x + y = 6$

Algebra Second-degree equations

Determine the value of $x^2 - y^2$.

(1) This indicates that $(x - y)^2 = 9$. It follows that $x - y = -3$ or $x - y = 3$, which gives information about the value of $x - y$ but not specific information about the value of x, y, or $x^2 - y^2$. For example, if $x = \dfrac{9}{2}$ and $y = \dfrac{3}{2}$, then $(x - y)^2 = \left(\dfrac{9}{2} - \dfrac{3}{2}\right)^2 = 9$ and $x^2 - y^2$

$= \dfrac{81}{4} - \dfrac{9}{4} = 18$. But if $x = \dfrac{3}{2}$ and $y = \dfrac{9}{2}$, then

$(x - y)^2 = \left(\dfrac{3}{2} - \dfrac{9}{2}\right)^2 = 9$ and $x^2 - y^2 = \dfrac{9}{4} - \dfrac{81}{4} =$

-18; NOT sufficient.

(2) This indicates that $x + y = 6$ but does not give specific information about the value of x, y, or $x^2 - y^2$. For example, if $x = \dfrac{9}{2}$ and $y = \dfrac{3}{2}$, then

$x + y = \dfrac{9}{2} + \dfrac{3}{2} = 6$ and $x^2 - y^2 = \dfrac{81}{4} - \dfrac{9}{4} =$

18. But if $x = \dfrac{3}{2}$ and $y = \dfrac{9}{2}$, then $x + y =$

$\dfrac{3}{2} + \dfrac{9}{2} = 6$ and $x^2 - y^2 = \dfrac{9}{4} - \dfrac{81}{4} = -18$;

NOT sufficient.

Taking (1) and (2) together is of no more help than (1) and (2) taken separately since the same examples were used to show that neither (1) nor (2) is sufficient.

Alternatively, note that $x^2 - y^2 = (x - y)(x + y)$. From (1), $x - y = \pm 3$, and from (2), $x + y = 6$. Therefore, taking (1) and (2) together allows for both $x^2 - y^2 = (3)(6) = 18$ and $x^2 - y^2 = (-3)(6) = -18$.

**The correct answer is E;
both statements together are still not sufficient.**

DS01267

284. For each landscaping job that takes more than 4 hours, a certain contractor charges a total of r dollars for the first 4 hours plus $0.2r$ dollars for each additional hour or fraction of an hour, where $r > 100$. Did a particular landscaping job take more than 10 hours?

    (1) The contractor charged a total of $288 for the job.
    (2) The contractor charged a total of $2.4r$ dollars for the job.

Algebra Applied problems

If y represents the total number of hours the particular landscaping job took, determine if $y > 10$.

(1) This indicates that the total charge for the job was $288, which means that $r + 0.2r(y - 4) = 288$. From this it cannot be determined if $y > 10$. For example, if $r = 120$ and $y = 11$, then $120 + 0.2(120)(7) = 288$, and the job took more than 10 hours. However, if $r = 160$ and $y = 8$, then $160 + 0.2(160)(4) = 288$, and the job took less than 10 hours; NOT sufficient.

(2) This indicates that $r + 0.2r(y - 4) = 2.4r$, from which it follows that

$r + 0.2ry - 0.8r = 2.4r$	use distributive property
$0.2ry = 2.2r$	subtract $(r - 0.8r)$ from both sides
$y = 11$	divide both sides by $0.2r$

Therefore, the job took more than 10 hours; SUFFICIENT.

**The correct answer is B;
statement 2 alone is sufficient.**

DS17600

285. If $x^2 = 2^x$, what is the value of x?

    (1) $2x = \left(\dfrac{x}{2}\right)^3$
    (2) $x = 2^{x-2}$

Algebra Exponents

Given $x^2 = 2^x$, determine the value of x. Note that $x \neq 0$ because $0^2 = 0$ and $2^0 = 1$.

(1) This indicates that $2x = \left(\dfrac{x}{2}\right)^3$, so $2x = \dfrac{x^3}{8}$ and $16x = x^3$. Since $x \neq 0$, then $16 = x^2$, so $x = -4$ or $x = 4$. However, $(-4)^2 = 16$ and $2^{-4} = \dfrac{1}{16}$, so $x \neq -4$. Therefore, $x = 4$; SUFFICIENT.

(2) This indicates that $x = 2^{x-2}$, so $x = \dfrac{2^x}{2^2}$ and $4x = 2^x$. Since it is given that $x^2 = 2^x$, then $4x = x^2$ and, because $x \neq 0$, it follows that $x = 4$; SUFFICIENT.

**The correct answer is D;
each statement alone is sufficient.**

DS01169

286. The sequence s_1, s_2, s_3, ..., s_n, ... is such that $s_n = \dfrac{1}{n} - \dfrac{1}{n+1}$ for all integers $n \geq 1$. If k is a positive integer, is the sum of the first k terms of the sequence greater than $\dfrac{9}{10}$?

    (1) $k > 10$
    (2) $k < 19$

Arithmetic Sequences

The sum of the first k terms can be written as

$$\left(\dfrac{1}{1} - \dfrac{1}{2}\right) + \left(\dfrac{1}{2} - \dfrac{1}{3}\right) + \ldots + \left(\dfrac{1}{k-1} - \dfrac{1}{k}\right) + \left(\dfrac{1}{k} - \dfrac{1}{k+1}\right)$$

$$= 1 + \left(-\dfrac{1}{2} + \dfrac{1}{2}\right) + \left(-\dfrac{1}{3} + \dfrac{1}{3}\right) + \ldots + \left(-\dfrac{1}{k} + \dfrac{1}{k}\right) - \dfrac{1}{k+1}$$

$$= 1 - \dfrac{1}{k+1}.$$

Therefore, the sum of the first k terms is greater than $\dfrac{9}{10}$ if and only if $1 - \dfrac{1}{k+1} > \dfrac{9}{10}$, or $1 - \dfrac{9}{10} > \dfrac{1}{k+1}$, or $\dfrac{1}{10} > \dfrac{1}{k+1}$. Multiplying both sides of the last inequality by $10(k + 1)$ gives the equivalent condition $k + 1 > 10$, or $k > 9$.

(1) Given that $k > 10$, then it follows that $k > 9$; SUFFICIENT.

(2) Given that $k < 19$, it is possible to have $k > 9$ (for example, $k = 15$) and it is possible to not have $k > 9$ (for example, $k = 5$); NOT sufficient.

The correct answer is A;
statement 1 alone is sufficient.

DS05518

287. In the sequence S of numbers, each term after the first two terms is the sum of the two immediately preceding terms. What is the 5th term of S?

(1) The 6th term of S minus the 4th term equals 5.

(2) The 6th term of S plus the 7th term equals 21.

Arithmetic Sequences

If the first two terms of sequence S are a and b, then the remaining terms of sequence S can be expressed in terms of a and b as follows.

n	nth term of sequence S
1	a
2	b
3	$a + b$
4	$a + 2b$
5	$2a + 3b$
6	$3a + 5b$
7	$5a + 8b$

For example, the 6th term of sequence S is $3a + 5b$ because $(a + 2b) + (2a + 3b) = 3a + 5b$. Determine the value of the 5th term of sequence S, that is, the value of $2a + 3b$.

(1) Given that the 6th term of S minus the 4th term of S is 5, it follows that $(3a + 5b) - (a + 2b) = 5$. Combining like terms, this equation can be rewritten as $2a + 3b = 5$, and thus the 5th term of sequence S is 5; SUFFICIENT.

(2) Given that the 6th term of S plus the 7th term of S is 21, it follows that $(3a + 5b) + (5a + 8b) = 21$. Combining like terms, this equation can be rewritten as $8a + 13b = 21$. Letting e represent the 5th term of sequence S, this last equation is

equivalent to $4(2a + 3b) + b = 21$, or $4e + b = 21$, which gives a direct correspondence between the 5th term of sequence S and the 2nd term of sequence S. Therefore, the 5th term of sequence S can be determined if and only if the 2nd term of sequence S can be determined. Since the 2nd term of sequence S cannot be determined, the 5th term of sequence S cannot be determined. For example, if $a = 1$ and $b = 1$, then $8a + 13b = 8(1) + 13(1) = 21$ and the 5th term of sequence S is $2a + 3b = 2(1) + 3(1) = 5$. However, if $a = 0$ and $b = \dfrac{21}{13}$, then

$$8a + 13b = 8(0) + 13\left(\dfrac{21}{13}\right) = 21$$

and the 5th term of sequence S is

$$2a + 3b = 2(0) + 3\left(\dfrac{21}{13}\right) = \dfrac{63}{13}; \text{ NOT}$$

sufficient.

The correct answer is A;
statement 1 alone is sufficient.

DS01121

288. If 75 percent of the guests at a certain banquet ordered dessert, what percent of the guests ordered coffee?

(1) 60 percent of the guests who ordered dessert also ordered coffee.

(2) 90 percent of the guests who ordered coffee also ordered dessert.

Arithmetic Concepts of sets; Percents

Consider the Venn diagram below that displays the various percentages of 4 groups of the guests. Thus, x percent of the guests ordered both dessert and coffee and y percent of the guests ordered coffee only. Since 75 percent of the guests ordered dessert, $(75 - x)\%$ of the guests ordered dessert only. Also, because the 4 percentages represented in the Venn diagram have a total sum of 100 percent, the percentage of guests who did not order either dessert or coffee is $100 - [(75 - x) + x + y] = 25 - y$. Determine the percentage of guests who ordered coffee, or equivalently, the value of $x + y$.

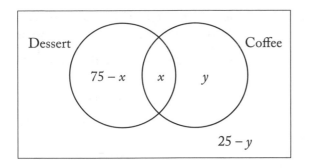

(1) Given that x is equal to 60 percent of 75, or 45, the value of $x + y$ cannot be determined; NOT sufficient.

(2) Given that 90 percent of $x + y$ is equal to x, it follows that $0.9(x + y) = x$, or $9(x + y) = 10x$. Therefore, $9x + 9y = 10x$, or $9y = x$. From this the value of $x + y$ cannot be determined. For example, if $x = 9$ and $y = 1$, then all 4 percentages in the Venn diagram are between 0 and 100, $9y = x$, and $x + y = 10$. However, if $x = 18$ and $y = 2$, then all 4 percentages in the Venn diagram are between 0 and 100, $9y = x$, and $x + y = 20$; NOT sufficient.

Given both (1) and (2), it follows that $x = 45$ and $9y = x$. Therefore, $9y = 45$, or $y = 5$, and hence $x + y = 45 + 5 = 50$.

The correct answer is C; both statements together are sufficient.

DS05302

289. A tank containing water started to leak. Did the tank contain more than 30 gallons of water when it started to leak? (Note: 1 gallon = 128 ounces)

(1) The water leaked from the tank at a constant rate of 6.4 ounces per minute.

(2) The tank became empty less than 12 hours after it started to leak.

Arithmetic Rate problems

(1) Given that the water leaked from the tank at a constant rate of 6.4 ounces per minute, it is not possible to determine if the tank leaked more than 30 gallons of water. In fact, any nonzero amount of water leaking from the tank is consistent with a leakage rate of 6.4 ounces per minute, since nothing can be determined about the amount of time the water was leaking from the tank; NOT sufficient.

(2) Given that the tank became empty in less than 12 hours, it is not possible to determine if the tank leaked more than 30 gallons of water because the rate at which water leaked from the tank is unknown. For example, the tank could have originally contained 1 gallon of water that emptied in exactly 10 hours or the tank could have originally contained 31 gallons of water that emptied in exactly 10 hours; NOT sufficient.

Given (1) and (2) together, the tank emptied at a constant rate of

$$\left(6.4 \frac{\text{oz}}{\text{min}} \right) \left(60 \frac{\text{min}}{\text{hr}} \right) \left(\frac{1}{128} \frac{\text{gal}}{\text{oz}} \right) = \frac{(64)(6)}{128} \frac{\text{gal}}{\text{hr}} =$$

$$\frac{(64)(6)}{(64)(2)} \frac{\text{gal}}{\text{hr}} = 3 \frac{\text{gal}}{\text{hr}} \text{ for less than 12 hours.}$$

If t is the total number of hours the water leaked from the tank, then the total amount of water emptied from the tank, in gallons, is $3t$, which is therefore less than $(3)(12) = 36$. From this it is not possible to determine if the tank originally contained more than 30 gallons of water. For example, if the tank leaked water for a total of 11 hours, then the tank originally contained $(3)(11)$ gallons of water, which is more than 30 gallons of water. However, if the tank leaked water for a total of 2 hours, then the tank originally contained $(3)(2)$ gallons of water, which is not more than 30 gallons of water.

The correct answer is E; both statements together are still not sufficient.

DS12752

290. In the xy-plane, lines k and ℓ intersect at the point $(1,1)$. Is the y-intercept of k greater than the y-intercept of ℓ?

(1) The slope of k is less than the slope of ℓ.

(2) The slope of ℓ is positive.

Algebra Coordinate geometry

Let m_1 and m_2 represent the slopes of lines k and ℓ, respectively. Then, using the point-slope form for the equation of a line, an equation of line k can be determined: $y - 1 = m_1(x - 1)$, or $y = m_1 x + (1 - m_1)$. Similarly, an equation for line ℓ is $y = m_2 x + (1 - m_2)$. Determine if $(1 - m_1) > (1 - m_2)$, or equivalently if $m_1 < m_2$.

(1) This indicates that $m_1 < m_2$; SUFFICIENT.

(2) This indicates that $m_2 > 0$. If $m_1 = -1$, for example, then $m_1 < m_2$, but if $m_2 = 4$ and $m_1 = 5$, then $m_1 > m_2$; NOT sufficient.

The correct answer is A; statement 1 alone is sufficient.

DS14588

291. A triangle has side lengths of a, b, and c centimeters. Does each angle in the triangle measure less than 90 degrees?

(1) The 3 semicircles whose diameters are the sides of the triangle have areas that are equal to 3 cm², 4 cm², and 6 cm², respectively.

(2) $c < a + b < c + 2$

Geometry Triangles; Pythagorean theorem

Given a triangle with sides of lengths a, b, and c centimeters, determine whether each angle of the triangle measures less than 90°. Assume that the vertices of the triangle are A, B, and C and that a is the side length of the side opposite $\angle A$, b is the side length of the side opposite $\angle B$, and c is the side length of the side opposite $\angle C$, where $a \le b \le c$.

Note that for a right triangle, $a^2 + b^2 = c^2$. However, if $a^2 + b^2 > c^2$, then the triangle is acute (i.e., a triangle with each angle measuring less than 90°). This is illustrated by the following figures.

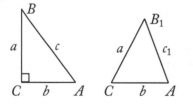

$\triangle BCA$ on the left is a right triangle with sides $BC = a$, $CA = b$, and $AB = c$, where $a^2 + b^2 = c^2$ by the Pythagorean theorem. The triangle on the right, $\triangle B_1 CA$, has sides $B_1 C = a$, $CA = b$, and $AB_1 = c_1$. Clearly $AB = c > AB_1 = c_1$, so $c^2 > c_1^2$. Since $a^2 + b^2 = c^2$ and $c^2 > c_1^2$, it follows that $a^2 + b^2 > c_1^2$, and $\triangle B_1 CA$ is clearly an acute triangle.

(1) This indicates that the areas of the 3 semicircles whose diameters are the sides of the triangle are 3 cm², 4 cm², and 6 cm², respectively. Then, because "respectively" implies that a is the diameter of the semicircle with area 3 cm², b is the diameter of the semicircle with area 3 cm², b is the diameter

of the semicircle with area 4 cm², and c is the diameter of the semicircle with area 6 cm², as shown below, then $3 = \frac{1}{2}\pi\left(\frac{a}{2}\right)^2$ from which it follows that $a^2 = \frac{24}{\pi}$. Similarly, $b^2 = \frac{32}{\pi}$, and $c^2 = \frac{48}{\pi}$.

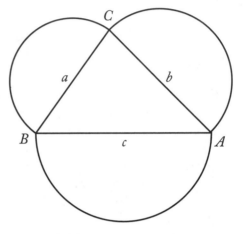

Because $a^2 + b^2 = \frac{24}{\pi} + \frac{32}{\pi} = \frac{56}{\pi} > \frac{48}{\pi} = c^2$, the angle with greatest measure (i.e., the angle at C) is an acute angle, which implies that each angle in the triangle is acute and measures less than 90°; SUFFICIENT.

(2) This indicates that $c < a + b < c + 2$. If $a = 1$, $b = 1$, and $c = 1$, then $1 < 1 + 1 < 1 + 2$. It follows that the triangle is equilateral; therefore, each angle measures less than 90°. However, if $a = 1$, $b = 1$, and $c = \sqrt{2}$, then $\sqrt{2} < 1 + 1 < \sqrt{2} + 2$, but $1^2 + 1^2 = (\sqrt{2})^2$ and the triangle is a right triangle; NOT sufficient.

The correct answer is A; statement 1 alone is sufficient.

DS00890

292. Each of the 45 books on a shelf is written either in English or in Spanish, and each of the books is either a hardcover book or a paperback. If a book is to be selected at random from the books on the shelf, is the probability less than $\frac{1}{2}$ that the book selected will be a paperback written in Spanish?

(1) Of the books on the shelf, 30 are paperbacks.

(2) Of the books on the shelf, 15 are written in Spanish.

Arithmetic Probability

(1) This indicates that 30 of the 45 books are paperbacks. Of the 30 paperbacks, 25 could be written in Spanish. In this case, the probability of randomly selecting a paperback book written in Spanish is $\frac{25}{45} > \frac{1}{2}$. On the other hand, it is possible that only 5 of the paperback books are written in Spanish. In this case, the probability of randomly selecting a paperback book written in Spanish is $\frac{5}{45} < \frac{1}{2}$; NOT sufficient.

(2) This indicates that 15 of the books are written in Spanish. Then, at most 15 of the 45 books on the shelf are paperbacks written in Spanish, and the probability of randomly selecting a paperback book written in Spanish is at most $\frac{15}{45} < \frac{1}{2}$; SUFFICIENT.

The correct answer is B; statement 2 alone is sufficient.

DS06683

293. A small school has three foreign language classes, one in French, one in Spanish, and one in German. How many of the 34 students enrolled in the Spanish class are also enrolled in the French class?

(1) There are 27 students enrolled in the French class, and 49 students enrolled in either the French class, the Spanish class, or both of these classes.

(2) One-half of the students enrolled in the Spanish class are enrolled in more than one foreign language class.

Arithmetic Sets

Given that 34 students are enrolled in the Spanish class, how many students are enrolled in both the Spanish and French classes? In other words, given that $x + y = 34$ in the diagram below, what is the value of y?

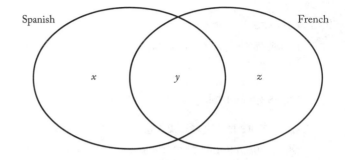

(1) It is given that $y + z = 27$ and $x + y + z = 49$. Adding the equations $x + y = 34$ and $y + z = 27$ gives $x + 2y + z = 34 + 27 = 61$, or $y + (x + y + z) = 61$. Since $x + y + z = 49$, it follows that $y + 49 = 61$, or $y = 12$; SUFFICIENT.

(2) Given that half the students enrolled in the Spanish class are enrolled in more than one foreign language class, then it is possible that no students are enrolled in the French and German classes only and 17 students are enrolled in both the Spanish and French classes. On the other hand, it is also possible that there are 17 students enrolled in the French and German classes only and no students enrolled in both the Spanish and French classes; NOT sufficient.

The correct answer is A; statement 1 alone is sufficient.

DS04910

294. If S is a set of four numbers w, x, y, and z, is the range of the numbers in S greater than 2?

(1) $w - z > 2$

(2) z is the least number in S.

Arithmetic Statistics

The range of the numbers w, x, y, and z is equal to the greatest of those numbers minus the least of those numbers.

(1) This reveals that the difference between two of the numbers in the set is greater than 2, which means that the range of the four numbers must also be greater than 2; SUFFICIENT.

(2) The information that z is the least number gives no information regarding the other numbers or their range; NOT sufficient.

The correct answer is A; statement 1 alone is sufficient.

295. Last year $\frac{3}{5}$ of the members of a certain club were males. This year the members of the club include all the members from last year plus some new members. Is the fraction of the members of the club who are males greater this year than last year?

   (1)   More than half of the new members are male.

   (2)   The number of members of the club this year is $\frac{6}{5}$ the number of members last year.

Arithmetic Operations with fractions

Let L represent the number of members last year; N the number of new members added this year; and x the number of members added this year who are males. It is given that $\frac{3}{5}$ of the members last year were males. It follows that the number of members who are male this year is $\frac{3}{5}L + x$. Also, the total number of members this year is $L + N$. Determine if $\dfrac{\frac{3}{5}L + x}{L + N} > \frac{3}{5}$, or equivalently, determine if $3L + 5x > 3L + 3N$ or simply if $x > \frac{3}{5}N$.

   (1)   This indicates that $x > \frac{1}{2}N$. If, for example,

       $N = 20$ and $x = 11$, then $11 > \frac{1}{2}(20) = 10$, but $11 \not> \frac{3}{5}(20) = 12$. On the other hand, if $N = 20$ and $x = 16$, then $16 > \frac{1}{2}(20) = 10$, and $16 > \frac{3}{5}(20) = 12$; NOT sufficient.

   (2)   This indicates that $L + N = \frac{6}{5}L$. It follows that $N = \frac{1}{5}L$. If, for example, $L = 100$, then $N = \frac{1}{5}(100) = 20$. If $x = 11$, then $11 \not> \frac{3}{5}(20) = 12$. On the other hand, if $x = 16$, then $16 > \frac{1}{2}(20) = 10$, and $16 > \frac{3}{5}(20) = 12$; NOT sufficient.

Taking (1) and (2) together is of no more help than (1) and (2) taken separately since the same examples were used to show that neither (1) nor (2) is sufficient.

The correct answer is E; both statements together are still not sufficient.

296. If a, b, and c are consecutive integers and $0 < a < b < c$, is the product abc a multiple of 8 ?

   (1)   The product ac is even.

   (2)   The product bc is a multiple of 4.

Arithmetic Operations with integers

Determine whether the product of three consecutive positive integers, a, b and c, where $a < b < c$, is a multiple of 8.

Since a, b, and c are consecutive integers, then either both a and c are even and b is odd, or both a and c are odd and b is even.

   (1)   This indicates that at least one of a or c is even, so both a and c are even. Since, when counting from 1, every fourth integer is a multiple of 4, one integer of the pair of consecutive even integers a and c is a multiple of 4. Since the other integer of the pair is even, the product ac is a multiple of 8, and, therefore, abc is a multiple of 8; SUFFICIENT.

   (2)   This indicates that bc is a multiple of 4. If $b = 3$ and $c = 4$, then $a = 2$ and $bc = 12$, which is a multiple of 4. In this case, $abc = (2)(3)(4) = 24$, which is a multiple of 8. However, if $b = 4$ and $c = 5$, then $a = 3$ and $bc = 20$, which is a multiple of 4. In this case, $abc = (3)(4)(5) = 60$, which is not a multiple of 8; NOT sufficient.

The correct answer is A; statement 1 alone is sufficient.

297. M and N are integers such that $6 < M < N$. What is the value of N ?

   (1)   The greatest common divisor of M and N is 6.

   (2)   The least common multiple of M and N is 36.

Arithmetic Properties of numbers

   (1)   Given that the greatest common divisor (GCD) of M and N is 6 and $6 < M < N$, then it is possible that $M = (6)(5) = 30$ and $N = (6)(7) = 42$. However, it is also possible that $M = (6)(7) = 42$ and $N = (6)(11) = 66$; NOT sufficient.

(2) Given that the least common multiple (LCM) of M and N is 36 and $6 < M < N$, then it is possible that $M = (4)(3) = 12$ and $N = (9)(2) = 18$. However, it is also possible that $M = (4)(3) = 12$ and $N = (9)(4) = 36$; NOT sufficient.

Taking (1) and (2) together, it follows that 6 is a divisor of M and M is a divisor of 36. Therefore, M is among the numbers 6, 12, 18, and 36. For the same reason, N is among the numbers 6, 12, 18, and 36. Since $6 < M < N$, it follows that M cannot be 6 or 36 and N cannot be 6. Thus, there are three choices for M and N such that $M < N$. These three choices are displayed in the table below, which indicates why only one of the choices, namely $M = 12$ and $N = 18$, satisfies both (1) and (2).

M	N	GCD	LCM
12	18	6	36
12	36	12	36
18	36	18	36

**The correct answer is C;
both statements together are sufficient.**

DS07575

298. Stations X and Y are connected by two separate, straight, parallel rail lines that are 250 miles long. Train P and train Q simultaneously left Station X and Station Y, respectively, and each train traveled to the other's point of departure. The two trains passed each other after traveling for 2 hours. When the two trains passed, which train was nearer to its destination?

(1) At the time when the two trains passed, train P had averaged a speed of 70 miles per hour.

(2) Train Q averaged a speed of 55 miles per hour for the entire trip.

Arithmetic Applied problems; Rates

(1) This indicates that Train P had traveled $2(70) = 140$ miles when it passed Train Q. It follows that Train P was $250 - 140 = 110$ miles from its destination and Train Q was 140 miles from its destination, which means that Train P was nearer to its destination when the trains passed each other; SUFFICIENT.

(2) This indicates that Train Q averaged a speed of 55 miles per hour for the entire trip, but no information is given about the speed of Train P. If Train Q traveled for 2 hours at an average speed of 55 miles per hour and Train P traveled for 2 hours at an average speed of 70 miles per hour, then Train P was nearer to its destination when the trains passed. However, if Train Q traveled for 2 hours at an average speed of 65 miles per hour and Train P traveled for 2 hours at an average speed of 60 miles per hour, then Train Q was nearer to its destination when the trains passed. Note that if Train Q traveled at $\frac{(120)(55)}{140} = 47\frac{1}{7}$ miles per hour for the remainder of the trip, then its average speed for the whole trip was 55 miles per hour; NOT sufficient.

**The correct answer is A;
statement 1 alone is sufficient.**

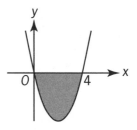

DS01613

299. In the *xy*-plane shown, the shaded region consists of all points that lie above the graph of $y = x^2 - 4x$ and below the *x*-axis. Does the point (a,b) (not shown) lie in the shaded region if $b < 0$?

(1) $0 < a < 4$

(2) $a^2 - 4a < b$

Algebra Coordinate geometry

In order for (a,b) to lie in the shaded region, it must lie above the graph of $y = x^2 - 4x$ and below the *x*-axis. Since $b < 0$, the point (a,b) lies below the *x*-axis. In order for (a,b) to lie above the graph of $y = x^2 - 4x$, it must be true that $b > a^2 - 4a$.

(1) This indicates that $0 < a < 4$. If $a = 2$, then $a^2 - 4a = 2^2 - 4(2) = -4$, so if $b = -1$, then $b > a^2 - 4a$ and (a,b) is in the shaded region. But if $b = -5$, then $b < a^2 - 4a$ and

215

(a,b) is not in the shaded region; NOT sufficient.

(2) This indicates that $b > a^2 - 4a$, and thus, (a,b) is in the shaded region; SUFFICIENT.

The correct answer is B; statement 2 alone is sufficient.

DS01685

300. If a and b are positive integers, is $\sqrt[3]{ab}$ an integer?

(1) $\sqrt{a}$ is an integer.

(2) $b = \sqrt{a}$

Arithmetic Properties of numbers

(1) Given that $\sqrt{a}$ is an integer, then $a = 4$ is possible. If, in addition $b = 1$, then $\sqrt[3]{ab} = \sqrt[3]{4}$ is not an integer. However, if, in addition $b = 2$, then $\sqrt[3]{ab} = \sqrt[3]{8} = 2$ is an integer; NOT sufficient.

(2) Given that $b = \sqrt{a}$, then $\sqrt[3]{ab} = \sqrt[3]{a\sqrt{a}} = \sqrt[3]{\sqrt{a^3}} = \sqrt{\sqrt[3]{a^3}} = \sqrt{a} = b$ is an integer; SUFFICIENT.

The correct answer is B; statement 2 alone is sufficient.

6.0 Quantitative Question Index

6.0 Quantitative Question Index

The Quantitative Question Index is organized by difficulty level, GMAT section, and then by math concept. All the numbers below are associated with the problem numbers in the guide and not the page numbers.

There are different ways you can classify and categorize each of the different types of problems. Below are the GMAC classification and categorization of the quantitative practice problems.

Difficulty: Easy

Data Sufficiency: Algebra

Applied problems: 198

Arithmetic operations: 201

Equations: 202

Exponents: 186

First-degree equations: 177, 204

Inequalities: 181

Linear equations: 199

Data Sufficiency: Arithmetic

Applied problems: 179, 184, 188, 189, 194

Inequalities: 190

Percents: 195

Properties of integers: 185

Properties of numbers: 182, 191, 196, 200

Ratio and proportion: 192, 203

Rounding: 180

Series and sequences: 178

Statistics: 69, 183

Data Sufficiency: Geometry

Coordinate geometry: 197

Coordinate geometry; Triangles: 193

Triangles; Pythagorean theorem: 187

Problem Solving: Algebra

Applied problems: 49

Applied problems; Substitution: 21

Exponents: 48, 53

Factoring: 3

First-degree equations: 10, 18, 25, 35, 51, 55

First-degree equations; Substitution: 45

Fractions: 30

Inequalities: 9

Operations on integers: 7

Operations on rational numbers: 28

Order: 20

Percents: 78

Ratio and proportion: 68

Second-degree equations: 2, 29, 71, 73

Sequences: 64

Simplifying algebraic expressions; Substitution: 31

Simultaneous equations: 46, 50

Statistics: 89

Substitution; Operations with rational numbers: 17

Problem Solving: Arithmetic

Absolute value: 41

Applied problems: 8, 13, 15, 23, 42, 56, 60, 63, 65, 82, 91

Applied problems; Operations with fractions: 62

Applied problems; Percents: 77

Applied problems; Proportions: 11

Estimation: 74

Factors, multiples, and divisibility: 5

Inequalities: 43

Interpretation of graphs: 84

Operations on integers: 24, 86, 88

Operations on rational numbers: 16, 47, 59

Operations with fractions: 80, 81, 85

Operations with integers: 79, 83

Operations with rational numbers: 54, 72

Percents: 12, 14, 27, 37, 44, 67, 90

Percents: Inequalities; Applied problems: 52

Place value: 40, 93

Problem Solving: Geometry

Difficulty: Medium

Data Sufficiency: Algebra

Data Sufficiency: Arithmetic

Data Sufficiency: Geometry

Angles: 205

Circles: 222

Quadrilaterals; Perimeter; Pythagorean theorem: 209

Simple coordinate geometry: 206

Triangles: 217

Volume: 208

Problem Solving: Algebra

Absolute value: 103

Applied problems: 120

Applied problems; Percents: 128

Inequalities: 97, 108

Inequalities; Absolute value: 112

Ratio and proportion: 115

Sequences: 129

Simple coordinate geometry: 116

Simplifying algebraic expressions: 117

Substitution; Operations with rational numbers: 104

Problem Solving: Arithmetic

Applied problems: 98, 102, 114

Decimals: 99

Estimation: 131

Exponents: 118

Exponents; Operations with rational numbers: 96

Inequalities: 94

Measurement conversion: 127

Percents: 119, 124, 132

Percents; Estimation: 105, 123

Place value: 106

Properties of numbers: 95, 109, 110, 121, 125

Statistics: 100, 113

Problem Solving: Geometry

Difficulty: Hard

Data Sufficiency: Algebra

Data Sufficiency: Arithmetic

7.0 GMAT Official Guide Quantitative Review Online Index

GMAT Official Guide Quantitative Review Online Index

ARE YOU USING BOTH THE BOOK AND THE ONLINE QUESTION BANK TO STUDY? If so, use the following index to locate a question from the online question bank in the book.

To locate a question from the online question bank in the book—Every question in the online question bank has a unique ID, called the Practice Question Identifier or PQID, which appears above the question number. Look up the PQID in the table to find its problem number and page number in the book.

PQID	Question #	Page
DS00890	292	166
DS01104	185	157
DS01121	288	165
DS01130	197	158
DS01140	282	165
DS01169	286	165
DS01267	284	165
DS01503	178	157
DS01613	299	166
DS01633	231	161
DS01685	300	166
DS02474	243	162
DS02589	188	157
DS02741	236	161
DS02779	183	157
DS02865	251	163
DS02899	233	161
DS02940	248	162
DS03006	192	158
DS03308	283	165
DS03503	272	164
DS03615	224	160
DS03678	246	162
DS03939	193	158
DS03989	209	159
DS04039	216	160

PQID	Question #	Page
DS04083	268	164
DS04468	221	160
DS04474	240	162
DS04510	184	157
DS04573	190	158
DS04636	182	157
DS04644	181	157
DS04910	294	166
DS05149	177	157
DS05172	186	157
DS05302	289	165
DS05518	287	165
DS05519	280	165
DS05637	265	164
DS05657	227	161
DS05766	210	159
DS05986	211	159
DS05989	202	159
DS06067	232	161
DS06368	237	161
DS06644	264	164
DS06650	195	158
DS06683	293	166
DS06785	226	161
DS06810	234	161
DS06842	274	164

PQID	Question #	Page	PQID	Question #	Page
DS07206	219	160	DS15618	257	163
DS07217	262	163	DS15863	223	160
DS07258	194	158	DS15902	247	162
DS07568	213	159	DS15938	218	160
DS07575	298	166	DS16034	269	164
DS07715	260	163	DS16044	263	163
DS07832	277	164	DS16050	279	165
DS08306	212	159	DS16277	242	162
DS08307	229	161	DS16456	241	162
DS08352	201	158	DS16461	271	164
DS08660	239	162	DS16464	278	165
DS08852	208	159	DS16469	273	164
DS09260	200	158	DS16470	266	164
DS09385	199	158	DS17095	258	163
DS09642	207	159	DS17107	256	163
DS10383	214	160	DS17110	275	164
DS11003	245	162	DS17112	254	163
DS11614	220	160	DS17136	276	164
DS12033	191	158	DS17137	249	162
DS12187	295	166	DS17147	250	162
DS12752	290	166	DS17150	252	163
DS12862	205	159	DS17151	253	163
DS13097	206	159	DS17153	255	163
DS13132	230	161	DS17164	261	163
DS13189	270	164	DS17168	259	163
DS13384	180	157	DS17181	267	164
DS13457	203	159	DS17319	196	158
DS13640	296	166	DS17503	225	161
DS13706	238	162	DS17543	228	161
DS13837	297	166	DS17588	222	160
DS13907	215	160	DS17600	285	165
DS14052	281	165	DS17640	187	157
DS14170	198	158	DS18386	217	160
DS14471	244	162	DS19208	235	161
DS14588	291	166	PS00037	46	66
DS15099	204	159	PS00111	83	72
DS15349	189	158	PS00335	37	65
DS15510	179	157	PS00774	99	74

PQID	Question #	Page
PS00777	87	72
PS00812	11	61
PS00817	76	70
PS00904	134	79
PS00918	40	65
PS00986	94	73
PS01099	56	68
PS01120	36	65
PS01285	125	77
PS01334	157	82
PS01443	57	68
PS01466	32	64
PS01564	168	84
PS01650	48	66
PS01656	61	68
PS01867	33	64
PS01875	98	74
PS01949	23	63
PS02019	15	62
PS02053	135	79
PS02256	77	71
PS02352	116	76
PS02378	110	75
PS02389	169	84
PS02402	52	67
PS02498	63	69
PS02528	154	82
PS02775	69	69
PS02934	119	76
PS02948	25	63
PS02955	152	82
PS02978	3	60
PS03036	13	61
PS03356	150	82
PS03439	1	60
PS03614	102	74
PS03623	127	78
PS03695	140	80

PQID	Question #	Page
PS03696	143	80
PS03774	158	83
PS03777	54	67
PS03779	139	79
PS03831	91	73
PS03887	5	60
PS03918	20	62
PS04009	66	69
PS04160	105	74
PS04254	159	83
PS04362	41	66
PS04765	88	72
PS04780	167	84
PS04971	65	69
PS04987	148	81
PS05008	39	65
PS05083	96	73
PS05109	38	65
PS05129	28	64
PS05146	142	80
PS05292	7	61
PS05413	120	77
PS05470	123	77
PS05616	70	70
PS05775	85	72
PS05916	86	72
PS05924	124	77
PS05965	104	74
PS05972	166	84
PS06135	121	77
PS06180	90	73
PS06189	153	82
PS06273	118	76
PS06288	59	68
PS06312	160	83
PS06555	24	63
PS06719	22	63
PS06726	49	67

PQID	Question #	Page
PS06913	108	75
PS06937	9	61
PS06959	163	83
PS07001	97	73
PS07058	128	78
PS07080	51	67
PS07117	175	85
PS07331	50	67
PS07380	35	65
PS07385	17	62
PS07386	55	67
PS07394	68	69
PS07397	34	64
PS07426	171	85
PS07659	27	63
PS07694	14	62
PS07771	147	81
PS07793	12	61
PS08011	18	62
PS08051	101	74
PS08375	4	60
PS08407	100	74
PS08416	174	85
PS08485	136	79
PS08572	146	81
PS08598	112	76
PS08654	164	83
PS08661	117	76
PS08729	145	80
PS08859	151	82
PS09050	115	76
PS09056	161	83
PS09294	114	76
PS09305	73	70
PS09322	44	66
PS09439	131	78
PS09820	106	75
PS09901	138	79

PQID	Question #	Page
PS09983	26	63
PS10174	82	71
PS10309	155	82
PS10339	78	71
PS10422	79	71
PS10493	72	70
PS10539	64	69
PS10810	89	72
PS10862	21	63
PS10921	74	70
PS11024	144	80
PS11042	2	60
PS11145	130	78
PS11430	137	79
PS11454	122	77
PS11468	8	61
PS11537	129	78
PS11647	109	75
PS11692	126	77
PS11738	80	71
PS11755	141	80
PS12450	113	76
PS12657	67	69
PS12759	93	73
PS12785	103	74
PS12857	92	73
PS12926	10	61
PS12934	42	66
PS13205	75	70
PS13426	53	67
PS13583	16	62
PS13686	31	64
PS13800	6	61
PS13829	58	68
PS13841	84	72
PS13882	71	70
PS13917	29	64
PS14037	19	62

PQID	Question #	Page
PS14060	107	75
PS14063	60	68
PS14087	95	73
PS14237	45	66
PS14267	162	83
PS14293	81	71
PS14397	165	84
PS15469	43	66
PS15538	149	81
PS15753	62	68

PQID	Question #	Page
PS15994	30	64
PS16963	176	85
PS16967	170	84
PS16977	172	85
PS16990	173	85
PS17036	47	66
PS17461	156	82
PS17708	132	78
PS17806	111	75
PS19062	133	79

Appendix A Answer Sheets

Problem Solving Answer Sheet

1.	37.	73.	109.	145.
2.	38.	74.	110.	146.
3.	39.	75.	111.	147.
4.	40.	76.	112.	148.
5.	41.	77.	113.	149.
6.	42.	78.	114.	150.
7.	43.	79.	115.	151.
8.	44.	80.	116.	152.
9.	45.	81.	117.	153.
10.	46.	82.	118.	154.
11.	47.	83.	119.	155.
12.	48.	84.	120.	156.
13.	49.	85.	121.	157.
14.	50.	86.	122.	158.
15.	51.	87.	123.	159.
16.	52.	88.	124.	160.
17.	53.	89.	125.	161.
18.	54.	90.	126.	162.
19.	55.	91.	127.	163.
20.	56.	92.	128.	164.
21.	57.	93.	129.	165.
22.	58.	94.	130.	166.
23.	59.	95.	131.	167.
24.	60.	96.	132.	168.
25.	61.	97.	133.	169.
26.	62.	98.	134.	170.
27.	63.	99.	135.	171.
28.	64.	100.	136.	172.
29.	65.	101.	137.	173.
30.	66.	102.	138.	174.
31.	67.	103.	139.	175.
32.	68.	104.	140.	176.
33.	69.	105.	141.	
34.	70.	106.	142.	
35.	71.	107.	143.	
36.	72.	108.	144.	

Data Sufficiency Answer Sheet

177.	208.	239.	270.
178.	209.	240.	271.
179.	210.	241.	272.
180.	211.	242.	273.
181.	212.	243.	274.
182.	213.	244.	275.
183.	214.	245.	276.
184.	215.	246.	277.
185.	216.	247.	278.
186.	217.	248.	279.
187.	218.	249.	280.
188.	219.	250.	281.
189.	220.	251.	282.
190.	221.	252.	283.
191.	222.	253.	284.
192.	223.	254.	285.
193.	224.	255.	286.
194.	225.	256.	287.
195.	226.	257.	288.
196.	227.	258.	289.
197.	228.	259.	290.
198.	229.	260.	291.
199.	230.	261.	292.
200.	231.	262.	293.
201.	232.	263.	294.
202.	233.	264.	295.
203.	234.	265.	296.
204.	235.	266.	297.
205.	236.	267.	298.
206.	237.	268.	299.
207.	238.	269.	300.

Graduate Management Admission Council®

Caution!

The penalties for cheating on the GMAT® Exam are severe.

The following is considered cheating:

- Hiring someone to take the test
- Taking the test for someone else
- Memorizing test questions
- Sharing answers with others

The penalties for cheating are:

- Cancellation of your scores
- Ban on future testing
- School notification
- Possible legal prosecution

Has someone been trying to get you to cheat?

File a report via email: **pvtestsecurity@pearson.com**

Pearson
VUE